Duress

Claire Spradling

*To Marsha,
Blessings to you!
Claire Spradling*

Copyright © 2012 by Claire Spradling

Duress
by Claire Spradling

Printed in the United States of America

ISBN 9781622309542

All rights reserved solely by the author. The author guarantees all contents are original and do not infringe upon the legal rights of any other person or work. No part of this book may be reproduced in any form without the permission of the author. The views expressed in this book are not necessarily those of the publisher.

Unless otherwise indicated, Bible quotations are taken from Zondervan NIV Study Bible. Copyright © 2008 by Zondervan.

www.xulonpress.com

Dedicated to

*M*y mother, Christine Trawick, who always said, "I wish someone in the family would be a writer."
Special Thanks to:
My husband, Stanley, who supported me in my ventures
And to:
Janice Trawick, Ginger Weimer, Bobby Cole and Bill Billington, who encouraged me

Chapter 1

Troublesome Kid

The Easter holiday ended on this unseasonably hot Sunday night in the small town of West Point, Mississippi. Most everyone had attended special services and hunted Easter eggs Friday through Sunday. Miles Arnold drank iced tea and relaxed in his comfortable den chair, channel flipping. His wife, Lottie, turned pages of magazines as she argued with her husband.

"You're not listening to me. Don't you care how badly she treats her children?" challenged Lottie.

"I know she's your sister, and I care, but they're not our children," said Miles.

"I'll do whatever it takes to ensure those kids have a happy childhood," declared Lottie.

"Well, you've got a husband and son that need you to ensure their happy-hood," laughed Miles. Lottie huffed at Miles.

"Quit trying to talk to Marilyn about her children," said Miles. "It won't help. She's too selfish."

"I should report Marilyn to Family Services," said Lottie in frustration as she re-twisted and clipped up her long honey-colored hair.

"You do, and Marilyn will move away and hire an attorney to slap a restraining order on you, Lottie Love," smirked Miles.

"We should take George and Victoria away from Marilyn," insisted Lottie. "She doesn't like her own children. She acts as if they're a curse."

"Well, we can't afford any more children," said Miles.

"If you can afford that new pickup truck, you can afford more children," said Lottie.

"Don't get too personal," joked Miles. "My pickup's a necessity. You know, man's best friend."

"That's a *dog*," refuted Lottie.

"Well, I don't own a dog; I own a truck that goes everywhere I go."

"Miles, be serious. Children are a blessing from the Lord!"

"I got all the blessing I want in that rascal son of ours," laughed Miles.

"We always said we wanted more children," said Lottie.

Miles flung himself playfully at Lottie on the sofa, smothered her with his chest, and tickled her face with his soft, trimmed beard and mustache.

"You want more children? I can arrange that." She grunted and pushed at him.

Suddenly emergency sirens rattled the house. Miles jerked up, and Lottie cried out.

They ran to the side door and stepped out to see policemen circling their house and firefighters attaching a fire hose to the hydrant and extending ladders to climb up to the second floor. Neighbors ran toward the house with buckets of water and blankets. A fireman asked Lottie, "Is anyone in the house?"

Lottie panicked. "My son! Little Rob! Little Rob!" She turned to rush into the house, but was pulled back. "He just turned five. He's a small boy," choked Lottie.

"Where did you last see him, ma'am?" asked the fireman.
"In his room, playing. At the top of the stairs," said Lottie in fear for her son.
"Don't worry, ma'am," said the fireman. "We'll get him." Firefighters disappeared into the house.

Warmhearted people surrounded Lottie and offered encouragement. "It's all right. They'll get Little Rob. He'll be okay. Don't worry about the house. We're here to help."

An hysterical bystander speculated, "I can tell that the smoke and flames are concentrated in the interior. Just watch! The roof will cave in soon!"

"I don't smell anything burning," commented someone else.

Several minutes passed as Lottie and Miles and their neighbors waited for the firemen to come outside with Little Rob. Terrified, Lottie repeated, "My son! My son! Oh, God! Oh, God, let them bring Little Rob out alive!" Neighborhood friends hugged and consoled the Arnolds.

Overcome with guilt, Miles said, "I should've grabbed Little Rob before I ran out. I had no clue the house was on fire."

Policemen lined up to keep people away from the house. Firemen came out the door, shaking their heads and mumbling. Moans of sorrow filled the air.

"Oh, no!" screamed Lottie. She fell to her knees in shock, crying. Miles dropped beside her and wrapped his arms around her. They sobbed. People in the yard wept and wailed and shook their heads in sorrow.

The last two firemen walked out the side door, weaving and dragging something. They pulled a young boy by his ears and prodded him down the steps. "Quit it! Quit it!" squeaked the boy.

"Little Rob?" gasped Lottie. She and Miles staggered to stand. Lottie ran to her son to hug him. "Little Rob! You're okay!"

Duress

The crowd stared at a fireman who railed and gestured in annoyance. Then he announced above the rumble, "No fire! The kid sent a false alarm. Everybody go home!"

The crowd's demeanor quickly changed. They muttered, "I knew I didn't smell smoke. . . . That boy's trouble. . . . I know what I'd do if my boy did such a thing. . . . Kids today . . . . All we need is a hoodlum in the neighborhood. . . ."

Firemen and policemen trudged to their vehicles. One complained, "I left steaks on my grill." Another said, "I threw down a royal flush and left my chips to come here." A patrolman fussed, "I left my woman. She probably didn't wait for me."

Police Chief Don Jenkins had been at home enjoying a quiet evening. He did not take time to change into his uniform, but rushed to the scene wearing a tight military green T-shirt. His robust chest and arms rippled under the dark shirt. He marched to Miles and Lottie. Rubbing his shaved head, he said, "Your kid signaled the station for immediate fire and police assistance. Dudley and his alarm people should've verified the emergency with you and canceled the alert. Dudley's probably riding horses and having a delightful holiday, unlike the rest of us," said Don cynically. Dismayed, he pursed his lips together.

Embarrassed, Miles apologized. "I'm sorry, Chief. We didn't know Little Rob sent the alarm."

"That's an unacceptable response. Get your boy under control. He's a minor and requires adult supervision. Do I make myself clear? This is the second time you've summoned us on false pretenses. You interrupted firefighters and policemen on a holiday. We had to drop what we were doing and race to your house. We didn't stop and ask questions. We responded swiftly with the intent to save lives and property. Don't let this happen again!" ordered the police chief.

"Next time I'll charge you with abuse of emergency services!" He abruptly turned and left Miles and Lottie humiliated. Bewildered, Little Rob rubbed his ears and asked, "Why's everybody so mad?" He gazed innocently up at his parents with his deep blue-green eyes and batted his long eyelashes.

Miles roughly jostled his son's messy curly head and said, "Buddy boy, you're in serious trouble." Miles looked at Lottie and asked, "And you want more children?"

Chapter 2

Empowered to Escape

*W*est Point was a tight-knit community of folks who supported local Little Leagues, family gatherings, and service clubs. However, forty miles away, the Claxton Mental Home kept this city on edge. An antagonistic workplace, this institution banked a sizable payroll that supported many of the citizens of Claxton.

Adhering to the usual schedule, a nurse came into Rastus Webber's room after lunch to give him a hypnotic barbiturate, phenobarbital, which would produce zombie-like sleepiness. He pocketed the capsule in his cheek, but swallowed the medicine cup of water. The nurse asked, "Did you swallow?"

Rastus replied, "Yes." He thought, *She's the worst nurse.* When she went to flush his toilet, he took the disintegrating, slimy capsule from his mouth and poked it into her plastic foam cup of Diet Coke, which the nurse always drank on her rounds.

He climbed into his bed as if to take a nap. The nurse left Rastus and pushed her medicine cart down the hall to the next room, sipping her drink as she continued her usual routine.

Empowered To Escape

Rastus avoided ingesting his medications at every opportunity because they poisoned his body and clouded his thinking so he could not hear the truth. Life in the mental home was an entanglement of aggravating side effects if he took his drugs, and of intolerable withdrawals when he did not take them.

He got up and opened the metal locker in his room. With uncoordinated tremors, he grappled far back on the top shelf to remove a backpack, which he had stolen from an inattentive employee who thought it was safely stowed. As he packed to leave, Rastus thought, *I go as I please, and nobody sees.*

He opened his door and looked to see if anyone was in the hall. He heard a rhythmic jangle of keys and chains and snapped back into his room as two hefty maintenance men walked down the hall and passed by. Again, he cracked his door and glanced both ways, and then he slipped out. He tiptoed toward the front of the facility, slithering his body close to the walls as if he were invisible.

Unexpectedly, a male aide appeared in the hall, flirting with another worker. Rastus pushed into a patient room, where a resident snored contentedly. Waiting restlessly, Rastus stared through a slight opening at the door and watched the couple turn the corner to go into the breakroom. The staff knew that Rastus had escape on his mind, and they considered Rastus hostile and hyperactive. Facility employees wanted Rastus to stay sedated.

They leave me unguarded. They think I'm retarded, thought Rastus. He could not let the workers catch him in the hall and suffer a humiliating attack. *They'll grab me and stab me with poison.* He paused at the swinging doors that separated the patients from the entrance. Loud laughter erupted from the front office, and a door slammed. Rastus jerked himself flat against the wall, daunted by the closeness of people who could sound an alarm and activate a confrontation.

Seconds later, he surged to the security keypad and pressed the correct numbers to open the locked doors. A rush of euphoria rippled through him as he fled from the mental institution, free again. He could tolerate the daily irritations for this moment of freedom.

With his backpack slung over his shoulder, he sneaked to the nearby subdivision, where he headed to the woods and disappeared into the dense pine trees. He followed a long path to his favorite hiding place: an old beam bridge that spanned a dirt road. It was a quiet place where no one forced him to talk or take pills.

Kudzu draped across the tunnel of the bridge. Rastus pushed aside the vines and climbed up on the rocks. He slung his stringy black hair to one side and let it fall back to cover his half-closed eye. He sat and contemplated the cleverness of his latest escape. A few days earlier, he walked passed the director of nurses' office and saw her purse open on the floor beside her desk. The plan for marking her flashed before his eyes.

He slipped her credit card out of her wallet and went directly to the facility library to place an online order. Afterward, he strolled back to the nurse's office and slid the credit card into her billfold. He joyfully said aloud, "Melinda's the one to be done!" He thought, *My quest is blessed. It's her turn for the burn.*

Then three days ago, the mail carrier delivered his merchandise to the mental home. Rastus had to create a distraction, so he pulled the fire alarm, even though the noise triggered his headache disorder and hammered him with pain. The disturbance worked, and he stole away with his package.

Now, he had to wait below the dim underpass until the time was right to be alone with Melinda. Rastus stared at the mildew and the cobwebs that crept over the ceiling of the bridge. At quiet moments like this, he thought about his dead father, his former schoolmates, and the facility personnel. They ridiculed him because he was different. He hated them all. There was only one girl, Lottie, with whom he had established a connection while growing up.

While squatting under the bridge, he rocked in silence. Then he shouted, "You commoners! You persecuted me! Only Lottie didn't hate me!" He snatched up a loose rock and slung it wildly.

His voice reverberated under the bridge, which brought on a dull headache. He rocked on the rocks and massaged his head. Then, he fumbled for his backpack and opened it. Pushing aside his rope and tape, he took out his woodburning instrument and fondly stroked it. It was an amazing tool; however, obtaining one was more challenging now than in the past.

Away from the facility, Rastus felt empowered to fulfill his destiny. He could hardly endure the monotonous questions and multiple medications . . . medications that harassed him with shakes, runs, and dizziness—medications that turned his skin gray and left him drooling and smacking.

Rastus believed that the people in the institution purposefully humiliated him and treated him like a mangy dog. *I hate them! They tell me I smell. Let them laugh at me. I won't mark them for eternity.*

He loosely rhymed his words, even in his thoughts. Rastus believed his poetry was an intellectual gift. His physician postulated that his poetic affinity flowed from his schizophrenia, a diagnosis that urged freedom of expression and exempted him from responsibility.

He believed that Melinda, the newest director of nursing, deserved the mark. She always smiled at him, asked how he was doing, and didn't seem to mind his company when he showed up at her office. She spoke kindly to him, unlike the other nurses. Rastus was anxious to seal Melinda with the mark, but he knew he would have to wait until she went home at five o'clock. He fantasized looping a strand of rope around her wrists and tying the rope to her left thigh with her left inner wrist exposed.

As Rastus continued to wait for his time to leave, his thoughts scattered to the fateful moment that his doctor repetitiously called the beginning point of his problems: the day his father got rid of his mother. During therapy sessions, Rastus's psychiatrist insisted that he regurgitate this past event to help him overcome his emotional pain. Repeating what happened never brought peace or relief to Rastus.

He shook Mama and pushed Mama. He hit Mama with all his might in a fight. Ripped from his mother, Rastus was left to find his way in life under the control of a cruel father.

Every day my father said to me, "I'll dump you in a pit and cover you with dirt." I hate him! I wasn't even his kid. He got rid of Mama.

During his school years, Rastus latched on to two allies, who provided havens away from his father. His first solace was Lottie, who expected nothing but his friendship and overlooked his disruptive tendencies. The second refuge was the local library, where he spent hours on the computer or in the books, until the librarian told him to leave.

Life was unfair and meaningless to Rastus until one night in the library. When he was reading about the Nephilim in the Holy Bible, something extraordinary happened that changed his life. A voice in a radiant light whispered his true heritage and told him that he was a descendant of the Nephilim. Rastus eagerly read about the Nephilim, the remarkable beings that came to earth to cohabit with humans.

No one believed him, but he found the evidence in Genesis chapter 6. The Nephilim were people of vast size and strength who fell out of heaven's favor because they saw beautiful women on earth and married whomever they chose. The Bible calls them "heroes of old, men of renown." Heroes of old, men of renown.

Rastus believed that the almighty God sent the great flood to destroy every living creature on the earth because He was angry with the Nephilim. However, the Nephilim left their earthly wives and rose back into the celestial heavens. They contended with humans as they wished through visions and earthly encounters, and appointed Rastus to go and save those of worth. Commoners dismissed the presence of these marvelous beings as mythological, but Rastus knew the truth.

Chapter 3

Mark the Mortal

*R*astus had told his physician some of his past, but there were secrets he could not tell Dr. Affle. Rastus believed he must carefully plan which private matters to reveal to his doctor. As an adolescent, Rastus discovered that when he explained his purpose to other kids, they ridiculed and insulted him more. Only Lottie did not criticize him.

He regretted telling his father that he was not his son because afterward, his raging father would wait until Rastus was sound asleep at night on his mattress and wildly strike his son with a stick.

Rastus's paranoia led him to believe that if he divulged confidential things to Dr. Affle, his doctor would interrupt his divinely appointed getaways and tell a nurse to plunge a needle of poison into his body.

As Rastus reflected on his past, an isolated afternoon thunderstorm rolled darkly across the sky and shook the ground with strikes of lightning and blasts of thunder. Rastus was elated. *It's a sign!* After the storm passed, he re-packed his tool in his backpack and walked toward town.

On the shoulder of the road, he picked up a broken soda bottle with razor-like edges. Intrigued by the irregular sharp spires, he held it in the sun to admire the rays shining through. "I like it. I'll pack it and take it back." He opened his pack, pulled out T-shirt strips, carefully wrapped the spiked-glass remnant, and placed it in his bag.

He walked to Melinda's apartment complex, which was less than a mile from the bridge. She was a diabetic, obese nurse with heart problems who lived alone in apartment 6A. Rastus lightly tapped on her door and heard no response. He knocked again. Anticipation stirred emotions inside him. He knocked harder.

"I just got here! Door's open! Come in!" she yelled from her kitchen. "Is that you, Debbie? I'm looking for something to eat. You want to go eat supper with me?" She closed the refrigerator door and looked toward the entrance threshold, expecting to see her friend. She gasped.

"Rastus! Why are you here? How do you know where I live?"

He rushed to Melinda, who stood in her nursing scrubs with her mouth gaped. Rastus said with excitement, "It's not time to dine. Zeus sent me lightning as a sign that it's time. It's time for me to bind you and mark you."

"What are you talking about?" asked Melinda, who was hired three months earlier. She never felt threatened by the mental home patients since they were heavily tranquilized. Melinda always smiled at Rastus when they passed in the halls, saying her customary, "Hello. How are you?" She tolerated his bothersome surprise visits, but typically, she avoided him.

Out of the facility, Rastus appeared frightening. Strings of greasy hair flopped across one drooping eye, and his slobbery tongue involuntarily thrust in and out like a snake.

"I can't believe the things they say you do to people," whined the nurse. "How did you get out of the facility? They'll be in lockdown looking for you!" she said.

"Don't you see? I'm here to be near, my dear."

Melinda rolled her eyes and snubbed her nose. "Don't be ridiculous."

Rastus half closed his eyes at Melinda, sensing her disdain. "I can see in your eyes, you despise me," said Rastus, tensing his fists and floating his stiff arms upward.

Rastus's strangeness troubled Melinda. She rapidly spoke, "You shouldn't be here, Rastus. You don't have permission to be out of the institution. This isn't an approved outing. I can't allow you to stay." She resolved to control the situation and to dismiss her anxiety and his foolish talk.

"I say how long I stay," said Rastus, grating his teeth at her rejection. "I thought I'd find you to be kind."

Raising her voice, the nurse said, "I'll drive you back to the facility now." With quivering hands, she picked up her car keys and purse.

"I can't go back yet—until you let me do my part and burn on the mark." He lunged at Melinda's upper arms and dug his long fingernails into her biceps. She dropped her purse and keys and screamed. Rastus screamed. Her shrill screech shot pain to his head.

"Take your hands off me!" she shouted. They were face to face. He smelled like sewage and drooled. He refused to release his deep grasp on her upper arms. Melinda crumpled and moaned, "Stop, Rastus. You're hurting me. You're scaring me. I have a bad heart!"

Rastus narrowed his eyes and wrinkled his mouth at her. He reluctantly released his hold and cradled his head with his hands to ease his headache.

Melinda rubbed the fingernail slits on her arms in disbelief. "You freak!"

He looked up and closed his eyes. "I've come to the one you said to come to. Use your might to strike her with lightning! Silence her! Evil upheaval!"

The nurse felt uneasy but asserted her supervisory role. "Rastus, we have to go to the facility. They're looking for you. Follow me to my car." She picked up her keys and purse off the floor and grabbed a garbage bag to put on the seat of her car for Rastus to sit on. She walked shakily toward the door, glancing over her shoulder to see if he was following her.

"Don't reject the sign. Now is the time." Rastus raised his head and looked up. "Should I burn her with the mark and save her from eternal dark? No? Yes? I know it's so. I'll never refuse the great Zeus!"

Perplexed, Melinda asked, "What are you talking about?"

Rastus opened his backpack, pulled out ropes and duct tape, and laid them neatly on the floor beside a chair.

Melinda was startled. "Where did you get that stuff? What do you think you're doing? Don't touch me again."

"Shut your mouth, you ungrateful snake! You want to hurt me? I'll hurt you instead. Pain passes fast!" He shoved her backward, and she tripped to the floor. In shock, she gulped for air and strained to push herself up with her fleshy arms. Melinda was terrified. She didn't care if Rastus got back to the mental home or not; she just wanted to get away.

"Get up," Rastus ordered her. He pinched her arms where he had pierced her with his fingernails and pulled her. She yelled, "Stop, you insane idiot!"

"Shut your mouth, you betrayer! Sit in this chair! You dare refuse me, too?"

Melinda stammered to reason with Rastus. She wanted to regain control. "I . . . you . . . uh . . . I care about your well-being. It's . . . it's important that we return to the facility. What do you want? I can't help you unless I know what you're thinking." She wanted to stall Rastus for time to decide what to do.

"You liar!" Rastus pushed her into a chair, got in her face, and shouted, "Sit still!" She felt paralyzed looking into his wild eyes. Melinda trembled as he tied her to the chair. He wrapped the rope around her wrists, but she resisted.

Duress

However, he twisted one of her arms and pulled her hair to subdue her. "Help! Help me! Somebody help me! Help! Aaaahhh!" she screamed. "Help! Help!"

Rastus found a scrap of dirty T-shirt in his backpack and stuffed it into her mouth. Struggling to maintain control, he ripped off a small strip of duct tape and slapped it on her lips. He shook his arms tensely, passed the free strands of rope through a loop, and tied her hands to her left thigh, with her left palm facing up. He plugged his wood-burning tool into an electrical outlet to let the temperature surge.

She thrashed about in the chair and bounced the legs. Rastus laid his instrument down on the floor beside her and shook her shoulders. He spewed words into her face. "You, you! Stop what you do! Be still. No pill for you!" Her bold insolence and outright rejection enraged him. People previously selected for this elite ritual physically and psychologically froze and submitted to him. They did not fight back.

Melinda's heart pounded. Her body emptied sweat through every pore. Rastus picked up his electrical tool and meticulously applied the rounded heated point to burn dots on Melinda's arm. She moaned in agony as the metal seared her arm and released the odor of burning flesh. Dizziness and nausea weakened her momentarily. Rastus changed the tip to a cone point. He intently drew lines on her arm. Melinda rocked violently in her chair. Her jaws hurt. The filthy rag in her mouth sickened her, but no vomit could escape even with the tape loosely in place. She futilely pushed the T-shirt wad with her tongue to force it out, but the poorly affixed duct tape held.

With his free hand, Rastus shook Melinda's shoulder. "You, you! Stop what you do!" Her excessive movement in the chair perturbed Rastus, but he was determined to finish. He carefully applied the scorching metal point to her arm. In a panic, Melinda rallied all of her strength to thrust her tied-up body at Rastus to make him stop; however, her powerful lunge forced the burning point deeper through the layers of her skin. In a reflex motion, her body jerked back, and Rastus's hand and the tool flew toward her face. The fiery tip struck her left eyelid and burned through.

The agony to her eye was secondary to the ominous tight squeeze in her chest and the erratic ripple up her throat. She felt a gallop inside her chest, followed by a painful contraction. Her head flew backward as she gasped for air. Her stuffed mouth strained to stretch open under the small loose square of duct tape.

"Finished! She's saved from hades!" Rastus sighed in relief that his work was over. "Her noncooperation ruined my constellation."

She stopped moaning and resisting. "Finally, the beast ceased whining," said Rastus aloud. He did not realize Melinda had suffered a fatal heart attack.

Chapter 4

Prosecute the Psychopath

A few days later, Dr. Affle, the medical director of the mental home, pushed his way into the office of the Claxton police chief, Mike Cantile, and accused him: "You stepped over the line! You mistreated a mentally disabled ward of a certified state mental home."

Mike Cantile stood and said, "What about the victims that he mistreated? He has assaulted innocent people, and the laws *do* apply to him! Webber stalked that nurse in your facility and, due to your negligence, escaped. He's a disturbed psychopath. Webber's responsible for her death."

"Police Chief Cantile," began Dr. Affle calmly. "Rastus is a delusional, paranoid schizophrenic with a neurotic personality disorder. He also suffers severe headaches from noise anxiety, which your men ignored, which exacerbated his mental distress. I cannot talk to you any longer. I have an important meeting at the courthouse. Here's a signed document that authorizes temporary release of Rastus to me for medical supervision and treatment."

Mike snatched the paper and read it. He stroked the short, stubby hair on the side of his balding head, visibly frustrated at the forced release of Rastus Webber. "He's going to the pen this time," said Mike. "I have evidence to prove he committed a sociopathic crime."

Ignoring the police chief's threats, Dr. Affle smoothed his hand over his graying head of long hair, which ended in a wavy ponytail. "My patient's cognitive stability has been compromised in your ill-equipped jail. I must expeditiously reassess him and recommence his chemical restraint medications and mood stabilizers to diminish his atypical behavior. Without his carefully prescribed medications, he goes at manic pace. I'll wait at the door for my patient."

As the police chief walked out the door of his office, he said under his breath, "Psycho-nonsense."

Dr. Affle went outside to get a wheelchair and Baron, the certified nursing assistant who was assigned to care for Rastus. An oncoming commotion erupted as Rastus gravitated toward Dr. Affle with two jailers on either side. Rastus shoved and pushed the old men escorting him. He wrestled one man to the floor in a gnashing reckless frenzy. The little man wailed in fright, "Oh, God, help me! Don't send me to hell! I'll stop drinkin'! I'll stop smokin'!"

Baron, the stout certified nursing assistant hired specifically to care for Rastus, locked one arm under Rastus's rib cage, grabbed his hair, and pulled his head back. Dr. Affle swiftly injected his patient with a highly potent sedative. Baron held Rastus until the drug eased his mania.

The spooked jailers scrambled toward the holding cells, grimacing and staring over their shoulders.

As Baron pushed Rastus to the van in the wheelchair, the Claxton police chief yelled to Dr. Affle, "He didn't sneak in and out of my jail like he did your institution!" After the aide and the psychiatrist restrained Rastus, they locked his wheelchair in the facility van and drove away.

"Baron, I'll have to let you and Rastus out as soon as we get to the home," said Dr. Affle. "I have to meet with the judge." At the mental institution, Baron unloaded Rastus and rolled him up the wheelchair ramp and through the large glass door entrance.

Dr. Affle sped away to his meeting with the prosecutor and the judge. Although a small-statured man, the psychiatrist's arrogance invigorated him to ascend the marble stairs of the courthouse and rush up the winding wooden staircase to the court area as if he were an athletic giant. The psychiatrist knocked on the door to the judge's chamber. "Come in," replied the judge.

"Greetings, Your Honor. My attorney is unavoidably delayed due to a family emergency. I'm here in his place." The judge nodded. Dr. Affle extended his hand to the young assistant prosecutor, who said, "Good afternoon, Dr. Affle. My name is . . . ."

Before the prosecutor could introduce himself, Dr. Affle interrupted. "My name is Dr. Affle. You say waffle and drop the 'w' for the correct pronunciation." He turned to the judge and to flatter him said, "My client and I appreciate your granting us this meeting before the preliminary hearing. Your sense of justice and knowledge of the law is unequaled.

"As you know," continued the doctor, "the prosecution has filed a criminal complaint against my patient. My lawyer has exchanged information with the prosecutor's office that counters their evidence."

The prosecutor stated, "Your Honor, my office has studied the criminal implications and believes that the charge should rightly be downgraded from murder to manslaughter."

"Judge Strickland, if I may, let me be the first to dutifully save the county the expense, trouble, and embarrassment of taking this case before a grand jury and to trial," said Dr. Affle. "I request a motion to dismiss the charges because the case doesn't have a legally sound basis."

"I object, Your Honor!" blurted the prosecutor. "The Claxton police arrested Webber the night of the murder and detained him properly."

"They used excessive force, and we will show evidence of injuries my patient sustained the evening of the casualty," affirmed Dr. Affle. "One policeman, pretending to be a master in karate, kicked my patient's hand with excessive aggression to dislodge a tool that Rastus held and fractured a bone in my patient's hand."

"Law enforcement uses as much force as is necessary to bring a combative criminal under control," argued the prosecutor.

Dr. Affle rebutted, "Witnesses will testify they saw police misconduct the night of the incident. An officer was seen on top of my unarmed patient, roughly handcuffing and wrestling him. The other policeman was yelling, 'Taze him! Taze him!' My patient suffers from situational psychosis, which will evoke sympathy from a jury, especially after they hear the unprofessional, prejudicial slur from the lips of a policeman, calling my patient a 'monkey nut.' Moreover, we can show that the police are guilty of denying proper medical care."

"That's not true," disagreed the prosecutor. "The policemen called for an ambulance to safely transport Webber to the hospital."

"I'm talking about the nurse. The police officers decided for themselves that she was dead and called for the coroner. They did not untie her and administer CPR, as police policy says they should do. They left her tied up and hanging by ropes in a chair, assuming she was dead."

"I have an expert witness that will testify that Webber is a psychopath and deserves to be incarcerated for killing that nurse," asserted the prosecutor.

Dr. Affle argued, "I have numerous expert witnesses who will prove that Rastus is afflicted by mental disability, schizophrenia, and noise-induced anxiety headache. The court cannot prosecute him due to his disturbed mental perception. He doesn't know the difference between right and wrong.

"Furthermore, we will subpoena the medical records of the nurse to prove that her preexisting medical condition precipitated her ill-fated demise. The death of the woman was inevitable because she was extremely high-risk for a heart attack. Statistically speaking, she was due to die any day."

"Your Honor," protested the prosecutor. "The accused felon in this case has a history of executing planned assaults on innocent victims that cannot be ignored or go unpunished."

"Judge Strickland, let me explain," said Dr. Affle. "My patient is in treatment for his psychological and antisocial impairment. He must be protected from manipulation and abuse of the legal system."

"Your legal shenanigans are improper," stated the prosecutor. Turning to the judge, who remained pensive, he said, "Your Honor, I object to the irrelevant evidence that he proposes to introduce at trial. I can win a conviction of manslaughter. I can prove Webber's guilty beyond a reasonable doubt."

The judge rubbed his forehead and closed his eyes. Then he spoke. "The inevitable inconsistencies and contradictions in this case will pervert justice and result in a legal fiasco. There's an undeniable risk for a mistrial. I rule to accept the motion to dismiss the charges. Case dismissed."

Chapter 5

Security Blunder

*N*ot far away in the small town of West Point, Lottie Arnold and four girlfriends got together and tried to prod their former high school class president or vice president into coordinating their class reunion. However, the former class officers lived far away and weren't interested.

The girls decided that they could plan the reunion and voted Lottie as chairwoman. They agreed to do whatever she told them to do. They set the date for the Saturday before Labor Day because many people returned home that weekend to visit family and to attend the community Prairie Arts Festival.

To simplify the reunion project, Lottie assigned tasks to each committee member, appropriate to their individual dispositions. For example, Mary Cecil was nosy in high school and relished her assignment to fearlessly search for the whereabouts of everybody. The graciousness of Trudy made her the perfect hospitality chairwoman. A natural party girl, Lucy, was assigned food and entertainment responsibilities. Katherine was the class secretary-treasurer in high school, so she retained that position for the committee.

On this hot morning in June, Lottie sat in her office above the garage and studied the roster of classmates, for which Mary Cecil had tirelessly snooped. Lottie was bored entering names and addresses into her computer. She was tired of waiting on her best friend, Lucy, to show up and help as she had promised. Lucy would provide little assistance, but her lively camaraderie would make time fly and dissolve Lottie's fatigue.

Exasperated, Lottie thought, *Why did I agree to be chairman of the high school reunion? Will I have to do everything for everybody? Lucy Jenkins and I made a deal: She promised to help me get these letters ready if I would go to that ridiculous self-defense class that her police chief husband taught last week.*

Lottie leaned back in her old chair and blankly stared at the address labels lagging out of the printer. *Don told us, "Don't worry about getting hurt during self-defense." What a joke. I'm still sore from Lucy's shin kicks and knuckle strikes.*

In a daze, Lottie folded the letters and registration forms and stuffed them into envelopes. A paper cut jolted her attention back to her monotonous job. *Where's Lucy? Probably getting her hair highlighted or a manicure. I've written the reunion letter and printed all these labels by myself. I'm the chairwoman. I should've delegated this chore to Katherine. She sits at her computer all day in the library, and she could've finished the notices and walked them across the street to the post office this morning. I'll let Katherine handle all communication after today. Why did I agree to be chairwoman of this committee?*

The sound of sirens in the distance interrupted Lottie's lamentation. *Hmm. I hope there's no problem in our neighborhood.* The emergency sirens grew louder and closer. Lottie took an elastic band off her wrist to wrap around her long hair.

Below Lottie's home office at the bottom of the stairs, her rambunctious five-year-old son had climbed on his red stool and had crawled his fingers up to the alarm keypad. Happy to amuse himself, he punched the fire and policeman pictures with his index fingers and chanted, "Fie-uh, cop, cop! Fie-uh, cop, cop!"

Police cars and a fire truck raced up the hill to the two-story white house that serenely stood with hanging ferns and rocking chairs across the front porch.

Lottie looked out the window. "Oh, no! Not again!" She dashed out of the little study and down the stairs and saw her son perched on his stool, pressing the alarm touch screen.

Lottie screamed, "Stop it! Now!"

Little Rob jumped and crashed the stool into the door. He muttered, "I got to hide! I got to hide!" and ran around the corner.

Frantically, Lottie keyed in the code to disarm the flashing alarm. She kicked away the stool, rushed out into the hot garage, and slapped the door opener. Sweat trickled down her neck as she waited on the garage door panels to slowly rise. Although she dreaded what she would encounter, she stooped to rush out and then abruptly stopped. Flashing red and blue lights clicked quietly. Fully equipped firemen and somber policemen suspiciously squinted their eyes and pursed their lips at Lottie.

Oh, no! This can't be happening again! Lottie's face flushed. She felt sick.

Chief of Police Don Jenkins, dressed in a starched shirt with shoulder patches and a shiny badge, marched toward Lottie, crunching the driveway with his thick-soled boots.

"Oh, Don. I'm so sorry."

"Hello, Lottie," said the police chief as he wiped perspiration off his face and neck. Then he neatly folded the white handkerchief and returned it to his back pocket. He rhetorically asked, "Is there a problem here?"

"Oh, no. Little Rob accidentally set off the alarm. I . . . ."

Grievously annoyed, Don interrupted, "This is the third time Little Rob accidentally set off the alarm." We can't spare time or manpower for bogus emergency signals. I'm charging you with repeated false alerts."

The West Point police chief, his men, and the firemen were aggravated over a pointless run to Lottie's house. She dropped her head and burned with embarrassment. Perturbed, Don retained his frown.

Miles Arnold jerked his large pickup truck to a stop at the bottom of his blocked driveway. He jumped out and sprinted toward Lottie. "Is everybody all right? The security company called and said there's an emergency!"

"Miles, your son set off the emergency signal *again*," said the police chief. "We responded immediately with the intent to save lives and property. A security system safeguards innocent people, but it's not a toy."

"My son can't reach the keypad and punch in the code! Are you sure Little Rob set off the alarm?" asked Miles.

The police chief ignored his question. "Miles, I'm glad there's no fire or other danger. But we don't have time for prank calls. It's your responsibility to provide adult supervision for a minor. Do I make myself clear? I'm arresting you both for repeated false alerts and abuse of emergency services. Can you make arrangements for your boy, or do I need to call Child Services? Your son will grow up knowing that his parents were jailed for his foolishness." Don slapped his hands on his hips and stood with outstretched legs.

Chapter 6

It's Her Fault

"*P*lease don't file charges," begged Lottie. "We'll never let this happen again."

"I apologize for the inconvenience," said Miles. "My son will never touch the alarm again. I'm asking you as a special favor to not charge us. It was an honest mistake." Don glared at Miles and Lottie and shook his head.

Then Miles looked at Lottie to blame her. "I can't run a business if I have to run home all the time to check on you and Little Rob. And now, I have to hire a lawyer, which we can't afford, to get us out of this mess because you can't keep our son out of mischief."

Irritated at her husband, Lottie snaked her head from side to side and said, "I *do* keep Little Rob 'out of mischief.' You're not the only one with deadlines and work to do."

"I've had to lay off people from work, which means I have to fill in when we're short-handed, like today. You need to hire a sitter or put Little Rob in day care if you can't watch him at home."

"Uuugh!" Lottie shifted her head at Miles. His criticism distressed her. "I stay at home to take care of our son because I don't want to be too busy like my mother was, or leave him at home by himself like my sister does with her children. I was here, taking care of Little Rob. While I worked on the reunion letters, he watched one of his favorite movies."

Don widened his eyes and sighed at the petty bickering between Miles and Lottie. "Excuse me . . .," Don started.

But Miles continued to scold Lottie. "You can't leave a five-year-old unattended. You have to be more responsible!"

"Don't call me irresponsible!" refuted Lottie.

"None of this would have happened if you had canceled the alarm. Why didn't you stop the alarm when you heard it?"

"Little Rob and I didn't hear anything." Lottie stretched her neck and said, "It was *your* idea to change to a silent alarm. Don't you remember?"

"I don't remember that." When making a decision, Miles identified a quick remedy with no thought for secondary consequences.

Lottie huffed a full-throated sigh, "Huhh! You asked Dudley to switch us to a silent alarm because *you said* you were afraid Little Rob would hide if he's scared, and we wouldn't be able to find him."

"I can't believe we changed to a silent alarm. That makes no sense. What was I thinking?"

"Ah-hem," coughed Don to get their attention. "Ah-hem!"

Without heeding the chief, Miles riveted Lottie one more time. "You should've been watching our son. Now, we've got problems because of *you*."

His repeated reproach incensed Lottie. She bobbed her head sideways and put her hands on her waist. "I'm tired of this. I don't want to talk about the alarm anymore."

Vexed at their verbal sparring, Don approached them indignantly and said, "The boy is a minor. I'm giving you one last chance to discipline your boy and get him under control. Don't let this happen again! Now, if you good folks will excuse us, we have to get back to the station."

With an about-face, he turned sharply. "Let's go, men!" Under his breath, he said, "Maybell was right; she told me this was a false alarm."

All of the vehicles backed down the driveway one by one and left.

Provoked by her husband's reprimand, Lottie wanted to justify herself. "How dare you talk to me like that! I'm chairwoman of my class reunion, which takes place in three months!" Miles absently ignored Lottie. Sticky sweat dripped under his arms. He walked through the garage and into the air-conditioned house to get out of the heat. Lottie followed. At the corner of the hall, Little Rob timidly stuck out the toes of one bare foot.

"Robinson Miles Arnold, don't you dare run away! Don't you dare play with that alarm again! Do you hear me? The chief of police, the fire department, and your daddy left their work to come here because of you!"

"That's enough, Lottie. He's only a little boy. Hey, Buddy, come see your daddy." Miles delighted in his son.

Little Rob ran to his dad's open arms. Miles lifted him high to touch the ceiling. On his way down, he bumped his daddy's forehead in fun. Miles set Little Rob down and began his ritualistic game. Miles put his hands out with palms up for Little Rob to slap before Miles withdrew his hands. He let Little Rob smack his hand, and then, in turn, the boy timidly extended his hands for his dad to slap. Miles tapped one of Little Rob's hands and cackled, "Gotcha!" Then Miles poked his son's chin and stomach to prompt jerks and giggles.

Frustrated, Lottie said to Miles, "I can't stand how you talked to me. I'm trying to be a good mother and the best committee chairwoman I can be. I didn't know Little Rob had sent an alarm. I didn't hear it. I was printing reunion letters and address labels, and stuffing envelopes. I wish I'd never agreed to be chairwoman. Somebody more qualified, with more time than I have, should've spearheaded this event."

Miles realized his insensitivity to his wife. He switched his attention to Lottie and apologized. "I'm sorry, Lottie Love. I shouldn't have been so harsh. I guess I was looking for someone to blame. I've been under stress at work. I'm short of help and was in the middle of a big order with a new customer when the security company called about this emergency. I shouldn't have talked to you like that in front of the police chief. I'm sorry. Okay?" He pecked her lips and smiled.

"Okay. Well, don't say things like, 'You have to be more responsible.' My mother and my older sister called me 'irresponsible' all the time when I was growing up, which bothered me."

Miles put his arms around Lottie and hugged her. "I know the reunion is important to you. It's in good hands with you in charge."

"Thanks, Miles."

Anxious to resolve the alarm dilemma, Miles said, "We should disconnect the alarm. We don't need a security system here in West Point. And the next time, the police chief *will* press charges against us. Then, we'll be the talk of the town, which could hurt my business."

"You're right," Lottie agreed. "We never have burglars. We're wasting our money. Will you ask Dudley to discon nect it?"

"Yes," said Miles. "I'll call him this afternoon and cancel it."

Lottie remembered her reunion duties and said, "It's such a short time until my class reunion. I'm getting the letters ready to mail by myself since Lucy didn't show up to help."

"Sounds like Lucy is the irresponsible one. Don't worry. I'm sure you'll plan the best reunion ever held in West Point." Miles patted her shoulders.

Miles held his son's hand and walked toward the door. "Well, Buddy, I've got to go back to work." Lottie and Little Rob paused at the door to tell Miles good-bye. The calm moment was interrupted by a deafening roar and a cannonball blast.

Chapter 7

Duress Extraordinaire

*L*ittle Rob jumped when he heard the boom, and his daddy picked him up again. "What was that?" Miles asked as he smacked heads with his son.

Lottie looked out the door. "Oh, it's Dudley. You can tell him *now* to disconnect the house alarm."

"Sounds like he's still driving that piece of junk," said Miles.

She leaned outside and watched the lanky young man get out of his dented red van and plop his cowboy hat on his head. Lottie yelled, "Hi, Dudley. Come inside out of the heat!"

Dudley Stevens of Stevens Security Systems trudged to the door. He looked like an Old West cowboy with his handlebar mustache, thin body, and bowlegs. Wearing a red bandana, he scuffed his boots on the sidewalk and seesawed his shoulders up and down with each step. Dudley was an honest, hardworking fellow who worked for his successful father.

Miles let his son down and walked outside to shake Dudley's hand. Miles liked Dudley, and he liked to nickname people. He called his wife "Lottie Love" and his son

"Buddy." His pet name for Dudley was "Dud." "Get that van tuned up, Dud, or better yet, tell your father to buy you a new one. I thought I'd been shot when you drove up."

"Yes sir, Mr. Arnold. My van needs an adjustment or two. I got all my stuff in special places in that van. I don't need no new one," said Dudley in his country drawl. He stopped and turned his head to spit in the yard.

Miles shook his head and raised his eyebrows. He continued to tease Dudley. "Dud, you're late. The fire was put out, and the burglars, put in jail while you were riding horses."

"Okay. Okay. Very funny," said Dudley, ashamed that he had not come out at the same time as the police and firefighters. He did not like people commotion and decided to wait a mile down the road until he saw the firefighters and police officers coming back to town. He was afraid the alarm might be false.

Deep wrinkles fanned from his eyes to his hairline. He rotated his shoulders back and stood straight. "Yes sir, down at Central Monitoring, Deb said that direct alarms was sent to the police and fire departments. They should've known that a house owner calls for one or the other, not both at the same time. Hmmp. I suppose if your house was on fire and all the neighbors came to gawk, then you'd need police for crowd control. Well, in a big city, maybe, but not here in West Point. Yes sir. Deb's supposed to call and ask, 'Is this a real emergency?' and then ask for your password."

"Nobody called me, Dudley. I feel terrible. Little Rob set off the alarm while I was upstairs on my computer. I didn't know the alarm was sent."

"Uh, I don't know why Deb didn't check with you first, like she's supposed to do," lamented Dudley.

Miles guided Dudley down the hallway. "Listen, Dud, I need to talk to you. Lottie and I decided that we don't need a security system. And since you're already here, we want you to disconnect it. We want to terminate our alarm services."

"Terminate?" choked Dudley. "Ter-ter-terminate ser-ser-services?"

Dudley fumbled to untie his bandana to wipe the sweat that popped out on his throat and forehead. He struggled to not break down. Rejected and embarrassed, he managed to say, "Oh, Oh. Okay. Okay, Mr. Arnold. That's a serious matter. Real serious." Dudley's face flamed, and he thought he better say something to change Miles's mind.

"I'd feel real bad if you had a fi-fire or some robber br-break into your house while you was out of town or while your ki-kid and the missus was here alone." Dudley was worried about losing a customer, but more apprehensive about what his father would say. He nervously rubbed his neck and throat.

Miles perceived that Dudley was sweating over the loss of a client. Since Miles was in business for himself, he understood the importance of maintaining clientele. He remembered that Dudley and his father generously charged supplies at his store every month. Miles smoothed his soft mustache and beard with his fingers and reconsidered. "Let me see . . . All right, Dud. Never mind. We'll keep the alarm. Don't disconnect it."

Lottie cocked her head at Miles and whispered, "What?" as she heard her husband back down on his declaration to cancel the alarm.

"Thank you. Thank you, Mr. Arnold," said Dudley. Relieved that his father wouldn't lose the account, he continued to dab his face and neck with his bandana and to breathe short, shallow breaths. Dudley was anxious to get back to work and forget about Miles's request to end security services with his father's company.

Irritated with her husband, Lottie complained, "We can't hear a silent alarm. What good is it?"

Duress Extraordinaire

"Uh, Mrs. Arnold, you didn't hear no alarm because Mr. Arnold asked me to make your alarm silent, which ain't much alarm, if you ask me."

Lottie looked at Miles and agreed loudly with Dudley, "Uh huh!"

"Most people want loud sirens and beeps to scare a thief into runnin' for the hills," explained Dudley.

"All right, Dud. You made your point," said Miles. "I want an intruder to 'run for the hills.'"

"Yes sir, Mr. Arnold. I can change your control panel to activate an au-di-ble alarm. To dee-activate the alarm, go to the keypad, and enter your four-number security code, and then press 'off.'" Explaining technicalities gave Dudley a sense of pride. He enjoyed the minimal stress of his job. Many people subscribed to his father's business, even though burglaries were rare. Stevens Security Systems responded most often to accidental alarms.

"Now Dudley, let me be sure I understand," said Lottie. "After you fix the alarm, I can push the police or fire picture, and the alarm will sound loudly?"

"Yes ma'am. You'll hear it blarin' loud. Then you got fifteen seconds to enter your four-digit security code numbers and press 'off,' if it's a false alarm. If you don't do nothin', then a signal's sent to the police or the fire station, and, of course, to Central Monitoring. Anytime your alarm makes a racket, Deb at Central Monitoring will be callin' to see if everything's okay and ask for your password."

"All right, Dud; do it!" said Miles. "Change the alarm to roar." He picked up his son and said, "Now listen, Buddy. If the alarm goes off, you find Mommy or Daddy and help us get out. All right? And you better not ever touch the alarm keypad again. Do you understand?"

"Yessur," said Little Rob.

Dudley hesitated to add, "Uh, you're gonna still have the silent 'duress' alarm."

Duress

"What's that?" asked Miles.

"I saw the 'duress' description in the booklet you gave us when you installed the alarm system, but I never understood it," said Lottie.

"Uh, yes ma'am, Mrs. Arnold. It's never used, but it's an added feature found in all up-to-date systems. If a trespasser comes in your home, you enter the 'duress' code to leave the impression that the alarm's off. But in actuality, a 'duress' code triggers a silent panic message to Central Monitoring, the police station, and to my little black box. That means to 'call out the cavalry!' There's a hostage situation!"

"You're right, Dudley. We'll never need that code, not here in West Point," said Lottie.

"Uh, yes ma'am, but you need to know how it works. Okay. Okay. I'm not supposed to ask, but tell me your security code number."

"It's four, six, four, six," said Lottie.

"Okay. Okay. You add one to the last number of the code. Your last number is six. One plus six is seven. You punch in four, six, four, seven; that sends a silent emergency signal that you're a hostage or that an intruder has you under duress. None of the sirens will sound." Dudley was titillated as he explained the advanced "duress" code.

Miles was unimpressed and said, "It's so nice that we have that feature, but I have to get back to my business so I can pay Stevens Security Systems for its services."

"Uh, no sir. There ain't no extra charge for this."

"Thanks, Dud," said Miles as he set his son down and rubbed his head. "See you later, Buddy. See you at supper, Lottie Love." He lightly kissed her lips, pressed her breast to his chest, and walked out.

Lottie felt time pressure to get the reunion letters mailed. "Little Rob, you can look at Dudley do his work, or watch your movie. We'll go to the post office as soon as I get the addresses on the reunion invitations." Lottie hurried upstairs.

Duress Extraordinaire

Dudley went outside to his van and put on his tool belt. Little Rob inquisitively observed the cowboy bring in his paraphernalia. Dudley dragged his boots on the ceramic tile floor and stopped to hang his cowboy hat on a kitchen chair. Little Rob followed him back and forth from the master control panel in the kitchen closet to the alarm keypad by the door.

"Are you a cowboy?" asked Little Rob.

"No, kid. Leave me alone so I can do my work."

"You look like a cowboy," persisted Little Rob.

"Yeah, well, I'm not. I can't make a living around here being a cowboy. Don't you have something else to do?" asked Dudley.

Lottie walked into the kitchen with the box of class reunion notices and looked for Dudley and Little Rob. They were both in the kitchen closet, where Little Rob tinkered with Dudley's tools on his belt and pretended to fix the master control box along with Dudley.

"Dudley, how are your parents this summer? I haven't seen them in weeks," said Lottie.

"They went on a cruise and left me in charge." Dudley shook his head and puttered on the control box.

"Too bad you couldn't go with them. I'm sure they're enjoying their vacation."

"I don't care nothin' about going nowhere on a big boat."

"I wish Miles and I could go on a vacation. His building supply business ties him down. We never leave West Point," said Lottie. "Dudley, could Little Rob stay here with you and watch you work while I go to the post office? I'll be back in less than fifteen minutes."

Dudley looked at Little Rob. The boy grinned and put on Dudley's cowboy hat, which covered his eyes. Dudley pulled his chin to his chest and stammered, "Uh, uh. Yes ma'am. Uh, uh, I mean, no ma'am. He better not stay with me. I'm almost through. Central Monitoring might call me with an emergency."

"That's all right, Dudley," laughed Lottie.

"Little Rob, you and I will go to town. Let's put on your shoes." They sat on the kitchen floor, and Lottie put her son's socks and tennis shoes on his bare feet.

"Dudley, if you finish your work before I get back, will you lock the door when you leave? Don't worry about setting the alarm. I'll be back soon."

"Yes ma'am."

Lottie drove to the post office, which was on the corner directly across from the police station. She wanted to mail the reunion notices quickly, before a policeman or fireman recognized her. "Come on, Little Rob. Let's hurry inside before anyone spots us." She lowered her head and scooted Little Rob into the post office. They mailed the letters and rushed back to the car. She glanced across the street toward the police department parking lot and saw someone flapping his or her arms at her.

Chapter 8

Don't Invite Rastus

The sight of someone fervently shaking his or her hands in the police station parking lot aroused shameful feelings in Lottie. She squinted to see who was there. "Oh, it's Lucy," sighed Lottie in relief that her lifelong friend, Lucy Jenkins, the police chief's wife, was waving and not an ill-humored policeman venting hard feelings.

Lucy yelled, "Wait there! I want to see you, Girl!" She drove to the post office, parked her sports car, and strolled to Lottie with an exaggerated hip swing that shimmied her bright bangles. Her thick layers of yellow hair hung to her shoulders.

She leaned down to look in the window at Little Rob. "Hi, Little Rob." Then she strutted to Lottie's window and laughed. "Girl, you upset my husband's day." Lucy laughed louder. Her brown eyes danced with a friendly charisma that heralded her outgoing nature. "I was at the station when he came back from your house. If it weren't for your false alarms, his men could never practice racing to an emergency."

"I'm so embarrassed. Your husband and all of the firemen and policemen in West Point came to my house. Not one of them said a word to me except Don, and he promised to press charges against us if we have another false alarm. Miles and I decided to terminate our house alarm today, but Miles got soft, afraid he would lose Mr. Stevens' corporate business account. Miles told Dudley we would keep the alarm system. And we don't need it . . . or the problems it's caused."

"It's hilarious," laughed Lucy. "Don said that he would count the run to your house as one of their mandatory practice drills. Girl, why didn't you cancel the alarm before the policemen and firemen got there?"

"I didn't know the alarm had been sent. It was a silent alarm."

"Silent alarm! Why would you want a silent alarm? Nobody can hear it."

Lottie rolled her eyes. "Dudley Stevens is at the house changing it. Please, Lucy, I don't want to talk about the alarm anymore."

"Okay. You know, Don and his officers don't have much action here in West Point. I'm thankful for the few violators who make Don feel needed. I'm sure he misses the action of big city law enforcement. But he's resigned to stay here for me." Lucy raised her shoulders and bulged her breasts in pride. "I'm glad we live in a small town where I don't have to worry about muggers or kidnappers. However, if somebody attacks me, I know what to twist and where to strike." Lucy laughed.

"Yes, Lucy, you were the star student of the women's self-defense class."

"That was the most fun I've had in years. I wanted to practice against Don, but he refused."

"Yes, Lucy. You got stuck with me as a practice partner. I don't think you heard Don say, "If your force is excessive, then *you're* guilty of assault," and you become the attacker. You didn't exercise restraint in your punches and kicks. I'm still sore," said Lottie. Lucy threw her head and arms up and cackled.

Lottie shook her head at Lucy and then remembered why she drove to town. "Where were you this morning? You promised to help me. I had to write the letter, stuff envelopes, and put on the address labels by myself. That's why Little Rob and I have come to the post office, to mail the reunion notices."

"I was in the gym this morning. I thought you said that we would work on the reunion stuff *this afternoon.*"

"No. I said we had to get the invitations ready *this morning* to mail this afternoon. We're trying to do the impossible and host an impressive class reunion in three months. The information needed to be mailed early today."

Lottie softened her words and patted Lucy's arm. "It's all right, Lucy. Don't worry about today. I'll forgive you this time," said Lottie with a wink. "There's plenty for you to do, since you're in charge of food and entertainment."

"Girl, you don't have to worry about the food and entertainment. I can handle that easily," said Lucy, flicking her bangled hand at Lottie and flashing her happy smile.

"Mary Cecil located all of our classmates," said Lottie. "Nobody but Mary Cecil could have tracked down all of our former schoolmates. Do you remember Rastus Webber?"

"Rastus Webber! Do I remember Rastus Webber? Girl, I hope you didn't send him an invitation!" exclaimed Lucy. "Rastus was always breaking things. He did weird stuff, especially in science lab. I'll never forget the time Mr. Brown told us to dissect frogs and remove the skin to look at the leg muscles. Rastus straightened a paper clip and heated one end with the Bunsen burner and then burned little dots on the frog's leg muscles. Ooooooh," shuddered Lucy. "One time he grabbed my wrist and twisted it over to burn me with one of those hot paper clips. I screamed loud enough to shatter his brain," laughed Lucy. "He fell to the floor as if I had burned him. After that incident, I stayed away from Rastus."

"I don't remember that," said Lottie. "Well, Mary Cecil discovered that he's a patient at the Claxton Mental Home."

"I knew it!" said Lucy. "I knew he would end up in an institution of some sort, especially after Social Services took him away the last week of school. They said he was 'going away temporarily' due to his 'obsessive, destructive tendencies.' Hmmp. Well, he did set fire to the science lab and burn all of his lab partners." Lucy laughed. "After the principal told our instructor that he would have to be Rastus's partner, we stopped working in pairs. Mr. Brown demonstrated each experiment while we followed along in the workbook. I liked those short labs.

"Just think," said Lucy, "if Rastus were still in West Point, he would wander around, frightening people. Don could lock Rastus up with other offenders to scare them into acting right." Lucy laughed.

"You and everybody else were mean to Rastus," reflected Lottie. "You threw rocks and mud at him and called him awful names. You ought to be ashamed. He was smarter than everybody thought. One time in literature class, he helped me."

"What are you talking about, Girl?" asked Lucy.

"Don't you remember when we studied mythology? Rastus knew more than the teacher about the mythological characters. I couldn't keep those half-gods and full-gods straight."

"Oh, yes, I remember. We saw Rastus in a new light that semester. All those myths sparked his dormant imagination."

"Now Lucy, some of those stories *were* interesting."

"Yes, but Rastus acted as if the mythological people were real. He called me a 'commoner' and told me repeatedly that I was 'in the stark dark.'" Lucy mischievously fingered quotation marks in the air and laughed. "It'll be a bad scene if Rastus comes to the reunion. Don't invite him. You know, he didn't officially graduate."

"How do you know? Just because he didn't walk in the graduation ceremony doesn't mean he didn't graduate. He's entitled to an invitation like everybody in our class. He may have straightened out," said Lottie.

"Ha! Are you serious? That would be a miracle. He's in a mental facility for a very good reason. He was strange in school, and no doubt, he's strange now. If only Rastus had not rhymed his words," said Lucy, "and acted so *crazy*. Do you remember how the guys teased Rastus and would take his words and turn them into jingles that were funny?"

"I remember the rudeness and ridicule," said Lottie.

Lucy looked up to ponder school days of long ago. "I wish I could remember what Rastus said that day in Mrs. Harris' class. She called on Rastus, and he answered her with some nonsense that rhymed. What was it he said? Something like, 'Snakes part in the stark dark.' Somebody repeated something ridiculous that sounded like, 'Apes fart in the dark part.'"

Lucy laughed as she continued to reminisce. "Mrs. Harris burst out laughing and couldn't stop. The whole class roared for twenty minutes, until the principal opened the door and asked (Lucy drew quotation marks in the air again), 'What is so funny?' And that started the hooting all over again."

"He deserves to be treated like a normal human being. We're all different."

"Yeah, Girl, but not *that* different. If he's in a mental facility, they won't let him out to come here. You know, once a troublemaker, always a troublemaker."

Tired of defending Rastus, Lottie stretched her neck and said, "I invited Rastus, along with all of our classmates, except the ones in jail."

"Lottie, you shouldn't have been so nice to Rastus when we were growing up. He could have hurt you. I didn't like the way he looked at you, or the way he followed you around like a lost puppy . . . or should I say, a lost sick puppy?"

"Rastus looked at everybody the same."

Lucy shook her head.

"He followed me around because he was always hungry, and I shared my food with him. He needed somebody to be kind to him and treat him normally."

"He didn't talk normal or act normal. Who knows what happened to his mother? He probably inherited his insanity from his lunatic father. When I got my driver's license in high school, I used to cruise by that dilapidated house just to see Mr. Webber sitting on the front porch. He always shook a stick at me. I loved it!" Lucy laughed.

"You probably made faces at *him*. He thought *you* were crazy," said Lottie.

"Well, I did wave at him or stick out my tongue." Lucy laughed and laughed.

Lottie shifted her head from side to side, disturbed at Lucy's insensitivity to Rastus's childhood plight. "Nobody gave Rastus a fair chance or treated him like a regular person. That's why he's in a mental institution."

Lucy shrugged. "That was a long time ago. We were kids. We would do anything for a laugh. Hmm," said Lucy thoughtfully. "So Rastus is in the Claxton Mental Home. Girl, I know how to get my husband to come to the reunion. I'll tell him that a troublemaker may come."

Lottie bobbed her head in disgust. "Lucy Jenkins! Rastus wasn't the troublemaker! It was the other students who caused trouble for him. Some kids were so mean, they put sharp tacks in his chair."

Lucy held up her quotation fingers and said, "And some kids put car wax in his hair." She laughed at the rhyme she made, which reminded her of Rastus.

Lottie shook her head at Lucy's attitude toward Rastus. "You're terrible."

Lucy shrugged her shoulders.

"I hope Don will come to the reunion to have a good time and not be on police duty."

"Yes, Lottie," said Lucy facetiously. "Don needs a relaxing evening around normal people. I'm sure he won't miss the reunion, especially if Rastus comes."

"Lucy, I don't want to talk about Rastus anymore."

"Okay. Well, since you don't need me, I think I'll go to the tanning salon."

Lottie raised her eyebrows and shook her head at her vain friend. "I'll talk to you later, Lucy."

Lucy looked in the backseat at Little Rob and said, "Bye, bye, Little Rob." She prissed back to her convertible. As she drove away, she honked her horn and flashed her hand above the windshield.

Lottie sped away from the post office to avoid meeting a policeman or a fireman. "Let's go home, Little Rob. Dudley's probably still there, fixing our alarm system that we don't need."

Chapter 9

Psychotic Delerium

*T*he Claxton district attorney's office exhausted its appeals to prosecute Rastus. The case was closed, and charges, dropped. At last, Rastus was officially released back to the care of the Claxton Mental Home.

Rastus sat on the sofa close to the wall in the psychotherapy office. He watched his physician thumb through loose papers and wondered how long he could endure the pointless and irritating sessions with Dr. Affle.

The psychiatrist stopped to tap his sore fingertips together, deliberating if the harsh cleaner used by housekeeping in his office had caused an allergic reaction. The painful soreness was a nuisance that distracted him from his work. He spun his desk chair around and tilted his head up and down to adjust his vision of Rastus in his glasses. His thin, curly ponytail was pulled tight behind his head. He rubbed the smooth skin of his jaw.

"I see that you brought my freshly cleaned lab coats from the front and hung them in my office. You've confirmed your inclination for kindness, Rastus." The psychiatrist studied his patient and said, "We have a formidable task ahead of us, Rastus. The results of your last episode mean that I must postpone your placement in a group home until you achieve complete rehabilitation. I'll revise your plan of care to develop your competence to live in a peer group setting with others like yourself."

"I want to live alone in my own home. I want someone dear to be near. I want to go as I please, and nobody sees," said Rastus in a dejected state.

Dr. Affle wanted to stay on task with his methods and continued his therapy session. "Rastus, I need you to move to this chair in front of my desk so we can talk about your problems face to face."

Rastus felt safe on the couch that was close to the wall. He squirmed anxiously, not wanting to leave the security of the walls. He did not want to talk to Dr. Affle. He did not trust his physician.

"I see you feel uncomfortable with my request to move away from the wall, so I'll come to you, Rastus." Dr. Affle sat on the sofa with his patient, but stared at his tender fingertips. Obsessed with the puzzling pain, he rubbed his fingers together to ease the soreness that had recently returned. He habitually slid his hands into his lab coat and then flapped the pockets.

Dr. Affle inhaled deeply, stroked his head, and refocused on Rastus. "I know this is a hard time for you after your legal ordeal. I want you to know that I'll use my expertise and talent to reverse your neurological trauma."

Rastus did not make eye contact with Dr. Affle or speak a word.

"I believe your inner conflict continues because you've suppressed vital information. Something you haven't revealed to me delays your progress and impinges on your goal of independent socialization."

Dr. Affle fixed his eyes on Rastus, accepting his patient's abnormal appearance and mannerisms. Rastus's tongue involuntarily darted in and out of his drooling mouth while

Duress

he slung his stringy hair across his squinting eye. Rastus's face was mottled gray, a side effect of a psychotropic drug. The mental home medical director savored his institutional utopia, where he practiced psychotherapy and prescribed a merry-go-round of medications for patients.

"You must tell me when you hear voices. What are you thinking, Rastus? What do you want?" asked Dr. Affle. He paused to let Rastus organize his thoughts and express himself.

Rastus felt coerced to speak. "I want to be . . . a hero of renown . . . with no fear in town."

"Yes, Rastus. We all want to be a hero to someone," said Dr. Affle. "Who do you feel is a hero? Is it some significant person in your life who's been there to listen to you and give you advice?"

Rastus stared. Dr. Affle patronized him, but Rastus needed someone to intervene for him every time he roamed out of the facility and returned. He despised Dr. Affle and hated talking to him. The psychiatrist insisted that Rastus speak freely of his hurtful memories, although it was exhausting and tedious. Dr. Affle never grew tired of hearing what happened. Rehashing that day never diminished Rastus's anger and hatred. He believed that Dr. Affle was cruel and controlling like Rastus's father.

"Remembering will help you cope and understand the truth so that you can become a whole person again. Do you recall that pivotal moment when your father provoked you and forced your mother to leave?" asked Dr. Affle in a soft voice.

Rastus exhaled in frustration as he again was forced to scratch open the scar of his childhood hell. "I loved Mama. He shoved Mama down on the rug. He knocked me down on the floor. He locked me behind the closet door. He got rid of Mama. He hid Mama from me."

Psychotic Delerium

Rastus's hostility increased. He raised his voice. "I hate him! I hate him! He wouldn't let me see Mama." Sweat popped out on Rastus's face. He cried in grief, "Mama! Mama! Hold me! Hold me!"

Dr. Affle peacefully said, "You must avoid emotional retaliation to past stress. It activates your headache disorder, Rastus. You'll always look for a hero to replace your father who did not fulfill his duty. Be calm, Rastus. I'm qualified to help you work through this grievous memory."

"My father bothered me." *I hate him. I hate you.*

"He made you feel unworthy. He did not affirm your self-worth. You can overcome the unworthiness he instilled in you," assured Dr. Affle.

"People think I'm unworthy and dirty. People in town don't like the way I sound."

"You have a paranoia of people that's misdirected. People don't want to ridicule you or discriminate against you," said Dr. Affle.

"They do. They hate you. They hate me, too. I'm accursed because I speak in verse." Rastus stood, projecting and retracting his tongue and erratically flailing his arms up and down. "Set me free! Zeus gave me a plan for man." In an outburst, he yelled, "Zeus! Zeus! Only Zeus knows the truth!"

"Rastus, lower your voice. There're no threats here." Dr. Affle arose from the sofa and walked to his phone to call the charge nurse. "Rastus Webber is experiencing emotional instability. Send his aide to my office immediately."

Rastus rigidly flailed his arms, yelling, "Zeus! Zeus!"

Baron, the certified nursing assistant assigned to Rastus, boomed into the office. He wrestled Rastus into a wheelchair and strapped on a waist restraint with Rastus wailing and jerking. "Baron, put Rastus in seclusion to quell his agitation and excitement." The strong nurse aide nodded and rolled Rastus out of the office and down the hall.

Duress

When Dr. Affle's office was quiet, he phoned the administrative assistant and said, "Bring me the resumes of those applicants interested in the director of nursing position left vacant by that last nurse. Also, tell the activities director to get new art supplies for Rastus to allow him to freely express his inner hostilities."

"Yes, Dr. Affle," replied the secretary. "Anything else?"

"Yes, tell maintenance to check the burglar bars on the windows and to change the entrance and exit code. I need you to post the new numbers for employees."

"Okay, I will. Is that all?"

"One more thing. Tell housekeeping to stop using the current chemical disinfectant on my desk and in my office. I'm experiencing hypersensitive soreness to my fingertips again. I can't tolerate the sanitizing solution they use."

"I'll tell them, Dr. Affle."

Dr. Affle called the charge nurse to redundantly clarify the condition of Rastus. "Rastus suffered a minor setback in his psychodynamic treatment. I need you to give him an Ativan to relax him and increase his Risperdal to four times a day. Write in his medical record that he experienced delirium with acute anxiety."

"Yes sir. I'll note that in his medical chart."

Over the loudspeaker blared the alert, "Code Zeus! Code Zeus! Nurses' station! Nurses' station!" When Dr. Affle heard the peculiar signal designated for Rastus, he rushed out of his office to attend to Rastus. Explosive voices echoed through the halls. "He broke loose! Grab his hands! Get a straitjacket! Watch out! Don't let him touch you!"

Rastus had freed himself of his wheelchair restraint and stood inside the nurses' workplace with institution employees spread far away from him. Nurses held medical charts in their hands, ready to swing or throw them at Rastus if he got close. Other workers shook vases, food trays, and boxes at Rastus to defend themselves.

Although not a muscular man, Rastus swung an iron rod at staff and swept charts and plastic foam cups off the built-in worktables. Rastus felt people closing in and darted down a hall, pushing a chair at employees he thought were chasing him. He stopped to shatter the glass on the fire alarm with the metal bar. The loud siren prompted severe pain in his head.

Rastus retreated into a patient room, waving the metal bar. He beat the docile resident in bed and raked the water cup and pitcher off the nightstand. Raging, he went into the small bathroom and smashed the toilet with the iron pole until water flowed over the floor.

The staff exclaimed in a panic, "Where's Baron? Where is he? Go get Baron!"

"I'm here," said the nursing assistant. "I had to go to the bathroom."

Sighs of relief billowed through the employees. Nobody wanted to touch Rastus. The staff wanted Baron to handle the facility's problem patient. Rastus felt intimidated and threatened when the employees and Dr. Affle crowded into the room.

Dr. Affle spoke firmly to Rastus. "I can see you are distraught, Rastus. You must refrain from ravaging residents and property. This is objectionable behavior." The psychiatrist extended his hand to touch Rastus's arm to relax his patient.

Rastus exploded. "Don't touch me! You're like the rest! You're the one I detest! You don't hear my cries. I don't hear your lies!"

The psychiatrist reached to grab the metal bar, but Rastus pulled away, beating the wall, smashing the mirror, and turning on his physician. He raised the rod high and then hammered Dr. Affle, who defended his head from the blow with his left arm, but his hand collapsed, and the rod struck his eyeglasses and nose, breaking them both. The Claxton Mental Home medical director fell to the wet floor in pain and groaned loudly, "Use rapid tranquilization! Rapid tranquilization!"

"Can I use the Compazine this time?" asked a new, anxious nurse.

"Yes!" yelled Dr. Affle. "Or the Chlorpromazine! Full dose!"

The nurse ran to get the drug.

"Shut your mouth!" ordered Rastus. He dropped beside the physician and rolled him over. Rastus clawed the doctor's biceps through his lab coat and sunk his teeth into the psychiatrist's pectoral muscles.

Nurses and aides watched the uproar. Baron pulled Rastus away and bear-hugged him while the nurse stabbed his arm with a hypodermic syringe, plunging the powerful antipsychotic tranquilizer into his body.

Chapter 10

Nab Rastus

*T*wo days later, Rastus resumed his customary mental home maneuvers. Always watching for opportunities, Rastus found a large black satchel-like purse under the desk of an office worker while she was on break. He slyly stole the bag and sneaked down the hall. He went into a patient's room and shook the personal belongings into a garbage can. Stuffing the purse under his shirt, he ran on his tiptoes to his room. He flattened the bag and hid it under the head of his mattress. With his pillow in place, the slight rise in his bed was hardly noticeable.

The staff accused Rastus of taking her purse and searched his room and the facility thoroughly. When the contents of the bag were found, the employee was relieved to have her wallet, with her credit cards and driver's license, returned. She vowed to wear a fanny pack from that day forward.

Rastus learned to use the facility routine and the negligent staff to his advantage. For example, during lunch Rastus walked to the nurses' station bulletin board to see if the entry and exit code had changed. Nurses and aides left the area unattended during mealtimes and breaks, and never noticed Rastus staring at the numbers posted on the bottom right corner of the corkboard. The workers assumed that all of the patients were incapable of understanding how to use the security code to exit the building.

After lunch every day, the nurses gave sedatives to active patients like Rastus. He avoided swallowing his sleeping med, which freed him most afternoons to organize his plans for his next outing.

Today, the urge to slip away overpowered Rastus. With subtlety, he went to the laundry room unnoticed to swipe a white T-shirt, which he tore into strips. In the maintenance area, he found duct tape and rope hidden in large popcorn tins on a top shelf. A new maintenance guy concealed his backpack in a box behind the emergency generator, but Rastus found it. He emptied the contents back into the box and stuffed the pack under his large shirt. *I'll hide it for next time*, thought Rastus. Back in his room, he pushed the bag far back on the top shelf of his metal locker.

He waited impatiently for the employees to settle for their long afternoon break. He packed his tape, rope, and T-shirt strips into the square black bag he had found in the front office. Rastus cracked his door to see if the halls were clear. Staying close to the wall, he stealthily tiptoed to the front entrance, touched the correct numbers on the keypad, and passed swiftly out the secured doors. "Zeus made it easy to get loose!" he told himself.

Rastus cut through the adjacent subdivision and followed the wooded pathway through the pine trees to his hiding place under the bridge. After a while, he left the bridge and wandered through neighborhoods, picking up items of interest on his way to the hardware store to find a wood-burning tool. *I know they'll try to hide it. I'll find it*, thought Rastus.

When the Claxton Mental Home employees discovered that Rastus had disappeared, they initiated a lockdown, hoping to find Rastus in the facility. However, since he could not be found, they informed Dr. Affle, who alerted the local police.

Cpl. Taylor and Officer Dalgo were on duty when the alert for the missing patient was announced. They knew for whom to look. The two policemen checked the downtown hardware store since it stocked the wood-burning tool that Rastus wanted. They looked through the large glass windows and saw Rastus sneaking around in the store.

One officer spoke quietly on his radio to the dispatcher. "Cpl. Taylor reporting on the escaped mental patient. He's in Handy Hardware. We need backup. Call the shrink, and tell him to come down here. If I touch his patient, he'll cry 'police brutality,' and I'll be the one brutalized."

"Ten-four," replied the clerk.

The crouching policemen watched Rastus flap his arms apprehensively and mutter, "It's not fair. I don't know where .... It's not fair. I don't know where ...."

"He's going destructive," said a jittery Officer Dalgo.

"We can't wait any longer for backup," said Cpl. Taylor. "Let's go get the monkey nut!"

They tackled Rastus to the floor and handcuffed one arm. Rastus kicked, pinched, and bit the policemen. Officer Dalgo jabbed Rastus's jaw, which stimulated hyperactivity in the mental patient. Rastus bubbled loudly, "You snakes! Snakes forsake!"

Policeman Dalgo said, "He's seeing snakes! Taze him! Taze him! He's going psycho!"

Rastus pulled himself up a store shelf and raked glass bowls, coffee pots, and a blender to the floor, all the while wildly fanning the loose handcuff to strike the policemen. The cashier and the few customers continuously screamed and zipped back and forth in the store, since Rastus and the police were blocking the front door.

Police backup and Dr. Affle arrived. The psychiatrist ordered, "Do not provoke my patient to hostile behavior or use excessive force on him, or I cannot guarantee your safety."

Rastus stared at Dr. Affle, his tongue going in and out of his wet mouth. "I hate you!" said Rastus. "I hate you!"

The psychiatrist approached Rastus and said, "Rastus, I object to your reprehensible behavior. Be calm, Rastus. I'm here to help you."

Rastus violently threw at Dr. Affle whatever tool or appliance he could reach. The policemen stood back in hesitation. Then Dr. Affle addressed the officers, "If you will hold him firmly, I will quickly sedate him."

Two policemen shoved Rastus flat on the floor, face down, and the other two officers grasped his legs and arms. The physician injected a fast-acting tranquilizer into Rastus's right buttock. "Hold him still for a few seconds," ordered Dr. Affle. "Now, help me put him in this straitjacket. I need you to transport him to the mental home while I go to the police station to work things out."

After Dr. Affle left, Cpl. Taylor told two of the backup policemen, "I need you to haul him to the institution in your cruiser. I need to go change and clean up."

"No way," protested one of the men. "He's not stinking up my car. You can take him yourself and then go clean up. We'll help you load him. You found him. He's yours."

On the way to the facility, Officer Dalgo said, "Why do they keep letting him out? Why? Why?"

Chapter 11

A Psychopath's Collection

Dr. Affle telephoned the facility and told the charge nurse, "Lift the restrictive measures at the facility since Rastus is in police custody. I'll resolve the legalities while you prepare for his return."

The LPN assembled his medications in anticipation of promptly dispensing them to Rastus. She paged Baron, his certified nursing assistant. When Baron appeared at the nurses' station, she advised him, "You better be ready to grab Rastus at the front door. Dr. Affle said he's on his way."

Baron, the heftiest and strongest aide at the facility, was a likeable, jolly person, with shiny gold front teeth. His daily job was to care for Rastus, the institution's problem patient. Baron was the only one willing to handle Rastus during his demented tantrums.

The aide went to the front entrance and stood diligently, holding the handles of the wheelchair as he waited for his designated patient. However, he grew tired of standing and sat in the wheelchair. Half asleep, he watched for Rastus through the large glass doors.

Duress

He stared at the museum-like entrance to the building. He thought, *Man, Doc sure built a flashy front. Who was he tryin' to impress?*

The outside had a three-step base that extended across the front with obscured wheelchair ramps on both ends. Six marble-clad Corinthian columns grandly decorated the exterior. Above the columns were painted tiles of mythological gods at war with each other.

Finally, Baron saw the flashing lights of the police car. He hopped up and entered the access code that would allow the doors to open.

The patrol car drove around the semicircle drive and stopped at the prestigious entryway. The officers unloaded Rastus, who was bound in a straitjacket. One policeman held his shoulders, and the other dragged his feet. The officers slung his motionless body into the wheelchair.

Rastus's shoulder-length black hair hung in greasy strings. His tongue fell to the side of his mouth. His face, which usually was gray and splotched, appeared yellow and lifeless.

"He looks dead. Is he dead?" asked Baron.

"Hardly," said Cpl. Taylor. "We couldn't subdue him until the doctor incapacitated him with that shot."

"I need a break," said Policeman Dalgo. "He resisted arrest and wore me out."

"There's blood all over him," observed Baron.

"He's lucky he's not a bloody pulp. We wanted to break off his grabbing fingers and his handcuffed slugging arm," said Cpl. Taylor. The policemen waited at the secured doors for Baron to key in the exit code so they could quickly leave.

Baron situated Rastus in the wheelchair to prevent him from falling over. "Rastus, my friend, you did it again. I'm glad they don't fire someone every time you slip outta this place like they used to. I wouldn't have a job."

He wheeled Rastus through the warmly decorated foyer, lavished with an Oriental rug, a leather sofa, and an accessorized coffee table. Plantation shutters trimmed the window and hid the outside burglar bars.

Past the vestibule on opposite sides of the hall were two prominent heavy doors, each brandishing gold nameplates. One said "Director of Nursing," and the other was engraved with "Dr. Irvin M. Affle, Medical Director."

The designer facade ended as Baron pushed Rastus through the swinging doors that separated the grandiose entry from the institution. They rolled through the dappled halls as orderlies and nurses stared at Rastus and murmured. A few zombie-like patients walked around or stood, aimlessly babbling in the hallway.

"You're gonna get killed if you don't quit your scary stuff," Baron said to Rastus. "You're like a snake in the grass. You're gonna show your head to the wrong person, and they're gonna take you out, and I don't mean to dinner."

Baron held his tranquilized patient up with one hand and pushed the wheelchair with his other hand. As they approached the nurses' station, Baron waved to the nurse, who jumped up and came out of her nursing post to meet them.

"Rastus ought to be dead from so many high-dose injections," she said.

"How can anybody smell so bad?" asked Baron.

"You'd have problems with diarrhea if you took as many meds as he does," said the nurse. She checked his vital signs and recorded them for his medical chart. "Did you notice any severe cuts or contusions, Baron?"

"Well, he's got blood all over himself. Looks like they popped him hard on his jaw." The nurse looked at his jaw and pushed his chin up and down. "He's okay," she said. Then they peeled off Rastus's straitjacket and unbuttoned his shirt to remove it.

A snake fell to the floor. "Aaahhh!" screeched the nurse.

"It's not real," said Baron as he picked it up and hung it over the back of the wheelchair. "I'll add this one to his collection."

"Why can't he collect things like medicine cups, toilet paper rolls, or string like the other patients?" questioned the nurse.

"Yeah!" responded Baron. "Some kid or gardener will miss this snake this week. The day Rastus brings in a real snake is the day I quit."

"Me, too," said the nurse.

"There's blood on his chest. I wonder . . .," said Baron as he reached in Rastus's shirt pocket with a latex-gloved hand. "Yeah, I thought so." Baron removed pieces of glass.

"What is that?" asked the nurse.

"Rastus started a new collection. It's kinda been our little secret. Whenever he goes outta the facility, he doesn't just look for rubber snakes and that tool. He looks for broken glass bottles. He thinks the shapes and points are cool. Doc wants us to encourage creative stuff. Rastus likes to talk about what he sees in the curves and spikes. I told him he couldn't cut himself or anybody else with that glass. He's been good to keep a broken bottle a few days and then get rid of it."

"He's a mental patient, Baron," said the nurse. "He could easily mutilate his body with broken glass or, in a depressed state, try to kill himself."

"He wouldn't do that," argued Baron.

"If he throws sharp glass into the garbage or into the laundry, somebody who works here could get cut," said the nurse in great concern.

"Yeah, don't worry. I told him. He said he wouldn't throw pieces of glass in the garbage or laundry, but would wrap up the glass real good before he got rid of it. Doc wants us to build trust and stuff like that, so I thought I'd let him prove I can trust him."

"Baron, I don't think we should allow Rastus to keep broken bottles."

"Hmmp," said Baron, not willing to oppose Rastus or the nurse. "There're not many broken bottles on the side of the road. Most people throw out paper cups or plastic bottles. He *could* collect more dangerous items than broken glass and rubber snakes."

"I don't want him hurting anyone or cutting himself and making a mess. The glass shattered on impact and cut Rastus's chest. He's lucky it's just superficial."

Chapter 12

Rastus Repents

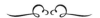

"Okay, Rastus, let the nurse see your arms and legs." Baron completely removed Rastus's shirt and pants so the nurse could examine him. She pressed on his ribs, stomach, abdomen, and spine. "He's okay. He has multiple bruises and cuts, but they're relatively minor," said the LPN. "He doesn't need stitches this time." The nurse cleansed Rastus's cuts and taped them.

As she bandaged Rastus, the nurse talked to Baron. "That new employee in maintenance said somebody took his backpack but dumped everything out of it into a box. Rastus probably stole it."

"Yeah," said Baron. "I tell every new employee, 'Don't bring in a backpack, or it'll disappear.' They never believe me. They all think they'll hide it in a safe place."

"Rastus knows all the hiding places around the facility," said the nurse. "The police caught Rastus quickly today; they're figuring out *his* hiding places in town."

"One of the policemen said that he resisted arrest," said Baron. He leaned down to Rastus's ear and said, "That officer has some cuts and bruises, too, huh, Rastus? You know how to put up a fight, don't cha?"

Rastus Repents

"I crushed his medicines and mixed them in applesauce," said the nurse. "If you'll help me get him to swallow, this will be the quickest and easiest med pass he's ever had."

"He's almost comatose. Won't that medicine be too much on top of what he already got?"

"No. The injection the doctor gave him is temporary. It'll wear off soon."

Baron slapped Rastus's face and squeezed his cheeks to rouse him enough to open his mouth. The aide wiped the drool for the nurse as she force-fed the applesauce to Rastus.

"Thank you, Baron. You can take him to his room."

"You sure these meds won't sedate him more? He looks dead."

"We all need a break from Rastus. These meds won't affect him for one or two hours. He probably needs to sleep awhile. Don't worry about him, Baron."

"Well, I guess he won't remember anything from this afternoon. I think I'll hose him down in the shower. He's nasty, and I'm tired of wrestlin' him every time I bathe him."

The nurse nodded in approval. Baron rolled Rastus to his room to get clean clothes. Rastus began to stir and moan. "Let's hurry, Rastus. You don't like me to give you a bath any more than I like to give you one. Man, you stink."

Baron wheeled Rastus to the shower room and undressed him. The aide strapped Rastus on the plastic bath stool, showered him thoroughly, and toweled him dry. The shower rejuvenated Rastus, who awkwardly batted his arms and resisted Baron's efforts to dress him.

Baron said, "Yeah. We're done! That's the quickest bath you've ever had. Let's go to your room. That nurse said you need to sleep awhile." He positioned Rastus in the wheelchair to prevent him from falling. Rastus cocked his head sideways and hung his tongue involuntarily out of the side of his mouth. They stopped by the nurses' station to let her re-tape his chest, arms, and legs.

Duress

Baron talked as he rolled Rastus to his room. "I wanna know how you get outta this place, and nobody sees you. They change the security code every time you escape; it's a pain to keep up with the new numbers. You gotta show me how you shoplift so easily. They nabbed you quick today, before you could steal one of those burnin' things."

Rastus licked his lips and bubbled spit. He garbled a noise in his throat.

"If you wouldn't scare people to death, you could get away," said Baron. "You terrify people with your hot hand." Baron wiped Rastus's protruding tongue with a hand towel. Then the aide threw the towel over his own shoulder.

"Well, you're back home," said Baron as he pushed Rastus into the room. Hung on the walls were pencil drawings of lightning bolts, tridents, and constellations. On his nightstand was a gallon jug stuffed with rubber snakes. "Here's another one to add to your collection," said Baron as he pushed the snake in the neck of the full jar. Baron opened Rastus's closet to see if the previous broken bottle was on the shelf; it was missing.

"What's this?" asked Baron as he picked up a letter on the bedside table. "Did you get mail? Yeah. This is real mail, and it's addressed to you. It's open! Did you read it?"

Rastus grunted and struggled to lift his scrawny hand, but he was still groggy. However, the shot's shackling effect was dissipating. Rastus did not want his aide to touch his mail. "Ahh. Ahh, don't touch," were the only words Rastus could muster, with a negative shake of his head.

"Lemme read it to you. You never get mail. Yeah. You're invited to a high school reunion. Well, you're not gonna go to this party."

Agitated with his aide, Rastus blew spit on him. Baron wiped his face with the towel thrown over his shoulder. Rastus tried to claw Baron's arms with his lengthy fingernails, but Baron dodged him.

"I should've cut those fingernails while you were in a coma."

Rastus did not like Baron telling him that he couldn't go. He heaved the words, "No. No. Go, go," and continued to open and close his long pincher fingers at Baron.

"Watch out!" said Baron as he backed away to avoid Rastus's peculiar pinch. "Good gosh, Rastus. You don't want me to touch your letter? I'll put it down."

Rastus exerted himself to speak. He moved his mouth. "Ah want Lot-tay. Ah want Lot-tay." His words rolled on his thick wet tongue.

"You wanna what? A lotta what?"

"Lot-tay. Lot-tay!"

"A lotta what? Some kind of food? You need to eat some food. You're too skinny. You wanna milkshake?"

Rastus was aggravated that his aide didn't understand and that Baron was flippant about the reunion. He struggled to breathe and huff his words. He wanted to communicate to Baron, but the earlier sedation impaired his speech.

"Need Lot-tay. Need Lot-tay."

"You mean you wanna coffee latte? When did you pick up a coffee habit?"

"No. No. Need Lot-tay. Ah waited my life for Lot-tay."

"I might be able to get cha a cup of coffee from the breakroom. I hafta check with the nurse to see if Doc will let cha have it. You take so many medicines that I don't think you're supposed to drink coffee. I can't believe you wanna coffee latte." Baron stood behind Rastus and combed his hair.

"Doc will wanna see you soon. He'll wanna reevaluate you and reassess you. You'll have a stress management session again. I need the stress management help, not you." Baron put the comb on the side table and walked to the front of Rastus to look at his hair and to finish buttoning his shirt.

Rastus raised his arms up and down and tried to stand. Baron pushed him down into the wheelchair. Rastus's bony fingers reached for the biceps of Baron and locked on. He pinched Baron hard enough that the male aide yelled loudly, "Lemme go, you snake brain! Lemme go! I'll kill you!"

The nurse buzzed the room intercom. "Are you okay? Do you need assistance?"

"Yeah! I'm gonna break this yo-yo's arms if he don't let me go!"

The nurse rushed into Rastus's room. She approached Rastus from behind and shook his arms until he loosened his pinch on Baron.

The noise of Baron's yelling set off a pain in Rastus's head, and he pressed his skull to ease the stress and pain.

"Good gosh, Rastus!" exclaimed Baron as he pressed his arms and grimaced in pain.

The nurse asked, "Did he break the skin?"

Baron looked. "Yeah! He knifed my arms with his gross fingernails."

"Come to the nurses' station when you get through, and I'll put an antibiotic and a dressing on each arm. You'll need to get a tetanus shot if yours isn't current." She walked out and left Baron with Rastus.

"Good gosh, Rastus. You're gonna make me quit. And I need to work."

Rastus lamented, "It's time to sign up. I must be free to see. See . . . ." His chin was wet with drool. He lifted a hand that he seesawed up and down.

"See what? What cha want me to see?" Baron picked up the letter on the nightstand. "This letter? Is that what cha want me to see? The letter?" Baron shook the envelope in irritation at Rastus. "I saw this letter. It's an invitation to a high school reunion."

Rastus rocked up and down and growled. His tongue projected from his open wet mouth. "I know I must go!"

Calming down, Baron said, "Okay, my friend. I see this reunion is important to you. Don't try to escape and go. It's too far to walk to West Point." Rastus bobbed his stiff head up and down. In agony he croaked, "I can't bear to not go there."

Baron tried to humor Rastus. "You wanna see an old flame of yours?"

Rastus clicked his tongue on the roof of his mouth, thrust it out, and encircled his lips with it. He showed his unkempt teeth in a semi-smile.

"Yeah! Rastus had a girlfriend!"

"There's none like the one . . . Lot-tay."

Baron didn't try to understand Rastus. "Hmm. The return address is from somebody who lives at 213 Deer Tail Drive in West Point. Well, Doc's not gonna let cha go. You can't act right."

"I'll act right in her sight. I hated I waited. I want to see her. I want to sear."

"You talk like a man in love, Rastus, if I heard you right. Lemme look at this letter. The reunion is about two and a half months away. You can't complete Doc's rehabilitation program in that short time. He thought you were making progress, and then you ran off. There's not enough time for you to persuade Doc to let cha go. Besides, it's a holiday weekend, and nobody'll wanna go with you. Doc won't let cha go by yourself."

Rastus reached for Baron's arms to pinch him again. "No, Rastus. No!"

"My life's in strife," said Rastus as saliva dribbled out of his mouth. "Help me go. Don't tell me no." He pleaded for Baron to help.

Skeptically, Baron offered his advice. "Okay. I'll tell you what cha gotta do before Doc will let cha go to a weekend party. First of all, don't sneak off. Don't pinch people. Don't scare people with your flaky words. You hafta swallow your pills and not spit them out. You hafta brush your teeth and take your baths without a fight.

Duress

"Doc can't trust you to quit slippin' off and stealin' that thing you're obsessed with. It's mud on his face when the police hafta find you and bring you back. When you meet with Doc, show him your letter, and tell him about the reunion. You ask him, 'What have I gotta do so I can go to the reunion?' Tell him you wanna do better. He'll come up with a plan for your life. He'll try to teach you how to be sociable and how to act normal. Maybe he'll drive you to West Point. You follow what I say?"

Rastus nodded as if he understood.

Baron helped Rastus into his bed for a nap.

"You gotta act like an upright saint. You gotta eat your meals and not throw stuff. You gotta do what I say." Baron rattled the reunion invitation in Rastus's face. "You wanna go? You gotta shape up. Maybe Doc will let you go. I don't know. Good gosh, Rastus. You've got me talkin' in rhymes."

"Lot-tay. Lot-tay."

"Yeah. If you wash your stin-ky bo-dy, you'll get a lat-te." Baron laughed at the silly verse he concocted.

"The upright saint might faint."

"Naw. You won't faint. The people who see you or smell you might faint."

"I'll get Lot-tay. I'll get Lot-tay."

"Yeah, I hope so," said Baron sarcastically as he walked out of the room, shaking his head. "I need a break."

Chapter 13

In A Bind

*S*ummer had drifted into the middle of July with no reunion responses.

Lottie's Service Society was meeting at the library that night. Since Miles was busy counting inventory at his store, Lottie took Little Rob with her. She left him in the Children's Reading Room, which was dotted with small round tables and surrounded by shelves of children's books.

"I won't be in my meeting long, Little Rob. You stay here and look at books until I come and get you."

"Okay, Mommy," said Little Rob.

Lottie hurried to the meeting room, where Katherine, the librarian, greeted guests. Katherine, the reunion treasurer, beamed, "I've received twenty-three responses to the reunion!"

"How exciting!" exclaimed Lottie.

"I'll deposit the checks tomorrow and keep a tally of who registers," said Katherine.

Trudy Lee, who was also on the committee, heard them talking and said, "Did you say some of our classmates returned the registration forms?" Trudy had a son who was

Little Rob's age. She worked at the pharmacy gift shop downtown."

"Yes," said Katherine. "The forms are coming in now."

"I see Mary Cecil sitting in the front row," said Trudy. "Does she know?"

"No," said Katherine. "Mary Cecil arrived thirty minutes early to make sure I had things under control. She sat down while I was busy setting up the room."

Mary Cecil sat perfectly straight in her fitted pantsuit and low heels, studying the Service Society program, which she had prepared. She managed the office of a local engineering firm.

Trudy sat beside Mary Cecil to bubble enthusiastically about the reunion, but Mary Cecil tapped her fingertip to her mouth to indicate that time for talking was over.

Fifteen minutes after the meeting started, Lucy Jenkins burst into the room. Lottie waved from the back of the room, where she had saved Lucy a chair. Lucy flipped her hand, jangling her bracelets in response, and laughed. As Lucy sat down, she explained to Lottie why she was late. The meeting stopped while everyone turned to look at Lucy and to wait for her to be quiet.

After the meeting, Lottie told Lucy that they had received numerous responses to the reunion. "We need to have a committee meeting," said Lucy.

"You're right. Let's get together at my house tomorrow night at seven-thirty," said Lottie. "Will you call the other girls on the committee for me?"

"Yeah, Girl. I'll let them know. Is Little Rob with Miles tonight?"

"Oh," laughed Lottie. "I almost forgot him. Miles is counting inventory at the store and couldn't watch Little Rob. He's in the Children's Reading Room." Lottie and Lucy hurried to look for Little Rob. Not seeing him, Lottie called, "Little Rob! Little Rob!"

In A Bind

"I'm over here, Mommy."

In a corner of the room under a window by a child-sized bookshelf sat Little Rob, surrounded by a heap of books.

"Little Rob, why did you drag out so many books?" asked Lottie as she sunk to the floor to gather them.

Katherine walked in and said, "Just leave the books on the floor. The summer intern can shelve the books in their proper order tomorrow."

"Thanks, Katherine. Let's go, Little Rob."

"Can we stay home tomorrow night, Mommy?" asked Little Rob as he stepped over books.

The next day, Little Rob, Lottie, and Miles slept late. "What time did you come in last night?" Lottie asked Miles.

"Late," responded Miles, "but I finished counting inventory."

"My class reunion committee is coming here tonight at seven-thirty. Will you watch Little Rob for me during the meeting?"

"Let me see," joked Miles. "Sure."

Miles quickly showered, dressed, and went to work. Lottie and Little Rob leisurely ate cereal for breakfast and then dressed for the day. Little Rob played while Lottie made a to-do list. She telephoned Lucy to remind her to call everyone about the meeting.

Lottie said, "Let's go to town, Little Rob." First, they visited Miles at his business and then left because he was busy. As Lottie backed out of her parking space, her mobile phone rang. She fumbled in her large purse to feel her phone. Annoyed that she was unable to fix her grasp on the ringing tone, she pulled back into the parking spot to look for her cell phone.

"Hello. How are you, Marilyn?"

Lottie looked at Little Rob and whispered, "It's Aunt Marilyn."

Little Rob turned up his nose and looked out the window in disaffection toward his aunt. He didn't know why he disliked his Aunt Marilyn, but deep inside, he believed she was a bad person. However, Little Rob liked his cousins, but sensed that they knew nothing about fun or play.

Lottie's older sister, Marilyn, had divorced her hometown husband because he lacked ambition and lived on the same pig farm that belonged to his grandfather. Marilyn worked at a satellite location of a large corporation. She focused on projects to glorify her image and shoved aside anyone in her way. Lottie labored to maintain peace with her sister and to provide happy childhood experiences for her niece and nephew.

"Are you in town, Marilyn?"

"Yes, Lottie. I got to work an hour ago. I ran home to change clothes and get ready for an important meeting. I asked Mrs. Edwards to stay another night with the children, but that old woman refused. She doesn't have anything to do but babysit old relatives and my children. And I pay her very well," bragged Marilyn MacGinnis. "I need to work late tonight to get a presentation ready for tomorrow, and I don't have time to fool with the children. I left them whining and crying; they need to grow up. Those kids only think about themselves. They don't care that I provide everything they need with my own two hands."

"They need fresh air, Marilyn. You should let George and Victoria go to the farm to see their daddy and grandmother. They cried because they missed you and needed some attention."

"Oh, please," said Marilyn derisively. "They don't need any more attention. I know I can trust Mrs. Edwards to do what I say and keep them clean, quiet, and inside."

Lottie pictured her bossy sister sitting behind her polished wooden desk in her office, stroking her dark bobbed hair that was long on the sides and short in the back. "Marilyn, I know that Mrs. Edwards is good to your children, but Buster and Mama Mac need to see the children. You need to get over your hang-up that Buster owns a pig farm."

Lottie thought to herself, *How many times have I said that to Marilyn?*

"Their father's name is Boyd, not Buster!"

"All right, Boyd. Nobody calls him Boyd, except you."

"I forbid my children to go to that nasty swine bog, which Boyd calls a farm."

"Farms are fun for children and can be very educational," said Lottie.

"If I want my children to have lessons on sex education or corn planting, I'll get them a library book. I don't want to expose them to a stinking pauper's trade."

"It doesn't smell bad, and Mama Mac keeps her house cleaner than yours or mine. I don't understand why you won't let them be with their father and grandmother."

"*I'm* the one who provides for my children. I don't want them around uneducated people who live in a country dump. My children have experienced only the finest things in life. I've bought them all the things money can buy to make children happy," boasted Marilyn.

"They don't need *things*. They need a mother and a daddy to give them time and love. You keep them cooped up in the condo while you work long hours and make lots of money."

"Are you giving me advice now? I don't need your parental suggestions. You take care of your happy life, and I'll take care of mine. I'm in a bind, and I thought I could depend on you," challenged Marilyn.

Chapter 14

Abused Children

"I'm sorry, Marilyn," said Lottie, succumbing to her sister's manipulative words. "You know I'll help with George and Victoria." Lottie hesitatingly seized the opportunity to advise her sister one more time. "I think your children should play with other children to become more . . . ."

Marilyn interrupted. "I won't allow my children to play with snotty-nosed kids that I don't know."

"Marilyn, you have to invite their friends over when you're off from work and meet the children and their parents."

"I don't have time to babysit ill-mannered kids. I wouldn't waste a day off to bother with children and chitchat with lazy adults. I have important pursuits in life. I've had enough of your small talk. Urgent deadlines demand my attention. My own flesh and blood sister is about to let me down!"

Lottie never won an argument with her sister, who was a master of verbal controversy. "Oh, I'm sorry, Marilyn. I can help you. Why don't you let the children stay the night? I'm already in town and can get them."

"Yes. I would like for you to pick them up. It's in my best interest that I work late tonight. I'll phone the children to be ready. Don't rush. George and Victoria can take care of themselves until you arrive. By the way, there's a package for you on the dining room table. I bought you an early birthday present while I was in Atlanta."

"You found the Melanie Groner vase?"

"Yes, I found it."

"Thank you, Marilyn. I know you paid a lot for it. You don't have to bribe me to take care of your children."

Marilyn ignored Lottie's remark. "Let me know what ceramic piece you want for Christmas. I'll return to Atlanta in a few weeks."

"All right. I'll think about it. Little Rob and I are leaving Miles's store. We'll go now to get George and Victoria."

"Thank you very much, Lottie."

"You're very welcome," said Lottie. She dropped her phone into her handbag.

"Little Rob," said Lottie, "your cousins will spend the night with us tonight."

"We'll have fun! We'll play outside! I'll show them tricks on the trampoline," said Little Rob.

Mother and son arrived at the only gated community in West Point. They parked and walked up to Marilyn's condominium door. Lottie pointed to the intercom button, which Little Rob pushed fervently. A boy, trying to sound like a man, answered. "Yes. Who are you, and what do you want?"

Little Rob pounded the door with both palms and shouted, "Let me in! Let me in!"

George MacGinnis opened the door slightly, and Little Rob pushed his way into the room past George. Little Rob's cousin looked like a little man with bucked teeth, slicked-down hair, a thick middle, and toothpick legs. He called out to Little Rob, "You must stop! Don't go farther!" Little Rob circled the den and dining room, scanning its layout, with George on his heels.

"Hello, George," said Lottie pleasantly.

George stopped following Little Rob. "Hello, Aunt Lottie. It's very nice to see you." George's bottom lip quivered, and his eyes filled with tears. Lottie agonized over their emotional confusion. George felt pressure to act like a man, not an adventurous ten-year-old boy.

Lottie knew that her sister's criticism and hard-heartedness had devastated George and Victoria. *Marilyn tramples over their feelings. They stay here by themselves. They have no friends. They aren't allowed to go outside.*

George was afraid of his mother and refused to consider the temptation to sneak outside and play. Lottie grabbed George and embraced him. Finally, he moved his stiff arms and hugged her. He whimpered, and Lottie tried to comfort him. "Everything will be all right, George. I love you." Lottie sometimes wished that Marilyn would go far away to another job and leave the children in her and Miles's care.

Lottie looked around. "Where's your sister?"

George pointed to the corner of the dining room. There was Victoria, pitifully thin and pale. She crouched on the floor like a starving child from an impoverished country, with her arms across her chest, squeezing her shoulders and looking down. Her light wavy hair fell unkempt on her shoulders. Lottie rushed to Victoria and cradled her.

The little girl was deprived of motherly love and affection; she felt isolated and alone. Lottie kissed seven-year-old Victoria and told her, "Don't worry, Sweetie. I love you. You're a good girl." Lottie held Victoria's head up to look directly into the sunken blue eyes of her niece.

I've got to get these children out of here. Dear God, this is child abuse! Victoria is so thin and unhappy. Lord, please rescue these children.

Little Rob distracted George from his dejected state of mind. George followed his cousin around the condo and said, "Don't touch that! Don't touch that! No! No! Put that back!"

Marilyn had infected the perfectly decorated residence with a contentious spirit. Lottie wanted to evacuate with the children and take them to the safety of her home. On the antique mahogany dining table, Lottie saw a brown package. "This must be the designer vase that Marilyn found for me in Atlanta. Come on, kids. Let's head to my house. We'll have fun," said Lottie.

"I'm the fastest. I'll beat you to the car," said Little Rob as he ran out the door.

Little Rob chattered all the way home. He pointed to every police car and motorcycle, and made sure that George saw them, too. Lottie conversed with her niece and nephew, but only George answered.

"I have to stop at the grocery store and pick up food for supper. Let's all go inside. We won't be long." While pushing her buggy in the supermarket, Lottie constantly told Little Rob, "Put that back. Stop running in the store! Don't knock those cans over! Stay beside me." George and Victoria obediently followed Lottie up and down the aisles and to the checkout, content to be away from their confinement.

When they arrived at Lottie's house, she unbuckled Little Rob to let him out of the car. He ran to the side door and pressed his face and hands against the windowpane, fogging the glass with his breath. George and Victoria waited in the car until Lottie opened the door and told them to get out. They rolled their suitcases along the sidewalk behind Lottie. Impatient to go inside, Little Rob pushed his way in first. Lottie carried her brown package and the grocery bags into the house and set them on the kitchen counter.

"You kids can play while I start supper. We'll eat early because I have an important high school reunion meeting here tonight with some ladies."

Chapter 15

First Meeting

*L*ittle Rob ran upstairs to play, while George and Victoria stood by their suitcases in the kitchen. They looked around cautiously. Lottie unwrapped her package.

"This is wonderful! Isn't this vase beautiful, Victoria?" Lottie's underweight niece stared blankly at her aunt. "Do you like it, George?"

"I don't know, Aunt Lottie."

"All right," sighed Lottie. "Take your suitcases upstairs, and put them in the guest room next to Little Rob's bedroom."

Lottie watched her sister's children drag upstairs. They showed no zest for life in comparison to her son.

Lottie listened for Little Rob's characteristic bumps and noises. She knew that if Little Rob did anything that he shouldn't, George would tell her. Lottie put place mats and bottles of salad dressing on the table, and continued her simple supper preparations.

"Is anybody home?" asked Miles as he walked into the kitchen and hugged and kissed his wife. While he flipped through the mail, Lottie walked to the stairs and announced, "Daddy's home!"

First Meeting

Little Rob ran down the stairs. "Daddy! Daddy!" He jumped into his father's arms and was lifted high and then set down.

"Hey, Buddy! You should be outside playing!"

George and Victoria slowly sidestepped into the room.

"I see we have some guests. How are you, George?" asked Miles. He reached for George's hand and shook it, and then poked him under his chin and then his stomach repeatedly until George laughed uncontrollably.

"Hey, Sweetheart," said Miles to Victoria. He held out his hand to her, but she clutched her hands tightly to her chest and would not look at him. "You're hiding something in your hand. I bet you're holding my pet spider."

Victoria opened her hands wide to look. Miles playfully slapped her palms with his hands and said, "Gotcha!" Then he grabbed Victoria's stiff skeleton body and lifted her high and then brought her down and hugged her.

"Come on," said Little Rob. "Let's jump on the trampoline!" Little Rob ran out the back door, leaving a trail of socks and shoes.

"All right!" said Miles. He led George with his hand and carried Victoria.

"Miles, don't try any stunts on the trampoline. It's men your age who are most likely to get hurt," said Lottie. Miles stopped and pouted at Lottie. She winked at him and then closed the door and picked up Little Rob's socks and shoes.

Lottie raised the kitchen window and listened to the happy sounds of children. She watched Miles make silly faces and jump on the trampoline. When the meal was prepared, Lottie yelled out the open window, "Supper's ready!"

George and Victoria immediately came in, washed their hands, and stood by the dining table. George looked at Lottie's built-in kitchen china cabinet and said, "Your things don't shine like diamonds like my mother's."

"You're right, George. Your mother likes crystal and fine china, but I like colorful ceramics. I can use them every day and not worry if I break one."

"Miles, did you notice the new vase that Marilyn bought for me?" said Lottie. She pointed to her new ceramic piece.

Miles glanced at the vase. "Yes, that's nice. What's for supper?"

"Hmmp." Lottie rolled her eyes at Miles, irritated at his lack of interest in her new vase. "We're having spaghetti and salad. Did you remember that I have a committee meeting here tonight at seven-thirty? Why don't you take the children to get ice cream and maybe to Kid Town to play?"

"Let me see. Who wants to get ice cream after supper and then go play at Kid Town?" asked Miles.

"I do! I do! I want to go!" said Little Rob. "We can all go. George and Victoria want to go, too."

George sheepishly grinned. Victoria raised her shoulders up and down with each breath. They were elated over the prospect of outdoor play.

The children ate their supper quickly and waited on Miles to finish.

"Let's go, Daddy. Can we go, please?" implored Little Rob.

"Yes, go!" said Lottie. "I hear someone driving up now."

"Good-bye, Mommy," said Little Rob, leading the way out the door.

The first committee member to arrive was Mary Cecil. Her commanding reputation and obsession as a punctual person was clearly established. At exactly seven-thirty, Katherine, the town librarian, drove up Lottie's driveway. She was highly organized but not as obsessive as Mary Cecil. Turning in behind Katherine was Trudy. She smiled a lot and was in charge of hospitality.

Conversation dragged as Lottie and the ladies sipped drinks and waited for Lucy Jenkins, who was habitually late.

First Meeting

Mary Cecil twitched uncomfortably and said, "How can anyone be so rude? Lucy Jenkins doesn't care if she's late and wastes our time. We should expel Lucy Jenkins from this committee. This project is above her capabilities, and I can't tolerate her incorrigible, thoughtless chatter!"

"I hear someone now. That must be Lucy," said Lottie, relieved that Lucy finally arrived before Mary Cecil burst into a frenzy.

"Hey, girls! Sorry I'm late. I had to get my nails retouched," said Lucy as she fluffed her hands up to admire her fingernails. Lucy cocked her upswept hair and touched the flower, clipped to one side.

Katherine and Trudy responded, "That's okay. Don't worry about it. We haven't started." Mary Cecil pressed her lips, crossed her arms, and forcefully grunted.

Lucy Jenkins entertained the ladies with lively conversation. "The assistant police chief pulled me over for speeding and told me to 'slow down.'"

"Did he give you a speeding ticket?" asked Trudy.

"No. He was working late and more interested in getting home for supper. He wouldn't ticket the police chief's wife!" Lucy laughed and continued talking.

Lottie picked up a ceramic dinner bell and rang it. Everyone looked at Lottie.

"I'm sorry to interrupt. I want to applaud Mary Cecil for organizing the contact information on the registration form and formatting it into a directory on CD."

The girls exclaimed, "Great idea! They'll love it! Way to go!"

Mary Cecil smiled. Her carefully applied blush formed a perfect circle on each cheekbone. In her deep voice, she elaborated, "Our classmates can reconnect even after the reunion. Katherine said that she can burn the CDs, and we'll distribute them at the Saturday night banquet.

"I also took the initiative and arranged for the city to hang welcome banners across Main Street to salute our class. I'll be at the information booth early that Saturday morning, where I think *all* of us should be. We can watch for out-of-town classmates who failed to sign up for an afternoon activity. We also can help Katherine collect money from anyone who hasn't paid. And Lottie may need help with unforeseen problems."

"Thank you, Mary Cecil. Your organizational skills are impeccable. You think of everything," said Lottie.

"Oh, yes," bragged Mary Cecil, "I located the whereabouts of *all* of our classmates. I found out that nine are dead, five are incarcerated, and one is in a mental institution."

Chapter 16

Compatible or Not

"*M*ental institution," gushed Trudy. "Mental institution?"

"Rastus Webber," explained Lucy. "Don't be surprised. He's still crazy."

"I was afraid of him in school," confessed Mary Cecil.

"You should have been in science lab with him. He was obsessed with the Bunsen burner and tried to burn me with a hot paper clip," elaborated Lucy.

"He was very animated in literature class," said Katherine.

"Ladies, we're not here to discuss Rastus Webber. Trudy, have you appointed people to help with hospitality?" asked Lottie.

"Yes. I've already planned who will welcome people at each of the Saturday afternoon activities and get them started so everyone can renew old friendships," bubbled Trudy. "My husband has agreed to videotape the afternoon activities and the banquet that night, and put it on a DVD for people to order! Isn't that wonderful?"

"Great idea! Cool! Yeah!" agreed all the women, except Mary Cecil.

"*What?*" exclaimed Mary Cecil. "I can't believe that you took it upon yourself to include a DVD as part of the reunion without talking with the committee first. Nobody told me. If I had known, I would have mentioned it on the registration form, and we could have included the charge. We . . . we have to let everyone know," said Mary Cecil, splaying her hands in frustration, short of having a panic attack. "I didn't expect such a major addition to our plans. It's too much . . . in too short a time . . . to coordinate a CD and a DVD. I didn't know . . . ."

Lottie assured Mary Cecil, "It's okay. Don't worry, Mary Cecil. I'm sure we'll have other options arise that we'll want to include. It's a good idea; it doesn't matter who thought of it. It's important that we work together."

Irritated at Trudy's DVD offer, Mary Cecil huffed short breaths and said, "Who's going to notify people and find out who wants one? Someone will have to take orders and money the night of the banquet."

Lottie asked Katherine, "Will you send everyone a message about the availability of a reunion DVD?"

"No problem. I'm downloading everyone's information. I'll send weekly updates and take orders," said Katherine.

Mary Cecil sat stiffly with her arms crossed and pouted in annoyance.

"Okay. We'll move on," said Lottie. "Lucy, tell us what you've planned for food and entertainment."

Lucy whined, "Mary Cecil and Katherine didn't ask for enough money to pay for everything. A sit-down dinner will cost more money than we asked for on the registration form. Maybe we should do a buffet. Or maybe we can afford to serve heavy hors d'oeuvres."

The ladies looked at Lucy in surprise. Mary Cecil grabbed her chair and flatly asked, "What? You haven't done anything, you gaudy floozy!"

Mary Cecil turned to Katherine. "I told you she would fail. She can't even count how many pennies in a dollar. And we trusted her to handle food and entertainment?"

"Lucy, you gave me the expected expenses a month ago," said Katherine. "Mary Cecil and I set the fees for the activities, dinner, and entertainment on your recommendations, which we assumed you based on price quotes."

"Lucy Jenkins," said Mary Cecil gruffly, "you're an irresponsible, empty-headed mannequin! Your foolishness is unacceptable. Lucy Jenkins, you obviously don't know what you're doing!"

Unmoved by insults, Lucy said, "Don't worry. We'll be fine." She sat back, crossed her legs, and swung her top leg back and forth vigorously. "I'm sure the chef at Anthony's Restaurant can provide some kind of fabulous feast for the reunion banquet."

"Have you arranged for refreshments for the people who sign up for the afternoon activities?" asked Lottie. "It's hot on Labor Day weekend."

"I'm not sure," said Lucy. "They serve from the snack bar for tennis and swimming, and the mobile food cart goes around on the golf course. But the club charges by member numbers and handles no cash."

Mary Cecil rolled her eyes and sighed antagonistically.

Katherine moved to the edge of her chair. Not hiding her testiness, she said, "I told you that Old Waverly Club wants us to pay upfront for an estimated number of guests. You should have already arranged to pay for refreshments."

Lottie felt disquieted. *Lucy said she could handle the food and entertainment easily.* "Lucy, we have to provide beverages for everyone participating in the outdoor activities. The temperatures can reach 100 degrees."

Trudy sweetly encouraged Lucy. "If it were me, Lucy, I would go back to the club manager and arrange drinks for our guests."

Duress

"Yes," said Katherine. "I don't want anyone to pass out from a heat stroke or to leave an activity early because they're thirsty."

"Lucy Jenkins," snapped Mary Cecil, "before I printed the forms, you assured me that the prices for the Saturday afternoon activities and the banquet at Anthony's were adequate and confirmed!"

"Well," said Lucy, "that's what you said. You said that hosting a class reunion in three months was impossible. I was waiting to see if anybody signed up."

Mary Cecil, Trudy, and Katherine were displeased, and Lucy was flustered. Uncharacteristically, Lucy did not talk the most. Lottie felt the start of a bad headache.

Mary Cecil stood up and said, "I vote to remove Lucy Jenkins from this committee. We've taken on a tremendous task to make a class reunion happen in a short time. We can't tolerate Lucy Jenkins's laggard actions. We can handle food and entertainment without her stupidity. All in favor of dismissing Lucy Jenkins from this committee, say . . . ."

Trudy, Katherine, and Lucy babbled erratically. Lottie put her hands on her hips and bobbed her head from side to side. She raised her voice. "Ladies. Ladies! Stop it!"

The women paused to look at Lottie. "We're in this together. The reunion . . . . This reunion will be unforgettable. The date is perfect. Many of our former classmates come home on Labor Day weekend for the Prairie Arts Festival, so the attendance should be high. Compatible or not, we *have* to put aside our personal differences. We have to work *together*. I'll help Lucy with the refreshments issue and the banquet meal."

"What have you done about entertainment?" asked Mary Cecil crossly.

Lucy ignored Mary Cecil's affront and responded with excitement. "You girls will love it! I've arranged for an amazing blues band to play."

"Have you ever heard them play?" asked Katherine.

"Are they a bona fide band? Are you sure they'll show up?" snarled Mary Cecil.

"Are they worth the money we'll pay them?" questioned Katherine.

Lottie thought to herself, *Oh, no. Here we go again. Why did I agree to be chairwoman of this committee?*

Chapter 17

Ignore His Advise

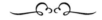

*L*ottie heard Miles and the children in the garage. She thought, *This is a good time to end the meeting.* She stood up and said, "I'll be in touch with everyone. Thank you for coming." She walked to the door and held it open for the ladies to leave.

"When will you schedule our next meeting, Lottie?" asked Mary Cecil.

Lottie sighed, "Next week. We'll meet weekly until the reunion. Katherine, keep me posted as you receive the registration forms and fees." Katherine nodded positively.

As the ladies exited the side door, Miles and the children entered through the door by the garage. Lottie rubbed her temples to ease her stress and headache.

Little Rob ran in the house first and headed to the refrigerator for a sports drink, with George and Victoria behind.

"How was the reunion meeting?" asked Miles.

"I don't want to talk about it," said Lottie, massaging her head.

"Let me see. It couldn't have been *that* terrible."

"It was *terrible*."

Ignore His Advise

"Well, we had a good time, didn't we, kids? Everybody fell down at least once, except Victoria." Little Rob giggled, and George smiled.

"Why don't we go for a swim tomorrow? Would you like to do that, George and Victoria?" asked Lottie.

"We don't have swimming suits, Aunt Lottie," replied George.

"Hmm. Never mind. When did you last see your daddy?"

"It's been a long time, Aunt Lottie," said George.

Miles raised his eyebrows at Lottie and muttered, "Uh huumm. They're not supposed to go there."

"Mother says that 'he piddles on his pig farm and does not have enough money' for us to visit," continued George.

"*Piddles* on his pig farm? Enough *money* for you to visit? I think I'll call tomorrow and see if your daddy and Mama Mac can afford some time for us to piddle on the farm."

Miles said, "Lottie, that's not a good idea." Lottie arched her chin away from Miles, ignoring his advice.

"Little Rob, would you like to go to the big farm tomorrow and see Uncle Buster and Mama Mac?"

"Yes! Let's go to the big farm! I want to go!"

Lottie changed the subject. "You kids can camp downstairs tonight." She spread sleeping bags and quilts in the den for the boys and covered the sofa with sheets and a blanket for Victoria. Lottie situated George close to Victoria so he could sleep by his sister, and then fluffed Little Rob's pillow and kissed them all good night.

She walked upstairs to get ready for bed. Miles was sitting up in bed, reading some papers. Lottie left the bathroom door open while she washed her face and put on her gown so she could talk to Miles.

"Lottie Love, you better not meddle in your sister's life. She has court papers that forbid Buster from seeing the children without her permission."

"The only reason she refuses to let her children see their daddy is because he owns and runs a pig farm. Oh, yes, and she told the judge that she makes enough money to support the children and he doesn't, as if Buster's making less money makes him an unfit father."

"I agree, Lottie Love, but George and Victoria aren't our children. We can't legally interfere. Don't take them to the farm without her knowing about it."

"Marilyn will never know. She won't call to check on the children. I'll have to call her when I'm ready to drive George and Victoria back to the condo. I don't understand why Buster didn't fight Marilyn's unreasonable demands. He and Mama Mac would spend time with the children and love them. Those kids deserve a life, too. Marilyn never takes them anywhere. She never plays with them. They have no friends. Marilyn doesn't let them visit us unless she needs a babysitter."

"The court awarded Marilyn control of her children," Miles reminded Lottie. "Don't go to the farm."

Lottie climbed into bed and sat with her pillow behind her back. "My sister has climbed the corporate ladder and pushed her children to the bottom rung. She spends all her time trying to impress her bosses and no time tending to her own children." Lottie heaved a heavy sigh.

"Umm hum," responded Miles, half listening. He directed his attention back to his papers. "I've looked over this information on the Builders Supply Convention, and it's scheduled the first week in September. I'll need to fly out on the Friday before Labor Day."

"That's the weekend of the Prairie Arts Festival and the class reunion! You can't leave Little Rob and me! I need you here for the reunion and the Labor Day holiday!"

"Lottie Love, *I have to go* to my convention. It's two weeks earlier this year. They changed the location to Seattle.

It's a long flight. And if I fly out early Friday, I save $500. I can't miss this trip."

"Do you have to go? I want you here for that weekend. We always go to the Prairie Arts Festival. I want you to meet some of my old schoolmates. You can miss the convention one year."

Miles assured her, "You'll be so busy with the reunion that you won't miss me. It's the biggest exhibition they've ever had. If I don't go and learn what's new, builders around here will go somewhere else to buy their supplies. This is an annual event that I can't miss."

"Well, I can't miss the reunion, especially since I'm the committee chairwoman. How irresponsible would it be for me to fly away to Seattle and leave the girls here to manage the reunion? If only your convention and the reunion weren't at the same time . . . ."

"I'm sorry, Lottie Love. I know you'll nail everything down without a hitch. With you in charge, it'll be great."

"I'm dreading the reunion. I should be excited. I've got to help Lucy with the food and entertainment. She hosted parties every other weekend in high school. I thought I gave her an easy job on this committee, but she couldn't make a decision or plan anything."

"A class reunion is a bit more structured than a weekend party. Lucy certainly knows how to make people feel welcome and can lure anyone into a conversation," said Miles.

"Lucy couldn't arrange the afternoon activities or the banquet meal. Her husband, Don, is very orderly and organized. Lucy and Don are a perfect example of opposites who attract," mused Lottie.

"Yes," said Miles. "His words are like cement that hardens after it's poured. Her words are like regular detergent that's added to a dishwasher: It's the wrong soap, and the bubbles run out the sides."

"That's not a nice thing to say about Lucy. We were best friends in high school. We have different priorities now. But she's been a faithful friend through the years."

"I wish you could go with me to Seattle. The weather will be cool there. We could walk to the outdoor markets, eat some good seafood. We haven't traveled together in a long time."

"You're mean. How can you talk about the good things you'll enjoy in Seattle without me?"

"I want you to go with me. I'd enjoy my trip much more if you would come."

"Miles, *I can't* leave town the weekend of the reunion. I have a responsibility to the committee and to my classmates. I can't believe you won't be here for my class reunion. I can't believe you'll be gone."

Chapter 18

The Secret Visit

*L*ottie tossed and turned all night long. She worried about the reunion. *I can ask Buster to help. He actually graduated with our class and probably would like to see everybody. Everything will be all right. Little Rob and I will be fine. I wish I felt better about the reunion. I mustn't fret about the reunion or be upset with Miles because he'll be out of town.*

Miles left early to go to work. Lottie got up tired. The children wandered into the kitchen, yawning, when they smelled the bacon cooking. Lottie served them crisp bacon and warm pancakes with syrup.

"Ummm. Ummm," said Little Rob as he sat down in his chair at the kitchen table.

George and Victoria stood stiffly beside the table. "Go ahead and sit," Lottie said as she sat down with her plate. "Little Rob, will you bless our food?"

Little Rob cupped his hands over his mouth and spoke quietly. Then he looked up, smiled, and started to eat. With each mouthful, George closed his eyes and sighed contentedly. Victoria slowly savored tiny bites.

Lottie watched her nephew and niece. *I'm not that good of a cook.* "Do you kids never eat pancakes and bacon for breakfast?"

"Never, Aunt Lottie," said George. "I like the way it tastes."

When they finished, Lottie told them, "Put on your play clothes, and we'll go to the farm."

"We're going to the farm! We're going to the farm!" squealed Little Rob as he ran upstairs to put on the clothes his mother had laid out for him.

"Aunt Lottie, we do not have any 'play clothes,'" said George.

"Okay, George. Just put on the clothes you packed."

Lottie quickly cleaned the kitchen and got dressed. After she gathered the three children and set the house alarm, they got into the car and drove away.

George asked, "Will Mother come to the farm?"

Lottie responded, "No, she will not."

"Aunt Lottie, may I please roll down the window to feel the fresh air?" asked George.

Lottie thought, *It's too hot to drive with the windows down. I'd rather have air conditioning. But Marilyn would never let the children ride with the windows open. And George would be afraid to ask his mother.*

Lottie unlocked the power windows and lowered them for George and Little Rob. The boys put their hands and heads in and out of the windows and were blissfully amused. The wind fluffed Little Rob's tight curls on his round head. Victoria clutched her elbows and looked straight ahead.

"I know your grandmother and daddy will be delighted to see you. Look! There's the white fence. We're almost there," said Lottie.

She turned off of the highway onto a long gravel road. Soon they reached the driveway to the house. Mums and daisies bloomed profusely.   Along the way, pecan and pear trees hung heavy with their harvest.

The children spotted Mama Mac's silver hair as she gently rocked in her chair. Wearing his rugged boots and jeans, Buster sat in the porch swing, watching for his children. When the car stopped, Buster walked to the car, opened the door for his children, and helped them get out. He fell to his knees and embraced his son and daughter.

"I'm so glad to see you. I could hardly wait for you to get here." Buster huddled over his children and wrapped his strong arms around them. "George, you've grown taller." Buster shook from sobs and moans. He patted their shoulders and heads and kissed their cheeks and temples. He stood up and rubbed his eyes with his hands and his nose with his sleeve. His sun-lightened hair was spiked short. Buster was a handsome, muscular man with a tender heart.

He picked up Victoria in his huge arms and held George's hand, then walked to his mother. Mama Mac reached for George and rubbed his head. "You've become such a fine young man," said Mama Mac. Buster set his frail daughter in his mother's lap, as she said, "Precious, precious child." The older woman wrapped her arms around them both and kissed them continually. Tears rolled down her cheeks. She spoke softly to her grandchildren and stroked their arms and hands.

The sight of such a family picture made Lottie cry. She wondered, *How long has it been since they've seen each other?*

The sentimental moment ended when Little Rob disappeared around the house to play on Buster's farm equipment. Little Rob rubbed his hands on the bars, straps, and tires. Then he ran toward the nearest building that towered to the sky, and everyone followed. The children took turns swinging on the handmade wooden tree swing that hung high on a limb of a massive oak tree.

Afterward, they walked to another barn, where Buster threw open the doors. He climbed into a huge tractor and pulled the children up into the cab. Victoria sat in his lap, and the boys held onto his shoulders as they toured the farm. The women strolled back to the house, where Lottie helped Mama Mac cook lunch. They prepared a country meal of pork tenderloin, fresh corn, butter beans, fried okra, red, juicy tomatoes, and corn bread muffins.

"I made a banana pudding for George," said Mama Mac. "I think he'll like it as much as his daddy does."

About an hour later, Buster and the children returned. It was obvious that Buster had let the children play at the horse barn because their shoes were dirty and smelly.

"Leave your shoes at the back door," said Mama Mac. "Your daddy will clean them after we eat. Now wash your hands, and we'll sit down for lunch."

When Mama Mac sat down at the table, she said, "Buster, will you please bless our food?"

After he prayed, Buster served his children's plates. He gave George extra large portions, which his son especially enjoyed. Victoria continually ate little bites. Little Rob finished his lunch quickly and walked over to Mama Mac to tell her, "I enjoyed it! Can I be excused?"

"Yes, Dear. You may be excused." Little Rob ran out the kitchen door, letting it slam behind him. Mama Mac attentively talked to George and Victoria.

Lottie asked Buster, "What's in that big green building?"

"That's my research barn. That's where I like to hatch my ideas. I just developed a product that has FOS, or fructooligosaccharide, added to the hog feed."

"Why would you add something else to hog feed? I thought hog feed was corn or pellets or something."

Buster laughed. "You're not a farm girl, are you? I found some good reasons to add this ingredient to the feed. And now, some city boys are trying to buy my idea and use my process."

"Wish I could sell some of my ideas," laughed Lottie.

"I'm not interested at the moment. I want to refine my product a little more."

"Well, if it's good for the pigs, I guess you should do it."

Buster was enthusiastic about his project and elaborated. "I figured out that this type of natural fiber can be added to hog feed to improve the nutrition, and as a side effect, it eliminates the bad odor from the hogs' excrement."

"Oh," said Lottie. She did not want to talk about hog feed anymore.

Chapter 19

Don't Tell Marilyn

"I think the kids would have fun riding my gentle horse," said Buster. "I'll walk beside the children so they won't be scared."

"Okay," said Lottie. "Then, we have to go back to town."

Buster and the children rode in the tractor to the barn while Mama Mac and Lottie walked to meet them. Buster saddled his tame horse, Dolly, and let each child ride around as he led it in the green grassy pasture. When it was time to go, Buster hitched his tractor to a flatbed trailer and gave the children, Mama Mac, and Lottie a hayride to the house.

"We have to leave now," said Lottie.

George and Victoria hugged their father and grandmother for several minutes. Victoria clung to her grandmother's arm with both hands. The MacGinnis children told Mama Mac and Buster good-bye over and over again. Lottie's eyes filled with tears, but Little Rob interrupted her reverie when he ran around the house to play. She chased him to the hay trailer. Out of breath, Lottie clasped Little Rob's hand and pulled him to the car.

The ride back to Marilyn's place was quiet. Little Rob fell asleep. George and Victoria rolled their eyes and heads around. They meditated on the relaxing day they had spent on the farm with their daddy and grandmother.

Lottie could not talk to the children on the way home because she was preoccupied with the woeful circumstances to which she had to return George and Victoria. The children were old enough to taste the sweetness of love and would surely crave more, but they must not tell their mother about their day on the farm.

She drove through the gate at the affluent complex in West Point and greeted the guard. Lottie felt as if she had taken the children from a warm wonderland into a shameful stronghold. She parked the car and unloaded the children. George and Victoria rolled their suitcases along the sidewalk, and Lottie carried her sleepy son. George tapped in the entrance access code and opened the heavy wooden door. Lottie laid Little Rob on the couch with his feet dangling over the side so he would not soil the sofa.

"I want to bathe you both before your mother gets in. I'll run some bath water while you pick out clean clothes."

George bathed first in their luxurious tub. As soon as he was through, Lottie gave Victoria a quick shampoo and bath, and then dressed her.

While in the den, Lottie brushed Victoria's hair. George stood by and timidly shared his feelings with Lottie. "I like to go to your house and to the farm to play outside, Aunt Lottie. Mother says that we have to stay inside by ourselves. We'll be here alone for a long time until Mother comes in tonight with our supper."

"We had a big lunch, George. Maybe you and Victoria won't get hungry for a while."

"I hope Mother is not angry tonight after work. Victoria always waits for Mother over there." George pointed to the dining room corner where Lottie saw Victoria the day before. "Sometimes Mother comes in mad and yells at us, and then Victoria wets herself, and Mother gets madder."

Lottie looked where Victoria often crouched. The area was stained and slightly darkened. Embarrassed, Victoria turned her head down and away from Lottie.

George continued to divulge family secrets and deep emotions to Lottie. "A lot of nights, Mother spanks Victoria and sends her to bed with no supper." Victoria inched over beside Lottie and stood stiffly, with her head hung in shame and her arms crossed tightly across her chest.

"Does Marilyn allow Victoria to eat her supper later? Or do you bring it to her room after your mother goes to bed?"

"No, Aunt Lottie. Mother throws her supper in the garbage and tells me not to touch it because she says, 'That's Victoria's punishment for bad behavior.'"

Oh, dear God! That's why Victoria is a skeleton! I can't believe Marilyn would starve her own daughter.

"I'll supply you both with boxes of food to hide in your rooms. If you eat something, throw the wrappers away after your mother leaves for work."

I can't believe I'm going to secretly give food to George and Victoria. I must talk to Marilyn about Victoria. She's only seven and doesn't intentionally wet herself and the carpet. Oh, God. How can I help my niece and nephew? This is child abuse.

"My father and grandmother gave me food with good taste today. My mother says that my father is not a father because he can't provide the things I need. What *things* does she mean?"

"Well, George, everybody needs food, clothes, and a place to live."

"My father and grandmother have those *things*."

"Yes. And they have love to give to you and Victoria." Lottie pulled Victoria close and continued to brush her hair.

"What is love, Aunt Lottie?" asked George.

"Hmm. Well, it's the warm feeling you had when Mama Mac stroked your arm and rubbed your head. It's the way you felt when your daddy played with you and hugged you."

"Today I felt so . . . so . . . I can't say what I mean. I don't know how to say it, but I liked the way my father and grandmother hugged me. Do you like to hug Little Rob?"

"Yes. I love to hug Little Rob, when I can catch him." Lottie winked at George, and he nodded. "Little Rob lets me hug him when he's tired or sleepy. I always hug Little Rob at night when I tuck him in bed."

"We put ourselves to bed," said George. Lottie inhaled a small gasp of sorrow as she fathomed the utter loneliness of George and Victoria.

"Little Rob likes to sit on my lap and hug me when I read to him."

"Mother doesn't hug us. She never reads to us."

I can't believe Marilyn neglects her children so miserably.

"Aunt Lottie, what do you read to Little Rob?"

"He has some favorite books that we read over and over again."

"Will you read one of Little Rob's favorite books to us next time we visit, Aunt Lottie?"

"I would love to read to you both." She hugged and kissed them.

"Mother and Father are very different," said George.

"Yes, George. They're different. That's usually the way it works when two people get married."

George said, "I wish Mother and my father could be together so that we could be a family. A real family. I want to go outside and play with my father again. Victoria and I don't like to stay here alone." Victoria turned her ear toward her brother and aunt, listening to every word.

"I'm sorry you and Victoria have to wait for your mother to come in late at night. I have an idea, George. From now on, whenever your mother gets home, no matter how late, you telephone my house and let it ring one time and hang up. I'll phone you back and let it ring once and hang up. Then I'll send up a prayer for you, and you send up a prayer for me. Have you ever heard of smoke signals?"

"Yes, Aunt Lottie, I know about smoke signals."

"We'll send 'phone signals' to each other. That will let me know your mother is home with you. I'll immediately return your call so that you'll know that I thought about you and prayed for you and Victoria. You can send me a 'phone signal' anytime you want me to pray for you."

"Thank you, Aunt Lottie. I will think of you sometimes and telephone a 'phone signal' to you. When I send you a 'phone signal,' will you pray that Mother and my father will come together so we can be a family? A happy family?"

"Yes, George. I'll pray for your mother and daddy. You can pray yourself, George."

"I don't know how. Whom do I pray to?"

"You pray to God. I close my eyes and talk to God. A verse in Ephesians says, 'We may approach God with freedom and confidence.'"

"What does that mean?" asked George.

"It means that you are free to talk to God. You don't have to be afraid to ask Him for help. You may ask God for anything, but I don't want you to be disappointed. Sometimes we don't get what we ask for in prayer because other people choose what God doesn't want, or they refuse to listen to God."

George shook his head positively, trying to understand. "Aunt Lottie, today was a very good day. I like my father and grandmother. I have never eaten food like I tasted today. I really enjoyed my father. I like him."

"I know, George. I'm glad we went to the country today to see your daddy." Lottie looked at Victoria. "Did you enjoy the day, Sweetie?"

Very shyly, Victoria nodded.

"Listen, George and Victoria. Today was a great day. I don't want to cause problems with your mother. You mustn't tell your mother about today."

"Tell me what?" asked Marilyn MacGinnis.

Chapter 20

Consequences of Deceit

*N*o one heard Marilyn come in. Lottie had not expected her sister to come home. George froze. Victoria became pale, grabbed her arms, and looked down. The hairs on Lottie's neck prickled. She choked to breathe and to speak. Dread and helplessness weakened her almost to the point of fainting. *Oh God! I'm caught!*

"Some idiot bumped into me at work and made me spill coffee on my suit. I had to come home to change. I have a presentation in one hour at the quarterly operations meeting. Now, what are my children not supposed to tell me?" asked Marilyn.

Lottie knew she couldn't hide what had happened. Marilyn was about to find out. Lottie's stomach fluttered. Her body trembled. Heat rippled from the small of her back up her spine to her face. She took a deep breath. She did not want to cower. "The children needed fresh air. They needed to go to the country and have fun. They needed to see . . . ."

"Don't tell me. Don't tell me you took them to that nasty pig farm. Is that where you took my children?"

"Marilyn, if you'll just listen. Let me explain."

"You did! You took them to that godforsaken pigsty. I am incensed at your trickery! What made you think you could take them there? My children are forbidden to go to that hog wallow! They aren't allowed to see their father without my permission. And I'll never permit them to see him. How could you take them there, you irresponsible sneak? And you told my children not to tell me!"

Lottie's heart hammered her chest and eardrums. "But Marilyn, they're Buster's children, too. The farm was beautiful; it didn't smell bad. They had fun on the swing that Buster made for them, and they rode a horse . . . ."

"Do you secretly take them to Boyd's mud hole when you have my children? Is that what you do? I can't believe my own sister would be so underhanded! You are so irresponsible."

"No, I'm not. No, Marilyn, you don't understand."

"Yes, I understand. You deliberately went against my rules. My children are of a higher class than a pig farm. I can't believe I spawned children with Boyd. I'm the one who buys them the best that money can buy!" shouted Marilyn. "I'm the one who keeps them clean and well-dressed! Boyd doesn't do anything but piddle with pigs and drive a tractor and coddle his old mother."

Lottie wanted her shallow breathing and quaking to stop. She responded quietly to offset the edge of the moment. "Buster can give them things that money can't buy. Fine clothes, expensive furniture, and fancy food don't make children happy. It takes more."

"You're right! It takes more than you'll ever know. Get your lying butt out of my house! Get away from my children! They would have been better off if they had stayed here by themselves without your interference in our lives. I can't believe I trusted you with my children. They will never set foot on that farm again! I forbid them to ever see their biological father again! They will never see you or your rotten family again! We don't need you. Now, get out of my sight!"

In tears, George shook. Victoria looked down, with her arms stiffened across her chest and her body straight as a pencil. Her bottom lip quivered. Urine ran down her legs and onto the carpet.

"Victoria MacGinnis! Can you not restrain yourself? I'm ashamed of you, acting like an infant. I don't have time to clean up you and the mess you made on my carpet! You stupid girl! I have to go to my meeting."

"I'll clean it up," said Lottie.

"No! You get out of my house! Get out of my life! I mistakenly thought I could trust you. You're a sorry, deceitful sister! You've corrupted my children."

"No, Marilyn. I was thinking of the children. I wanted to treat them to an outing with their father. He loves them."

Lottie courageously blurted her concerns to Marilyn. "I'm worried about Victoria. She's pathetically thin. She doesn't get enough food to eat. She needs love and affection. I'm afraid George and Victoria will develop emotional problems if they have to continue to live like this."

"What? 'Live like this'?" laughed Marilyn. "You're out of place telling me what I need to do. Victoria has problems, but it's not with eating. George is the one who eats like a slop hog. They have food to eat. And if they don't, I pick up something on my way home from work.

"I refuse to allow them to see their no-good father. You have intruded into my personal family matters. I shouldn't be surprised. I knew you wouldn't make anything out of yourself because you're ignorant and naive, and married that low-life builder, who has no ambition in life. I should've known not to entrust my children to an immature imp like you!" Marilyn was furious.

Lottie ignored Marilyn's hateful words; she was frantic to alleviate the friction. She felt crushed.

"I'll clean up the carpet and Victoria. You can go back to work." Lottie hoped that Marilyn would leave so she could comfort the children and talk to them.

"I told you to get out! And do you hear me, you fool? I never want to see you again! I've learned a valuable lesson today. I don't need a sister like you to lead my children astray." Marilyn got in Lottie's face and knocked her toward the door. Lottie tried to explain herself, but Marilyn shoved her into the dining table.

Little Rob roused from the sofa. He called out to Marilyn, "You're mean! You're bad! I hate you!"

Lottie brushed past Marilyn to pick up her son and to muffle his mouth with her hand. Marilyn grabbed at Little Rob and Lottie in a rage. "Take your idiotic ideas, and go!"

Chapter 21

Family Friction

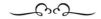

Marilyn pushed Lottie and Little Rob outside, and slammed the door. Lottie almost tripped backward while holding Little Rob. Her sister's blustering attack threw Lottie into emotional chaos. Shocked and disoriented, she stumbled to the car. Her hands and body shook in shame; she could hardly buckle Little Rob into his seat.

She collapsed into the driver's seat and bawled. "What have I done, Little Rob? What have I done? Oh, no, Little Rob. I should've thought about George and Victoria. How could I possibly think I could hide where we went today? I knew Marilyn didn't want them to go to the farm. George and Victoria don't deserve to be treated badly because of me. Oh, no. I've made things worse for the children." Lottie wept in despair. "She said we'll never see George and Victoria again. Oh, no."

Lottie buckled herself in the car and then spread her hands over her face and wailed. "What have I done? Little Rob, what have I done?"

"It was a good day at the farm. They like the farm. They like Uncle Buster. They like Mama Mac. I do, too. Don't cry,

Mommy. The farm's a good place to go. I want George and Victoria to live at my house. Aunt Marilyn's a bad mommy." Lottie sobbed in regret all the way home.

"Mommy, don't cry. Mommy, don't cry," repeated Little Rob to his upset mother. "I like the farm. It was a good day at the farm. George and Victoria had fun today. Don't cry, Mommy. Don't cry. Don't cry, Mommy. Mommy, don't cry."

The drive home was a grievous blur.

That afternoon at home, Lottie found paper for Little Rob to color, while she agonized over the predicament that she had caused for George and Victoria. Little Rob stretched out on the kitchen floor to be near his mother. He forcefully hit a picture he had drawn with the point of a crayon. Miles walked in to an uncharacteristically silent house. Lottie stood over the kitchen sink, staring out the window. Miles walked up behind Lottie, kissed her, and then spoke to Little Rob.

"I see we have a great artist at work. Let me see. What is it?" asked Miles as he bent down and picked up the drawing.

"George and Victoria should come here. They can live here. Aunt Marilyn's mean."

"I think I see Aunt Marilyn under the black scribbles. Is that right, Buddy?"

"She's bad. I hate her."

"Little Rob! Don't say that about your Aunt Marilyn," snapped Lottie.

"Let me guess," said Miles. "You went to the pig farm, and Marilyn found out." Miles shook his head.

"I like the pigs! I like the horses! I like hayrides! I want to go back," said Little Rob emphatically.

Turning to Lottie, Miles said, "I'm amazed that you took them to Buster's farm. You knew Marilyn didn't want them to go there. I told you not to go. You should've listened to me. She'll go to her lawyer for an order to ban you from her children. We may not see those kids again until they're twenty-one."

Duress

Lottie buried her head in her hands and drenched her face with tears. Miles wrapped his arms around Lottie to comfort her. Little Rob jumped up and clutched his mother's and daddy's legs. "Don't cry, Mommy. Don't cry, Mommy. We'll go get George and Victoria."

Finally, Lottie regained her composure and stopped her sobs. "A visit to see their father may have been wrong to Marilyn, but it was right for the children to see Buster and Mama Mac." Lottie choked her whimpers and rubbed her eyes. "If they don't ever see their father again, they'll never forget this day and the good time they had. I know their little hearts will burn to see their daddy. Miles, I wish you could have seen George and Victoria with Mama Mac and Buster. I've never seen the children so relaxed and happy."

Miles grabbed a tissue and dabbed Lottie's wet face. "Happy or not, you shouldn't have taken them to the farm. Things will be worse for George and Victoria. And do you hear me? If Marilyn legally prohibits *you* from seeing her children, you'll never get another chance to influence their lives."

Lottie again wept uncontrollably. Miles hugged his wife and patted her shoulders.

To lighten the moment, Miles playfully said, "You never understood the word 'no' growing up, did you?"

"Me? Marilyn was the one," sniffled Lottie. "She always wanted to play 'big company,' and I refused, but she made me sit still while she drew on posters and pointed to lines and pictures. My teddy bear and I would tell each other that she was a wicked witch. When I got enough courage, I ran and hid from her. She always insisted on doing things *her* way. She never played what I wanted to play."

Miles laughed. He picked up Little Rob and lifted him high, as if he would bump his son's head on the ceiling. Miles set his son down and held out his palms for Little Rob to slap. Little Rob smacked his dad's hands and said, "I gotcha!" Little Rob timidly opened his hands, which his dad immediately tapped. "Gotcha!" said Miles. Then he poked and tickled Little Rob, who jerked and giggled.

"Miles, I'm concerned about George and Victoria. Marilyn is too strict with them. She withholds food from Victoria. I'm upset because I've caused them more problems with their mother," lamented Lottie.

"Little Rob, come to the table, and eat supper," Lottie said.

The day's events and the class reunion details haunted Lottie. Sadness and stress weighed her down. She babbled to Miles, "Marilyn said she never wants to see me again. She said that the children would never see Buster again. I don't know how to undo the damage I've done."

Miles sensed her anxiety and said, "Things can only get better." He talked with Little Rob, helped him cut his meat, and encouraged his son to eat. After supper, Lottie asked Miles if he would bathe Little Rob. Miles filled the tub with water and tossed in toys. He settled into a chair to read his Builders Convention booklet while Little Rob played.

Meanwhile, Marilyn had returned from her work and threw a sack of fast food in front of George. "Eat that!" she ordered her son. George shook, holding back tears. "Don't you cry. Crying is immature."

"You go straight to your room, Victoria! No supper for a despicable, worthless child. You make me sick," said Marilyn. Victoria hung her head and clutched her elbows. She dragged her feet to her room and quietly closed the door.

"Hurry up and eat, George," said Marilyn, standing over him. "I have to work on my presentation for tomorrow. I want you to go to your room and go to bed as soon as you finish eating." She watched him stuff fries into his mouth and gulp down a soft drink.

George walked into his bedroom, closed the door, and sat at his desk. He laid his head down on his arms and cried.

He could hear his mother practicing her spiel for work and calling someone on the phone. "God. God. Are you there?" He rubbed his eyes with his hands and his nose with his sleeve. With his elbows on the table, he rested his head on his palms, his fingers spread in anguish.

"I don't have anybody to talk to," said George. "Aunt Lottie told me I could ask You for help. Me and my sister need help. I want my mother and father to come together. I want to have a real family. A happy family. Can You do that for me, God?"

George remembered Aunt Lottie's idea to send "phone signals." "She said she would pray for me if I would let the phone ring once and hang up." He waited until he heard his mother practicing her speech and quietly punched in the Arnolds' home phone number. He listened intently for the one ring and quickly hung up. *I'm sure Aunt Lottie will pray for me,* George assured himself.

The telephone rang once. Lottie remembered her pact with George to send a "phone signal." She returned the call, let the phone ring once, and hung up. Lottie bowed her head and whispered, "Oh, Lord, bless George and Victoria in their time of need. Dear God, please let me see them again."

The telephone rang again. Lottie stared at the phone. It rang several times, and she answered. It was Marilyn. "I forgive your intrusion into my personal family matters this time. You *are* my only living relative. I want you to understand that your opinions are incompatible with mine. You have to accept my authority and promise to abide by my rules."

Marilyn was a gifted communicator and manipulator. Lottie figured that she needed help with the children and was relieved that her sister had called. Marilyn was evidently willing to forget the earlier conflict. She had broken Lottie's heart when she declared that Lottie would never see George and Victoria again. Desperately, Lottie wanted to provide a few happy childhood memories for her niece and nephew.

"Lottie, Lottie? Are you listening to me? Are you there? I have an early flight to Atlanta tomorrow morning and a late return flight tomorrow night."

"Yes, Marilyn. Yes. Let the children stay here. Summer's almost over, and we'll have a good time. George and Victoria are no trouble. I can pick them up in the morning."

"I hate to inconvenience you, but Mrs. Edwards has to visit an aged aunt tomorrow and wouldn't agree to care for my children. Do not take them to that pig farm!"

"Marilyn, if only you could've seen how happy George and Victoria were at the farm."

"How can you imply that my children aren't happy? I provide them with fabulous clothes and the best housing in West Point. I told Boyd to forget about paying his pitiful child support. I'm the one who makes money. He grovels in the mud at that so-called farm. He took two extra years to graduate from high school because he piddled on cars and other people's farms. If he had finished college, he could have been a great veterinarian and made lots of money, but he didn't.

"He and his mother should have sold the farm to that real estate developer and moved up in the world. Boyd is penniless. *Why* should I let my children spend time with a man who can't provide financially for a wife and children?"

Lottie closed her eyes and whispered the answer to herself: "Because he's their father." Lottie wanted to avoid further strife. "Marilyn, don't worry about the children; I'll be glad to take care of them. Tomorrow I have to run a million errands for my class reunion. Little Rob will be a better passenger if he has George and Victoria in the car to entertain him."

The trauma from the earlier hurtful words was slow to lift, but Lottie sensed an incoming wave of relief. Lottie hung up the receiver. *Thank You, God.*

Little Rob ran out of the bathroom. Lottie and Miles followed Little Rob into his bedroom. They tucked their son into his bed, listened to his prayers, and kissed him good night.

On their way to the bedroom, Lottie told Miles, "Marilyn called me. She forgives my 'intrusion into her personal family matters.' And since Mrs. Edwards can't watch her children tomorrow, *she needs me!*"

Miles looked at her and smiled. "Well, you're out of the paint bucket this time since you have a sister who's willing to forgive and forget."

"Yes," laughed Lottie. "George and Victoria will spend tomorrow night with us. Marilyn has to fly to Atlanta in the morning."

"Do not take them to the farm!"

"That's exactly what my sister said." They laughed.

Miles quickly got into bed and sat up to study his trade show brochure.

"You're eager to go to the convention this year, aren't you?"

"I am, Lottie Love."

"I wish I could say the same about the class reunion. I have to finish Lucy's assignments tomorrow."

"You'll do an awesome job. I'll miss you in Seattle."

"Don't flaunt your upcoming grand vacation."

"I really want you to go with me to Seattle," pleaded Miles.

"Well, I would just *love* to go to Seattle, but I have a class reunion to attend *without* my husband." Lottie looked at Miles with raised eyebrows. He returned the gaze with begging eyes and his charming smile.

"I'm sorry I won't be here for your reunion," said Miles. "I didn't set the date for my convention. *I have to go.* I've gone every year since I've had my business. I'll be back Tuesday afternoon after Labor Day Monday."

"You'll be gone for the entire Labor Day holiday? I can't believe you will be out of town for the Prairie Arts Festival, my high school class reunion, *and* Labor Day!"

"Ohhh," sighed Lottie in disappointment. "I wish I felt better about the reunion. I thought if I led the committee, I'd find real fulfillment. But all the friction has been depressing."

"Hmm," said Miles. "Things will work out. You've got everything under control."

"I'm so tired," complained Lottie. "I don't want to talk about the reunion anymore tonight." She slid down in the bed and squirmed to get comfortable. "I should never have agreed to be chairman."

Miles leaned over and kissed her temple, and stayed up to read his Builders Convention pamphlet.

Chapter 22

Constructive Confession

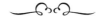

$\mathcal{F}$our weeks had passed since Rastus Webber began his accelerated rehabilitation program. Rastus demonstrated incredible progress to his psychiatrist, who believed his outstanding methods to treat the mentally ill were noble enough to be published in the *American Journal of Psychiatry*. Dr. Affle believed that Rastus's attendance at his high school reunion would be the grand finale to prove the doctor's expertise and propel the psychiatrist into circles of acclaim and prestige.

Dr. Affle was determined to teach appropriate social skills to Rastus to enable him to interact acceptably with a group of people at a genuine organized event.

Dr. Affle thought, I'll title my paper 'Societal Stabilization of the Schizophrenic.' I'll be invited to speak to university audiences and psychiatric symposiums!

As he fantasized about his future fame, the physician flapped his hands in his lab coat pockets and felt the pain in his split fingertips. He tapped together his sore fingers to comfort himself. The psychiatrist lowered his face to his desk and smelled and studied the surface for clues of a disinfectant allergen that had again triggered the bothersome symp-

Constructive Confession

toms. Then he thought, *What if my dermatological problem is a skin abnormality? I expose myself daily to contagious lesions and chronic skin disorders of my patients.* While Dr. Affle waited in his office for Rastus's scheduled counseling session, Baron hurriedly helped Rastus dress in preparation of meeting with the chief of staff. However, Rastus was in no hurry to meet with Dr. Affle.

"He wants to interfere and keep me here," complained Rastus to Baron.

"Naw. He wants you to go and prove he's changed you," said Baron.

"I know he doesn't want me to go," said Rastus, distrustful of Dr. Affle.

Baron knew he could not convince Rastus of anything when he was paranoid, so he stroked a comb through Rastus's hair and said, "Let's go see Doc."

Rastus clicked his long fingernails together and threatened, "If he tries to put me in a jacket, I'll whack at his eyes until he dies!"

"Rastus, have you been spitting out your pills again? You sound like the old Rastus, who thinks everybody's out to get cha. You gotta get along with Doc, or else he won't let cha go to the party."

Pretending to cooperate with the doctor had frazzled Rastus's wits. He was tired of Dr. Affle's debasing rehabilitation discussions. Rastus wanted out of the facility and could hardly restrain himself from sneaking away.

"I have to grab his lab coats!" blurted Rastus. "I put them back on the front rack."

"Okay, Rastus. We'll walk to the front and get Doc's cleaned lab coats, and then you can go to therapy. That's a nice habit of yours to bring Doc's lab coats to his office," said Baron to compliment Rastus. "When you get something on your mind, it becomes another obsession for Doc to figure out." Baron followed Rastus to the coat rack to get

Duress

Dr. Affle's lab coats and then down the gray halls to the psychotherapy office.

Outside the office door, Baron encouraged Rastus to knock. Rastus knocked once. "Come in," invited the psychiatrist.

The psychiatrist sat at his desk, thumbing through papers. "Ah, Rastus. I see you brought my freshly cleaned lab coats." Dr. Affle smiled, put his hands into his lab coat pockets, and flapped his hands. "Your good deed is appreciated.

"Come back later, Baron. We will finish in thirty to forty minutes."

Baron acknowledged Dr. Affle and backed out the door into the hall.

Dr. Affle studied Rastus through his eyeglasses and smoothed his tightly held hair.

"Sit down, Rastus. I like the way Baron combed your hair. Now, let's begin. Ten sessions ago, we began exploring your readiness for temporary release. I designed a plan of care to maximize your mental well-being and to prepare you to possibly attend a normal social event."

"I'm normal. Send me to the formal."

Dr. Affle chuckled. "Yes, Rastus. The reunion is not a formal function. Everyone will dress casually. I understand you want very much to go."

I will go, thought Rastus. "I must attend to see my friend. My life's in strife, with more in store." Rastus sputtered his words and then dragged his sleeve across his mouth.

"Use your handkerchief to wipe the sputum from your mouth." Dr. Affle spoke matter-of-factly to his patient. "Be aware of acceptable behavior, Rastus. It's too early to say if you'll definitely go." Rastus stared hatefully at Dr. Affle.

The psychiatrist turned on his digital voice recorder with his right pinkie since it was not as sore as the other fingers. Speaking into the device, he said, "This is the eleventh session with patient Rastus Webber. My professional counseling methods have produced astounding rehabilitative progress. I am examining the competence of the patient to participate in an out-of-town social event." Rastus glared at Dr. Affle, aggravated that his physician had not affirmatively granted him permission to go.

The psychiatrist addressed Rastus. "We want to ascertain if you're prepared for a monitored release."

"I'm prepared to go there," said Rastus in a deep-throaty voice. He thrust out his tongue, and it circled his open wet mouth. Saliva cascaded across his chin.

"I designed a plan of care to prepare you to network with others and to help you overcome your communal deficiencies. Your schizophrenic affliction is a direct result of your inappropriate upbringing. Your father was disturbed. He interfered with you and your mother's relationship and disallowed her to caress you and protect you, which are necessary to instill trust in a child."

"He knocked Mama down on the rug and wouldn't let her hug me. My earthly father bothered me." *I hate him.*

"Yes, I understand that you endured physical abuse from your father and tried to avoid him while growing up."

Weary of talking about his past, Rastus wanted Dr. Affle to talk about the reunion. "I know it's so. Free me to see Lot-tie. I know I must go." Rastus swirled his tongue around his mouth as if to lap up the excess saliva. Dr. Affle overlooked Rastus's rhyming associations, the drooling, and the clicking and thrusting of his tongue.

"You must speak in complete sentences. Learn to say, 'I would like to see Lottie and my old friends.' Do you understand? You must communicate with people plainly before we can allow you to go."

"I'll cast off the past and grasp my destiny at last."

"You have overcome your past and are more normal now. You survived your high school years in part due to this woman of whom you speak. She was a surrogate therapist

Duress

for you. You clung to her to satisfy your need for human contact and thus halted societal withdrawal."

"Let me see Lot-tie."

"An appropriate response when you see this woman is, 'Thank you for sending me a personal invitation.'"

"Hot tea is good for the body. Lot-tie is good for the body."

"You may have hot tea when you go to the cafeteria. Now, I understand that you believe you have feelings for this Lottie. When you see this Lottie, you will feel confused; she may reject you, and she may disappoint you. Since you haven't seen her in years, you must control the difficult feelings you'll experience when you reacquaint yourself with this Lottie."

"I'm grown. Send me home."

"Since you have continued to improve and to cooperate, I will meet with the Temporary Release Committee and present my recommendation. If we agree that you have successfully completed the criteria for your release, we'll allow you to go."

Dr. Affle stared at his sore, cracked fingertips and touched them to his tongue to soothe them. He shoved his hands down his lab coat, flapped his pockets, and said, "I'm glad you brought the invitation to my attention. This provides the opportunity for me to publicize my expert work in my professional journal and for you to prove your rehabilitation."

Rastus fought the urge to pinch and claw and bite Dr. Affle; the physician's degrading methods humiliated Rastus. Dr. Affle picked up the reunion notice. "This letter says, 'I want to personally invite you to come to the class reunion. I look forward to the time when we meet and remember old times.' And it's signed 'Fondly, Lottie.'"

"Let it be done. She's the one I want to see. You offend me. You hinder me."

"You must express your emotions constructively. It would be appropriate for you to say to her, 'I'm glad to see you again.' You have developed erotomanic delusions about this Lottie. You must not assume that she will reciprocate your feelings."

"The constellation illustrates my elation!"

"I sense your thoughts are adrift. You imagine something and think you see something. That is a hallucination; it usually lasts a few seconds and then vanishes. Do you need to confess something from your past?"

"No! Confession dooms my session. I won't confess unless I know you say I can go."

Chapter 23

Taxing Rehabilitation

*D*r. Affle leaned down to speak directly into his voice recorder. "Increase Rastus's lithium and Tegretol to stabilize his mood and to diminish paranoia and delusions."

Looking at Rastus, the physician said, "your compliance to swallow all of your special prescriptions is vital to maintain normalcy. Your medicines will enable you to control your perplexing desires."

"No more pills! You're still trying to poison me!" shouted Rastus.

"Medications will aid in your complete recovery," assured Dr. Affle.

"No!" bellowed Rastus.

"Block from your mind the despondency you feel," said Dr. Affle, moving his hands in circles to calm Rastus. "You are indeed fortunate to have a skilled counselor, such as myself, to ensure your betterment. After weeks of my systematic approach, you have developed confidence to interact acceptably with people."

Decisively, Dr. Affle said, "I believe you should be rewarded for your good behavior and your remarkable rehabilitation. A social outing that features your acceptable behavior will prove I have succeeded in rehabilitating you and will ensure the publication of my treatise."

Baron knocked on the door and opened it slightly. "We have not completed our session, Baron. Come back in twenty minutes." The nurse aide closed the door. Rastus sighed in weariness.

"Let's review the criteria for your reentry into a community. Number one is 'to control obsessive thought and compulsive actions.' You have not engaged in unauthorized facility exits. Your prescribed chemical restraint and antipsychotic drugs have helped you to manage your unnatural urges."

"I obeyed you and stayed here."

"You have progressed beyond hallucinations and delusions. You are more in touch with reality now. Use the 'mind-blocking technique' I taught you if you need to control your impulses." Dr. Affle demonstrated his technique to Rastus, who gazed in disgust at his psychiatrist. "Close your eyes and relax. Inhale deeply, and raise your hands slowly from your sides to above your head. Next, relax, exhale, and lower your arms."

Dr. Affle continued his long-winded discussion. "The second measure for your potential release is 'to accomplish daily living skills.' Baron informs me that you accept your medications and meals; you brush your teeth and take your baths without resistance."

"Pills keep me still. At meals, I stay in my seat and eat. I behave when I bathe." Rastus labored to communicate with Dr. Affle.

"Yes. You have acquired acceptable living skills." Dr. Affle noticed the saliva drizzling out of Rastus's mouth. "Wipe your mouth to be accepted."

"I'll wipe my drool and not be a fool," responded Rastus in a strain.

Duress

The third test for your competency in society is 'to acquire social and emotional standards.' This is confirmed by the cessation of your pinching assaults on the staff and other patients. Your verbal and nonverbal responses must be appropriate. Do you have uncomfortable feelings in regard to social interaction?"

Rastus was tired of expressing himself to his physician, whom he inwardly despised. Dr. Affle expected Rastus to speak clearly, but the physician spoke a mush of words, which Rastus had to decipher. Rastus's brain was clouded from his medications. He wanted to respond appropriately, but he was mentally and medicinally exhausted from the weeks of compliance with Dr. Affle's plan of care. Rastus understood that the final approval for his legitimate release would come from Dr. Affle, but approved or not, Rastus planned to go.

In frustration, Rastus said, "What must I do to be through with you?" He clicked his tongue on the roof of his mouth and thrust out his tongue.

Dr. Affle smiled. "I can see you are weary. Our session has extended beyond our usual time. However, let's complete our discussion.

"The fourth criteria for your temporary discharge is 'to achieve communal proficiency.' I understand that your table manners have improved. You've learned how to shake hands with other men. You've exhibited socialization with staff and patients. Rastus, you must deal with your fears and fantasies; otherwise, your rehabilitation is superficial and incomplete." Dr. Affle paused and waited for Rastus to respond. "Do you need to confess something from your past?"

"No. Confession dooms my session. I'm confused. I can't deal with how I feel."

"I understand that you feel confused. Feelings are hard to understand. It's all right to express your thoughts and feelings."

"I fear I won't be near to sear. I must see her." Rastus fought back tears. His mouth dripped.

"I can see that this reunion is important to you. If your release is granted, I'll mail the registration form and fee for the Saturday night banquet.

"If you go, I'll trust you to act maturely. Here are three of my personal handkerchiefs." The psychiatrist placed them in Rastus's shaking hands. "Use these to wipe your mouth often. Remember to speak clearly. Practice your social skills with staff. I want you to fit in and be helpful. Do you understand, Rastus?"

"Yes!" croaked Rastus, elated that his session was over. Rastus contemplated whether he should abandon his taxing cooperation with Dr. Affle and go to the reunion according to his own plans.

Chapter 24

Professional Decision

*T*he reunion was one week away, and Dr. Affle had not registered Rastus or said whether he could go. The morning therapy session, with Dr. Affle's repetitive exercises on shaking hands and speaking clearly, exhausted Rastus.

The psychiatrist diligently documented the progress of Rastus, developing graphs and tables to be included in his psychiatric journal paper. Rastus said and did whatever Dr. Affle wanted.

Later that same morning, Dr. Affle desired another session with Rastus and told the charge nurse to tell Baron to bring Rastus to his office. Baron escorted Rastus back to Dr. Affle's treatment office and chatted on the way. "You sure have impressed Doc. And you're still doing that act-of-kindness stuff, bringing his cleaned lab coats to his office. The rest of us have been taking bets on when you'll get tired of this crap and break out. It's been too quiet around here. Well, here we are. Knock on the door, Rastus." Baron motioned with his hand.

"Come in, Rastus," said Dr. Affle as he sat at his desk, thumbing through papers. "Baron, I'll meet with Rastus for

Professional Decision

about twenty minutes. I scheduled a Temporary Release Committee meeting this afternoon. I expect to see you there."

"Sure, Doc. I'll be there. Do you want Rastus to come?"

"No. I believe that we should have a closed meeting, with only staff present."

"Okay, Doc. Whatever you say," said Baron as he backed out and closed the door.

"Good to see you again, Rastus. Today is a momentous day in your progression toward normal function. I see you have thoughtfully brought my lab coats to me again." Dr. Affle flapped his hands in his pockets amiably and smiled.

Dr. Affle felt good. He anticipated that the reviews to his paper would acclaim him an innovator in the curative restoration of the schizophrenic patient. "When my article has brought attention to myself and to the facility, you can go with me to my speaking engagements." Dr. Affle tapped his fingers together; the soreness from the chemical cleaner allergy persisted.

"If you go to the reunion, you will mingle with people in a public setting. How does that make you feel, Rastus?"

"I feel it's real. Let me go."

"Yes, Rastus. I understand you want to attend your high school class reunion. After I meet with the Temporary Release Committee, I'll inform you of our decision," said Dr. Affle.

I will attend whether you send me or not, thought Rastus.

"You have met the criteria to reenter society," said Dr. Affle. "You deserve the opportunity to prove yourself. The logical person to accompany you on your outing is your certified nursing assistant, Baron. Will you be comfortable with Baron at your side?"

"Yes. He'll be my guide."

"Very good, Rastus. Let's end our session. I must expand my methodology for my paper and clarify my conclusions."

Dr. Affle paged Baron to come to his office. Rastus gladly ended his second session of the day with Dr. Affle.

Later that afternoon, the Temporary Release Committee met in the conference room. Arriving first was the administrative assistant, who wanted to busy herself setting up to record the minutes of the meeting and to avoid conversation with Dr. Affle. Next to arrive was the newest staff member, Nurse Dander, the director of nursing. Baron walked in with the activities director and the charge nurse; they sat down at the end of the table. The caseworker, who had retrieved records of Rastus for the doctor, arrived late and had to sit closest to Dr. Affle.

The psychiatrist stood to address them. "My fellow medical professionals, we are here to determine if the patient, Rastus Webber, may be granted a provisional release to attend a function apart from the institution. I have thoroughly assessed Rastus and attest that he is stable enough to manage this outing. His chemical restraint medications and mood stabilizers have diminished atypical behavior. He has satisfied the criteria to reenter a community and attend his high school class reunion."

The caseworker interjected, "I don't think he's ready to mix with regular people. He won't be accepted."

"He will be accepted in his hometown, which is the perfect setting to test his societal competence and rehabilitation," insisted Dr. Affle.

"His manner of speech is so peculiar. I can't talk to him and make sense of what he says," explained the activities director.

"A temporary release for Rastus is crucial to document his successful rehabilitation for my research. He will be warmly welcomed. Small-town people tolerate others who are physically and verbally challenged," said Dr. Affle.

"But what about his obsession, Dr. Affle?" asked the director of nursing.

Professional Decision

"Nurse Dander, you are the newest professional to join our staff. Please note that my name is pronounced *Dr. Affle*. Say 'waffle' and drop the 'w' for correct pronunciation."

The new director of nursing lowered her head to look at the psychiatrist over her eyeglasses frames. Indignant at his arrogant eccentricity, she said, "We can't be sure how he'll conduct himself. His previous ventures into our community were unacceptable. He's not prepared for a noisy, and probably rowdy, group activity over which we have no control. I don't think we should let him go."

"I perceive your cautiousness, Nurse Dander. Surely, you've noticed that Rastus has made no unauthorized exits from the facility during his period of rehabilitation. My expertise in adjusting his medications and implementing my techniques has resulted in his return to normalcy. To deny him this occasion to prove he's changed is reprehensible."

Baron spoke. "Doc, he stinks. Nobody's gonna wanna be around him. He doesn't cooperate with daily living skills. It takes me forever to get him to brush his teeth and use deodorant."

"That's perceptive of you, Baron. I expect you to bathe him and clean him thoroughly and to coach him in proper personal hygiene before you accompany him to his banquet Saturday night," said Dr. Affle.

"Say what?" asked Baron in surprise.

"Due to your close association with the patient, you are the obvious choice to escort Rastus. He trusts you," said Dr. Affle. "You may drive to West Point in the facility van. If you prefer, I'll arrange for you to stay overnight in a motel room with Rastus."

"Say what? Are you serious? I ain't gonna spend the night with Rastus. He's liable to pinch my eyeballs out while I'm sleeping. Anyhow, I already asked to be off this weekend. I got folks coming from Chicago."

"Baron, I don't think you understand the supreme significance of his release. You'll be well-compensated for your time and effort in the safe transport and return of Rastus."

"I'm sorry," said Baron, pushing his hands at Dr. Affle. "I ain't going with Rastus this weekend."

Dr. Affle turned to the director of nursing. "Nurse Dander, I need you to step up and agree to drive Rastus to his reunion and accompany him to the evening banquet. You will not have to stay overnight. Moreover, you are better equipped to observe his social performance and document it."

Nurse Dander dropped her jaw, incredulous at his presumption. "Dr. Affle . . . ."

"Nurse Dander, must I again remind you that my name is pronounced *Dr. Affle?* Say 'waffle,' and drop the 'w.'"

"Ah, hem," coughed Nurse Dander. "One of the benefits you promised me was that I would not work weekends, except in extreme emergencies. Attending an elective social event with a patient does not qualify as an emergency."

Dr. Affle's nostrils flared in disapproval at the director of nursing. "You miss the point of my weeks of validating my rehabilitation methods on a schizophrenic patient!"

"If the presence of the patient at this function is so important," contended the director of nursing, "I should think *you* would want to observe his behavior and record for yourself the results for your magazine article." Nurse Dander wanted to force Dr. Affle to be responsible for an activity that she intuitively believed was a bad idea. She deplored his attempt to railroad Baron or her into escorting Rastus on a Saturday night to another town.

The caseworker and the activities director looked down and shifted uncomfortably in their seats, fearful that Dr. Affle would call on them to take Rastus to the reunion banquet.

The director of nursing continued. "The reunion is a week away. You haven't mentioned to any of us your plan for a staff member to go with Rastus to West Point. We assumed

Professional Decision

that *you* would chaperone Rastus *if* he were permitted to go. No one other than yourself is familiar with your theories and exactly what you're trying to prove. You're the one who will be credited for the outcome of his release. If you accompany Rastus, you can meticulously document his behavior for your *research*."

Careful to correctly pronounce his name, Nurse Dander said, "Dr. Affle, you are the only one of us who approves of his release for this event; therefore, *you* should go with him and be prepared to incapacitate him, if needed."

The physician interpreted Nurse Dander's bold response as disrespectful insubordination and lashed out at her. "You mistakenly anticipate a negative schismatic result! I expected a unified collaboration! I upheld the best interest of my patient through my extensive social, emotional, and cognitive skills program. We, as a committee, cannot deny him this privilege and opportunity that will bring recognition and acknowledgment to me and to this institution!"

Dr. Affle slapped his folder shut and said, "I will take care of Rastus myself, without the participation of the professional staff of the Claxton Mental Home. I will annotate the opposition you have voiced to my exceptional endeavor. As chief clinical psychiatrist, I should not have to accompany my patient out of town on a Saturday night."

Nurse Dander and Baron hid snickers behind their hands.

Dr. Affle stalked out the door, straightening papers in his folder as he hastily deserted the meeting.

Chapter 25

Uncivil Conduct

*L*ottie daily regretted her decision to oversee her high school class reunion. The tumultuous weekly committee meetings grieved her. Mary Cecil brazenly harassed Lucy during every meeting. Lottie consoled herself, thinking, *The reunion will soon be over!*

Summer had ended, and school had started for the children. Moreover, the town of West Point was feverishly preparing for the renowned event of the year, the Prairie Arts Festival, which occurred the Saturday before Labor Day. Class reunions commonly occurred on Labor Day weekend, and this was the year for Lottie's high school class to meet.

Lottie had the reunion plans under control; she had coordinated activities and completed Lucy's assignments. It was the last night for Lottie and her committee friends to meet at her house before the reunion. Eagerly, Lottie anticipated the end of her stint on the contentious committee. Her gloom and depression would end soon. She longed for peace and the return to a regular routine.

"See y'all later," said Lottie to Miles and Little Rob as they went out the door. "Have fun playing at Kid Town!" Lottie stood on the doorstep and watched Miles back his pickup truck down to the street and honk at her. She waved to Miles and Little Rob as they drove away and to Lucy Jenkins as she turned into the driveway.

Lucy parked her sports car and tittered up to Lottie. She flaunted a sequined headband and swayed her hips in her usual way. "Hey, Girl!"

"Hi, Lucy. You're early!"

"I didn't want the others to talk about me. So I came early so I could talk about them." Lucy laughed.

"Come on in. I'll fix you a glass of tea."

"Lottie, why did you ask Mary Cecil to be on this committee? She is so negative. She sneaked behind you and me and checked on everything I did and faulted me because I didn't do it her way."

"Lucy, you know Mary Cecil is a perfectionist. She wants everything done correctly. Don't take it personally. All of us want the reunion to go smoothly. Besides, Mary Cecil, Trudy, Katherine, and you were the only ones who committed to help."

The doorbell rang. "That must be Mary Cecil. She's always fifteen minutes early," said Lottie.

"Come in, Mary Cecil. Lucy and I are having ice tea in the den. Would you like . . . ."

Mary Cecil interrupted, "Lucy Jenkins is already here? This is a first! Lucy Jenkins is always late. The beauty shop or the tanning salon must have burned to the ground. What's wrong?"

Lucy approached Mary Cecil. "Nothing's wrong, Mary Cecil," said Lucy. "I didn't want to miss out on the preliminary discussions."

"We never wasted our time on 'preliminary discussions.' We waited for you at *every* meeting for as long as it took you to get here before we started, you wastrel. Your immature tardiness delayed every meeting. I don't know why your slut butt is on this committee!"

Lucy opened her mouth in disbelief at Mary Cecil and exhaled an "Ahhh!" Lottie shook her head at Mary Cecil's uncivility.

"Let's go in the den. I hear Katherine and Trudy coming." When they rang the doorbell, Lottie yelled to them, "We're in here! Come join us!" Frustrated at Mary Cecil's contempt for Lucy, Lottie immediately started this last session hoping to avert further clash between Mary Cecil and Lucy.

"All right, ladies. We're in the final days before the reunion. It's this weekend! Let's focus on the last-minute details to make this occasion unforgettable. Our classmates will be treated to a memorable event, one they won't forget.

"Katherine, tell us how many have registered and if we've collected enough money to pay for the expenses."

Katherine opened her file. She turned through several pages and said, "Sixty-three classmates submitted their registration forms. All but two remitted their fees. I'll watch for them and personally ask them for the amount due. Several people signed up only for the evening banquet at Anthony's and no afternoon activity. I've made reservations for a total of ninety-one guests at the restaurant for Saturday night. The amount assessed will cover expenses, especially since Lucy forgot to reserve the softball field. Therefore, we won't have that outlay of money."

"How could a pea-brain remember to reserve anything?" asked Mary Cecil rhetorically.

Lottie bobbed her head in disapproval at Mary Cecil. "Katherine, exactly how many people signed up to play softball Saturday afternoon?" asked Lottie. She thought, *Why did you bring this up?*

"A total of seven people selected softball as their Saturday afternoon activity."

"We can't justify reserving the ball field and pavilion for two hundred dollars for seven people," said Lottie. "It's worked out well that we don't offer softball."

Lucy looked around the room at the women. She nodded her head proudly as if she had accomplished something.

"I think that Lucy Jenkins should personally contact the ones who wanted to play softball," said Mary Cecil. "Lucy Jenkins should apologize and invite them to participate in another activity of their choice."

Lottie took a deep breath. Mary Cecil had distressed her. Lottie wanted to shake Mary Cecil, but she retained her outward composure and said, "Only a few people signed up for softball, and several didn't sign up for an afternoon activity. We'll tell them Saturday morning when they check in at the information booth at the Prairie Arts Festival that softball is canceled.

"Besides, Buster MacGinnis has graciously invited our classmates and their families to come to his farm Saturday afternoon to fish. He said that he'll provide the tackle and supplies to catch catfish or bass."

Lottie was steadfast in her desire to moderate peacefully this last meeting. "You do have a good point, Mary Cecil." She turned to Katherine and said, "Will you list the softball people and their telephone numbers, and give it to Lucy?"

"Yes, I'll be glad to make a list and give it to Lucy," responded Katherine.

"Lucy, I want you to contact each one of them, and invite them to fish at Buster's farm or to participate in another activity." Lucy nodded positively. "Katherine, will you send out messages to everyone on your computer about Buster's offer to fish at his house Saturday afternoon?" Katherine nodded.

"Trudy, will you make a poster for the Prairie Arts information booth that lists the activities and where to go to participate? And phone numbers. List our cell numbers on the poster."

Duress

"Of course," said Trudy. "That won't be a problem. My husband and I plan to compile a PowerPoint presentation for the banquet of the Saturday afternoon activities."

"Trudy, that will be great!" Lottie wished that the rest of the women would be as enthusiastic as Trudy.

"You know," said Lucy, "most high school reunions don't offer golf, tennis, or swimming. They only have one big banquet or dance. I think our dinner and blues band would have been enough."

Trudy quickly responded, "Lucy Jenkins! We don't want to plan a class reunion that's dull and predictable like most high school reunions!"

Mary Cecil jutted her bottom teeth forward and said, "High school reunion committees with brain-disabled people like you can only manage to piece together a dinner and a dance."

Lottie stretched her neck in disgust and turned away from Mary Cecil.

Katherine added, "The afternoon activities cluster our classmates into small groups so they can reconnect and renew relationships with old acquaintances, which is highly unlikely to happen at a noisy, crowded banquet or dance."

Mary Cecil erupted in hostility: "If you had not been so inept and incompetent, we wouldn't have had so many problems. We repeatedly straightened out your mistakes, you vulgar ignoramus! Your doing nothing was better than your attempting anything."

Lucy had had enough of Mary Cecil. She stood over Mary Cecil with her hands on her hips and shouted in Mary Cecil's face, "You are a friendless skag!"

Mary Cecil looked at Lucy, puzzled. Lucy erupted into riotous laughter. "Ha! That's not in your highbrow dictionary! You're a streaky, snot scholar!"

Mary Cecil rolled her eyes and laughed at Lucy's unintellectual accusation.

"I'm not the one with problems. You are!" said Lucy to Mary Cecil.

Mary Cecil stood and lashed out, "At least I have a brain, and I can think!"

"If what you've got is a brain, I don't want it," countered Lucy.

Mary Cecil snapped. She lunged at Lucy to hit her. Lucy deflected Mary Cecil's clenched fists and laughed. Mary Cecil jerked Lucy's hair and neck. Lucy squawked. Mary Cecil slapped Lucy's face. Lucy cocked a one-knuckle fist and drew it back to fire at Mary Cecil.

Chapter 26

Fierce Disagreement

Katherine yanked Mary Cecil out of Lucy's line of fire. Mary Cecil shrugged away and swatted at Lucy with a tight fist. Lucy smiled as she grabbed Mary Cecil's wrist and prepared to take advantage of her defensive inadequacy. Lucy twisted Mary Cecil's arm until she squawked. Then Lucy zipped behind Mary Cecil, grabbed her shoulders, pulled her back sharply, and simultaneously kicked her legs forward. Mary Cecil fell to the floor, shrieking, "She attacked me! She attacked me!"

Lucy laughed and exclaimed, "It worked! Wait until I tell Don. Ha! This is great!"

"Stop it!" shouted Lottie. "I'm tired of your ridiculous bickering! You are too old to fight like little kids! Our classmates have entrusted us to plan the weekend precisely so that nothing can go wrong. Let's not wreck the reunion among ourselves. Now, sit down! Now!"

Mary Cecil and Lucy shifted their eyes and heads uncomfortably at each other, but did as Lottie commanded.

"Lottie," said Trudy, "I plan to enlist one or two people from each activity to report at the banquet about their afternoon with old friends. Is that okay?"

"Yes, that's a good idea," said Lottie, grateful that Trudy could guide their discussion back to the reunion agenda. "I know they'll tell some insanely funny stories."

Lucy uncrossed her arms and legs and slid forward in her chair. "We're paying the blues band to play for three hours. We shouldn't cut into their time, if we want to get our money's worth."

Mary Cecil moved forward from the sofa and said through her gritted teeth, "I think our classmates would rather hear what their former school friends have to say than listen to a loud blues band, of whom they've never heard. A lot of people don't like blues music."

Trudy bubbled, "I think it'll be fun for people to come to the podium and share their experiences with everybody at the banquet. If the band doesn't play the full time, I'm sure it won't be a problem."

"I agree," said Katherine. "The band gets paid no matter how long it plays. We want our classmates to reminisce about school days with each other and rekindle old friendships. People are coming to the reunion to see old classmates, not to hear a blues band."

"Should we try to get the single classmates together?" asked Lucy.

"No," answered Mary Cecil, Katherine, and Trudy in unison.

"The classmates who come by themselves will seek out other single classmates without help from us," said Lottie. "Besides, some of those who are single may not want to draw attention to the fact that they're here alone.

"Saturday is a big day. We're ready for the reunion. Thank you all for your hard work." Lottie walked out of the den to lead the ladies to the door. "Call me if you need anything or if you have questions. I'll see you girls Saturday morning at eight o'clock at the Prairie Arts Festival information booth."

Lottie opened the door for the women to leave and said, "Good night." After the last one departed, Lottie shut the door. She bowed her head, closed her eyes, and sighed loudly in frustration, "Thank You, God; this will soon be over!"

Lottie wagged her head and thought, *How can Mary Cecil trash Lucy so openly? Why can't Mary Cecil get along with Lucy?*

She heard the familiar rhythm of Little Rob running on the sidewalk. When he reached the threshold, he pounded his palms on the door to announce his arrival. Lottie let him in. He ran past her and said, "Hi, Mommy! We had fun!" He rushed into the den to watch television.

Miles walked in and looked at Lottie as she stood stationary by the door. He playfully stepped back. "Hi, Lottie Love. How was your meeting?"

"Thank God, it was the last one."

"Ummm. Let me see. That bad, huh?"

Lottie stretched her neck and punctuated her chin to one side and then the other. "I've had it with those girls! I'm sick that Mary Cecil spoke to Lucy so rudely. Lucy can tolerate anybody, but Mary Cecil absolutely abhors Lucy. Mary Cecil slugged Lucy tonight! Lucy was about to use a ferocious self-defense strike against Mary Cecil, but Katherine pulled her away. They kept on fighting!"

Miles raised his eyebrows in surprise. "Sorry I missed that," he said under his breath.

"Lucy could whip Mary Cecil in a fistfight, but Mary Cecil uses her words and intellect to belittle Lucy. I don't want to be on a committee with those girls again. And I definitely have not enjoyed the illustrious distinction of chairwoman."

"Probably if you had subtracted one person, things would have been more manageable and more enjoyable."

"I can't fire a volunteer. Besides, Lucy was my best friend in high school, and she's a good person. If I kicked

Fierce Disagreement

Lucy off the committee, I would lose her friendship. It's not worth that. I have no desire to go to this reunion. The excitement is gone. I dread this weekend," said Lottie.

"I'm afraid Mary Cecil may lose control Saturday and do something to Lucy. After Mary Cecil hit Lucy tonight, she offered no apologies to Lucy or to the rest of us, and showed no remorse. Mary Cecil upset me." Miles nodded his head as he listened to his wife vent her frustration.

Miles set the house alarm for the night. Lottie called to her son, "Little Rob, it's time for bed." He turned off the television, and the three walked up the stairs together.

Miles said, "I have to start packing tonight for my flight to Seattle. I can't pack the night before a trip like you do, Lottie Love." While Miles gathered his clothes and put them in his suitcase, Little Rob followed him around the bedroom and asked his dad questions about flying in an airplane and going far, far away.

Meanwhile, Lottie filled her son's bathtub with water. "Come take your bath, Little Rob." He gladly obeyed his mother but was disappointed that he had to get out so soon. Lottie helped her son dress in his pajamas. After she and Miles tucked him in bed and listened to his prayers, they went to their bedroom.

Miles sat up in bed to study his Builders Convention brochure. After Lottie climbed into bed, he leaned over and said, "It would be less stressful for you and more fun for me if you would come to Seattle."

"Will you stop talking about your trip to Seattle?"

"No."

"Hmm. It's refreshing to dream about flying away with you and leaving these women here to fuss without me," said Lottie. "You're wearing me down. But I can't leave the committee here to do all the work. That would be irresponsible to dump the last-minute reunion details on the ladies. If there were any way possible, I'd go with you. I have to stay here and suffer through the weekend by myself since you'll be leaving town."

"I checked airfares today. They posted a special rate. And the weather is a beautiful, sunny sixty-six degrees."

"You don't give up easily, do you? You have tried to get me to leave West Point this weekend. Don't worry about Little Rob and me. I'll arrange for Little Rob to spend Saturday with Trudy's son, Carey Lee, and his dad, so he won't have to tag along with me all day."

Miles got in Lottie's face and put his hands on her shoulders. "I want you to fly with me to Seattle. You can work things out for Little Rob."

"Why do you continue to ask me to fly hundreds of miles away with you? I can't go. I have to stay here. I'm chairwoman of the reunion committee." Irritated, she pushed his arms up and away.

"And a fine chairwoman you've been. You've completed your assignments and Lucy's with exceptional skill and diplomacy. You've done all the work. They don't need you now."

"Miles, be serious. How could I leave Trudy, Katherine, Mary Cecil, and Lucy to worry about the reunion while I go away on a vacation?"

"Those women can tell people where to go Saturday afternoon and meet everybody at Anthony's that night. They can *meet, greet, and eat* without you and tell you about it when you come home. You don't have to hold their hands. All you'll miss is the squabbling between Lucy and Mary Cecil."

"I don't know how Lucy and Mary Cecil will tolerate each other in the same room. And besides that, Lucy, Mary Cecil, Trudy, and Katherine would *never* forgive me if I left town."

"Everything has been planned and paid for, Lottie Love. Everything's done, except for the guests' showing up and

Fierce Disagreement

those women's pointing them in the right direction. If you aren't there, those women will figure out how to get along."

"Miles, I can't leave West Point this weekend. I'll go with you next year. I'm sorry you'll be gone. I'm glad tonight was the last committee meeting; I can't endure another one. Arbitrating disagreements and maintaining peace was exhausting. I need some rest."

"You said that you *dread* this weekend. Do you want to stay here and be miserable, or go with me and relax and have a good time?"

"I'd rather you stay here and be miserable with me." Lottie laughed in good humor to relieve her husband's strain.

Miles fixed his eyes on Lottie, intent on changing her mind.

"I don't want to talk about Seattle or the reunion anymore!" said Lottie. "I've got to go to sleep. Leave me alone." She slid down in the bed and punched her pillow to fluff it.

Chapter 27

Pain Not Fame

*T*wo days later, Baron walked into Rastus's room to take him to the shower. Not seeing Rastus, Baron called out, "Rastus. Rastus! Where are you? It's time to clean up." Baron looked in the halls for Rastus and thought, *I hope he didn't sneak off. Doc was takin' him to that party Saturday. Rastus is blowin' his chance for gettin' outta here.*

Baron checked with the staff members, who reported seeing Rastus at breakfast early that morning. The charge nurse told Baron, "I'll call the director of nursing and commence a lockdown."

"It's been like a vacation the last few weeks with Rastus hanging around here and cooperating with Doc," said Baron. "I shouldn't be surprised that he slipped off. I better start working out again so I'll be strong enough to stuff Rastus into a straitjacket. I guess this means Doc didn't change him after all."

The nurse pressed the intercom button to announce the lockdown.

"Wait a minute," said Baron. "Something's not right. Rastus never breaks out before lunch. He waits until the afternoon. Let me look for him a few more minutes. This weekend is too important to Rastus to ditch all that effort and blow his chance to go."

"Okay," said the nurse. "But hurry up."

Baron checked in other patients' rooms and facility closets. Employees speculated that Rastus had reverted to his former habit of sneaking away and complained about the imminent lockdown. As Baron passed by Rastus's room, he heard a muffled pounding noise. He pushed open the door. The hammering stopped. "Rastus, are you in here?"

The aide walked in and found Rastus hiding on the floor behind his bed. He held a stick-shaped object, wrapped in a torn sheet. In front of Rastus was Dr. Affle's freshly cleaned lab coats. The plastic was pulled up to the tops of the hangers.

"What are you doing with Doc's lab coats?"

"He's vain. He deserves pain."

"Say what? You talking about Doc? What pain? Are you up to no good?"

"You're in a plot to destroy what I've got."

Baron laughed. "You got nothin' here."

"I despise him. I devised a way to kill him, slowly. He needs to bleed, slowly. This way he loses a drop of blood every day. A small slash . . . a tiny gash . . . ."

"Rastus, my friend, you gotta take those pills. You're talking like a crazy person."

"In the end, you're not my friend! I know what to do. I'll kill you, too!"

"Doc won't let you go to the party this weekend if you talk that way."

"I'll attend whether you send me or not."

"I'm not the one who says if you go or not." Baron thought that Rastus was trying to hide what he was doing. The aide squatted beside Rastus to talk. Rastus swung his sheet-wrapped tool at Baron. Startled, the nursing aide fell sideways to avoid a blow.

"You moron!" Baron grabbed Rastus's weapon and uncovered it. "Where did you find this metal pole?" Rastus stared at Baron and breathed heavily through his nostrils. Baron placed the pipe behind his knee and thigh, out of Rastus's reach. Looking at the lab coats on the floor, Baron noticed bumps in the pockets. He looked in the pockets and saw pieces of glass.

"Nothing's the matter," said Rastus. "I need more to shatter. I'll finish in a minute."

Baron cautiously studied the contents of the lab coat pockets. "Whoa, Rastus. That looks like glass from those bottles. Is this what you been doing with those broken bottles you pick up on the side of the road?"

"Slivers of glass deliver pain fast."

"Why do you want to bring pain on people? Good grief, Rastus. You been gathering those bottles and crushing them in Doc's lab coat pockets, haven't you? No wonder his fingertips have been sore. He never noticed the sharp bits in his pockets. All this time, he thought he was allergic to cleaning stuff."

Baron pressed the intercom on Rastus's wall. "Rastus is in his room. Forget the lockdown," he told the charge nurse. Baron picked up the lab coat and held the metal rod.

"You, you, stop what you do!"

"Me stop? You stop!" retorted Baron. "You fooled me into believing that you had changed. This won't sit well with Doc."

"I won't tell him. You don't tell him."

"This is serious, Rastus. Don't bring any more broken bottles into your room. Don't crush any more glass in Doc's pockets. You got that?"

Rastus narrowed his eyes at Baron.

"I got to figure out what to do," said Baron. "That nurse told me not to let you bring broken bottles into your room. I trusted you not to hurt anybody."

"He deserves pain, not fame. Slow pain." Rastus laughed. Apprehensive, Baron stared at Rastus. "Umm, uhmm. I better see if my cousin can get me on at the convenience store. They'll fire me over this. I'm the one who let you bring glass into your room."

"I want you at my side when we ride to West Point," said Rastus.

"Say what? I'm not going with you Saturday. I got kinfolk coming from Chicago," said Baron. "If anyone goes with you, it'll be Doc."

"You have to go away with me Saturday. He said you would be my guide."

Ignoring Rastus, Baron said, "How will I get out of this mess? You're in trouble, too, Rastus. Doc's been working on his big research paper to prove you're cured. A normal person would not secretly put crushed glass in somebody's pockets."

"I'm normal. Send me to the formal."

"A class reunion isn't formal, and you're not normal." Baron stuck the metal pipe down the rear of his scrubs and then shook the glass fragments into the garbage can.

"I fear you'll interfere. I know what to do. I'll kill you," threatened Rastus.

Baron saw a sinister side of Rastus that intimidated him. "Umm. Ummh. I tell you what," said Baron, "you go to the party this weekend with Doc. He needs to see you act 'normal.' You can confess to him what you've been doing with that glass."

Rastus rushed at Baron with his pinching fingers. Baron pulled out the metal bar and waved it between Rastus and himself.

"I won't confess. I won't tell the past."

"Okay," said Baron. "I don't care if you tell him or not. I'm not telling Doc anything. I'll tell the girl in the office to send these lab coats back to the cleaners. No shower for you this morning. I'll see you in the cafeteria at lunch. You can just stink, so nobody will bother you."

"You'll never get the mark. You'll forever be in the dark!" warned Rastus.

Baron shook his head in perplexity and turned away from Rastus. "It's time I got outta this place."

Rastus threw a rubber snake at Baron as he walked out.

Chapter 28

Stop Harassing Me

The next night at bedtime, Miles refused to stop talking to Lottie about going to Seattle with him.

"Leave me alone," said Lottie. "I have to go to sleep. I have a lot to do this week."

He leaned his face directly above Lottie and stared at her closed eyes. "I want you to fly away with me this weekend."

His tenacity plagued Lottie, who felt depressed about the reunion and disappointed with Miles's absence from it. "Stop talking about your trip to Seattle. I want you to go by yourself and have fun. I don't want to talk about it anymore."

"I'm not talking about *me* going to Seattle. I'm talking about *you* and *me* going together."

"I can't go! Why can't you accept that? I'm chairwoman of the reunion. I have to be here. Don't say another word about it." Lottie flopped her head and body away from Miles.

"I need you more than the reunion committee needs you. I want you to go with me to rest and relax."

"You won't give up, will you? I'd rather go with you. I need some rest; I need to relax. I need you to leave me alone so I can go to sleep. Please."

"Come away with me, Lottie Love. You can work things out."

"I can't go with you, Miles. I can't go. Will you stop harassing me?"

"You *can* go. I need you to come with me."

"Miles, please. I don't want to talk about Seattle or the reunion anymore."

"Let me see. How many women are on the reunion committee?"

"Five, counting me," responded Lottie in irritation.

"Five? There are five on the committee? If you don't go, that leaves four. Four legs can hold up a table, and those four women can hold up the reunion without you. Surely, they can handle the few odd jobs left to do without you."

"Miles, give it up! I can't go to Seattle!" Lottie lay still, and then threw the covers back and sat up in bed. She drew her knees to her chest and stared straight ahead. "They'll call me irresponsible if I leave town."

"No, they won't. Your husband needs you more than they do."

"I don't know, Miles. I shouldn't leave West Point this weekend. I agreed to be chairwoman. I need to be here to ensure the success of the reunion."

"I need my wife to go with *me*. Those women can tend to the final minor chores just fine."

"Everyone will ask, 'Where is Lottie, the reunion chairwoman? Why isn't she here?'"

"Those women can tell everybody, 'Her husband needed her to fly away with him for the weekend.'"

"Okay. Okay. You're right. I need to get away. You need me more than the reunion does. I'll take fun over misery. The girls can handle the few things left to do. You've convinced me. I'll go with *you*."

"All right!" said Miles as he hugged his wife. "You can accompany me as my 'principal supply manager.'"

"Oh, yes. I'll supply you." She pulled away and winked at Miles. He kissed and embraced her, and then grinned as he put away the convention brochure.

His arms encircled her, and he whispered, "I've wanted the two of us to go away alone."

Lottie pressed her body against his and smelled the fragrance of his cologne. She scrunched her hands through the tight curls of his closely trimmed head. Lottie intertwined her legs with his and said, "We need some time together to relax."

Miles spread his fingers through Lottie's hair and massaged her scalp. He kissed her neck and tickled her with his short, soft beard. She kneaded his shoulders and arms and rubbed his chest. Their stress and tension melted away in the balm of closeness.

The next morning, Lottie felt energized and exhilarated about her decision. She called the committee members to inform them that she would be out of town for the weekend and gave them her final instructions.

Chapter 29

Kidnapped the Boss

*T*he flurry of preparations for her last-minute trip with Miles consumed the week. Friday materialized quickly. Early Friday morning, Mrs. Edwards rang the doorbell.

"Come in, Mrs. Edwards," said Lottie. "We appreciate your staying with Little Rob on short notice." Lottie detailed Little Rob's schedule with Mrs. Edwards. "Tomorrow morning at nine o'clock, Carey Lee and his dad will pick up Little Rob for the Prairie Arts Festival and bring him home after lunch.

"Today and Tuesday, you'll need to take Little Rob to school by eight o'clock and pick him up at fifteen till three. Little Rob can stay at home and play on Monday. Miles and I will return late Tuesday afternoon."

The elderly lady patted Lottie's shoulder reassuringly. "Dearie, don't worry. I'm sure my time with your son in your lovely home will be delightful. Everything will be fine while you're gone."

"I'll take your bags to the bedroom," offered Miles.

Little Rob walked into the kitchen in his pajamas and rubbed the sleepiness from his eyes.

"Hello, Dearie," said Mrs. Edwards, who bent over to hug him.

"We have to leave for the airport *now*," said Miles. "Vendors and out-of-town people have already started to pour into town to set up for tomorrow's festival. I don't want to get behind one of those vans or RVs."

Miles lifted up Little Rob in his arms and bumped his son's head playfully. "You're the man of the house while I'm away. You take good care of Mrs. Edwards and the tree house while I'm gone, all right, Buddy?"

"Yessur."

Lottie kissed Little Rob and told him to be good. Mrs. Edwards held the young boy's hand, and they followed his parents outside. The older woman and Little Rob watched Miles back his pickup truck down the driveway. "Good-bye, Daddy! Good-bye, Mommy!" said Little Rob. Miles honked the horn as he drove away.

"I feel like we're going on our second honeymoon," laughed Lottie.

At the stop sign, Miles leaned over and kissed Lottie. "I feel the same way."

On the way to the airport, Lottie itemized the arrangements she had made for Little Rob and Mrs. Edwards, and then proceeded to tell Miles who was in charge of what for the class reunion. "I planned things so that Lucy and Mary Cecil wouldn't have to be in the same location at the same time until the banquet Saturday night."

Miles indulged her anxious monologue of the weekend schedule since she had agreed to leave town with him and miss the reunion. Anticipation of their getaway to Seattle tantalized Miles.

"We're here," said Miles. "Let's hurry into the airport and get this luggage checked."

After their baggage was tagged and passed through security, Miles and Lottie sat down to await their boarding call.

Lottie again talked about the reunion and the committee members' assignments.

Miles put his arm around Lottie and said, "You need to forget about the reunion. I know you've taken care of everything. Those women are very capable—not as capable as you, but the reunion will come to pass as planned. You'll see Trudy's video and pictures when we get back. I want us to enjoy this time together. We never go away by ourselves."

"You're right, Miles. I'm sorry. I know you must be tired of my babbling about the reunion. I'm on vacation. I need a rest, and this trip will be great!" She touched his hand and squeezed it. "I'll forget about the reunion and concentrate on us."

"Ummm," said Miles, "you're beautiful." Lottie raised her shoulders and smiled at him.

The connecting flight to Seattle was announced, and passengers boarded. Miles and Lottie climbed the steps into the small airplane and walked down the narrow aisle. When they found their seats, Lottie sat by the window. Miles put their carry-ons in the overhead compartment and then sat down by Lottie. Once they were in the air, Miles took out his convention booklet and handed a smaller leaflet to Lottie.

"This is the Ladies Program. If you're interested, I can sign you up when I get there."

Lottie glanced through the brochure. "Oh, goodness!"

"What's wrong?"

"Nothing's wrong. They list a Pampered Lady Experience that sounds awesome! I can choose a pedicure, a manicure, or a massage. I can go to a cooking demonstration, an exercise session, or a 'latest fashion program.'"

"Hmm. Let me see. Maybe I'll sign up for your activities." They laughed.

Within a short while, they landed, exited their commuter plane, and switched to a large, comfortable jet. Once in the air again, Lottie took out the Ladies Program brochure to think about what she wanted to do in Seattle. Miles avidly talked about the exhibition of new building products. Then he showed Lottie the pictures of the hotel featured in his booklet. Lottie said, "Oh, I hope we have a good view of the skyline from our hotel window." After they had flown for several hours, they touched down at the airport. A shuttle bus transported them to the hotel.

Once in the hotel room, Miles said, "I'm starving. I'll shower while you find us a good place for dinner."

"I want to go someplace special." She looked through the telephone book and the room magazines, and then called the concierge for advice. Lottie changed clothes and freshened her makeup. She talked to Miles while he dressed. "The concierge recommended The Loon. He said that it's an exceptional candlelight dinner restaurant that serves the best steak and king crab in the city."

"Sounds good to me. What do you want to do after dinner?"

"I want to come back and soak in our giant hot tub." She winked at him.

Miles smiled. "Ummm. Sounds good to me." They laughed.

Since the restaurant was a short distance from the hotel, Lottie and Miles strolled there in the cool early evening. The hostess seated them by a window that overlooked a lighted fountain that sprouted water high into the air.

The excitement of the big city gave them a rush of energy. They studied the menu and selected a papaya salsa with pita chips appetizer. Lottie's exuberance gushed and then dried to a silent despondency.

After they ordered dinner, Miles observed his wife's onset of gloom. "Are you thinking about the reunion?"

Lottie nodded and tapped her glass with her fingernails.

"Are you sorry you came with me?" probed Miles.

Lottie blinked and then put away her melancholy and said, "Absolutely not. I'd much rather be here with you. It's such a relief not to deal with the committee. I feel no regret."

"Are you sure? Are you upset you're missing the reunion?"

"Actually, I feel guilty that I left the girls to carry on without me. But you're right; they're capable of doing the last-minute tasks. I'll look at Trudy's pictures and video when I get back. I'll have Mary Cecil's souvenir CD, so I'll be able to contact my old schoolmates. I can't believe your convention was scheduled during a holiday weekend."

Wanting to divert attention away from the conflict of his convention with her reunion, Miles said, "We never leave our dull little town, do we?"

"I think it's time we start family vacations," said Lottie. "We could go to your builders conventions every year and stay an extra day or two for fun. You always meet in impressive cities. We could bring Little Rob. He's old enough to travel with us now."

"Yes, he's old enough to enjoy a family vacation to someplace besides the farm." Miles raised his eyebrows at Lottie, who laughed.

"Miles, do you miss life in a big city?"

"No, Lottie Love. I grew up in a big city, but I think a small town is the best place and the safest place to raise a family. And business has been steady."

They leisurely ate their dinner and splurged on a flaming baked Alaska for dessert. Arm in arm, they savored the walk back to the hotel. When they returned to their room, Lottie filled the hot tub.

She undressed, eased into the water, and turned the jets on high. Miles stepped into the Jacuzzi and massaged Lottie's shoulders. "That's exactly what I need." She turned and pressed her body against his, and they relaxed in the foaming hot water. Afterward, they slid between the satin sheets on their comfortable bed. Lottie and Miles embraced and stroked each other tenderly and passionately. They indulged in the freedom to be close in the absence of the everyday demands and worries left at home.

The next day, Miles and Lottie toured the city of Seattle. They went up into the Space Needle and then to the open market to buy fresh apples and cherries. They meandered through the park, fed the ducks, and licked ice cream cones. Lottie bought souvenirs for everyone. When Miles felt blisters stinging his heels, he hailed a cab to take them back to the hotel.

Fatigued from their Saturday sightseeing and wearied from the previous day's travel, they called room service for dinner.

While they ate in their room, Miles reviewed his convention booklet and talked to Lottie about the schedule for the next day. "I'll go down early in the morning and register you for the Ladies Program. You can show up at ten o'clock at registration and go enjoy the day. I probably won't be back to the room until about five-thirty tomorrow afternoon."

Lottie suddenly remembered, "Miles, today is Saturday. The Prairie Arts Festival and the afternoon activities have ended. I was engrossed as a tourist all day. I can't believe I haven't thought about the reunion, except for last night in the restaurant. With the time zone difference, it's time for everyone to get ready for the banquet!" exclaimed Lottie.

"The girls should have decorated the restaurant by now and arranged the reception table with the souvenir CDs and the sports trophies that Trudy will present. I can't wait to see pictures of what everyone wears to the banquet. I wonder who's gained weight."

Irritated at herself, Lottie fretted, "I'm sick I forgot my phone charger. I could have bought one here. Then I could have talked to the committee."

"That would be a waste of money," lectured Miles. "We'll be home in three days. It wouldn't be a vacation if you talked to those women on your phone the whole time."

Lottie huffed at Miles's exhortation and disregarded his comments. She continued thinking about the reunion. "I know everyone will love the food and the band. I hope Lucy and Mary Cecil get along tonight. I'm confident that everything will go well, and if it doesn't . . . ."

"If nobody shows up or they have a brawling riot, it's my fault. I kidnapped the boss lady," joked Miles.

"Miles, stop it." She winked at him.

"All right," he said as he wrestled and rolled with Lottie.

"Today has been a good day for the two of us, hasn't it?" said Lottie. "I would've missed this wonderful trip if you hadn't been so persistent."

Chapter 30

Warped Plan

*E*arlier in Clink, Dr. Affle telephoned the charge nurse and told her to bathe and dress Rastus for his outing, since Baron had quit unexpectedly. When Dr. Affle arrived at the facility, he went to his therapy office and asked the charge nurse to bring Rastus to him. Irritated at the medical director's request, she flapped her arms to herd Rastus down the hall without touching him. She hammered on the psychiatrist's door. He calmly said, "Come in." After Rastus walked into the psychiatrist's office, she slammed the door and left.

"Rastus, your personal aide suddenly relinquished his responsibilities to you and to me," said Dr. Affle. "After careful contemplation of the circumstances, I have conceived a plan of action that will benefit me and you.

"Due to my enormous responsibilities as medical director, I must desist the burden to chaperone you. Furthermore, my research requires my attention. Since you have shown a propensity for self-reliance, I believe you are capable of going unaccompanied to the reunion banquet this evening and returning tomorrow morning," declared Dr. Affle.

"Going and returning independently would be the ultimate achievement for you. Do you feel capable of going alone?" asked Dr. Affle.

"I'm able," said Rastus, elated at the prospect of his sudden release.

"A bus leaves from Clink in one hour that will transport you to West Point. The West Point bus station is three blocks away from Anthony's Restaurant, where you will walk to the banquet tonight. You should have no trouble navigating downtown in your previous hometown. I told you how to ask someone politely for directions if you need them."

Dr. Affle flapped his hands in his lab coat pockets and drew them out quickly, lamenting, "Ohhhh. My fingertips are cracked and bleeding. Housekeeping must refrain from the use of harsh chemicals to sanitize my office. He plucked a tissue to blot his fingers."

The psychiatrist stared at his patient. "Rastus, you'll arrive after lunchtime. The cafeteria prepared a sack lunch that you may eat on the way. The nurse will package your medications, which you must take this afternoon and in the morning. On your walk to Anthony's Restaurant in West Point, you may stop in the library and read magazines and rest until it's time for the banquet.

"During the evening, I want you to talk to some friendly former classmates. Ask one of your old friends to drive you to the bus station after the banquet. Wait there in West Point for your bus to leave at 4:00 A.M., and I'll pick you up tomorrow morning here in Claxton. Are you comfortable with my schedule? Do you have any reservations about going by yourself?"

Excitement engulfed Rastus. He could not be more pleased that Dr. Affle was not escorting him to the banquet.

"You have not responded, Rastus," said Dr. Affle. "Tell me how you feel."

"I feel it's real. I know I must go home where I'm known."

"I trust you to act maturely, Rastus. Your good behavior is expected. I'll meet you at the Claxton bus station when you return tomorrow morning. Are my instructions clear?"

"Yes!" croaked Rastus.

"Here's your bus ticket and some cash for unforeseen expenses. Also, I printed a copy of your registration form and the check. Keep these in your pocket at all times, and present them at the banquet, if needed. I'll drive you to the bus station myself."

Chapter 31

Crazed Interruption

Meanwhile, Mary Cecil, Katherine, and Trudy were busy at the information booth at the Prairie Arts Festival, watching for classmates and providing information about the reunion activities. When the festival concluded that afternoon, the ladies oversaw the golf, swimming, and tennis at the Country Club, and the fishing at Buster's home.

They were exhausted by late afternoon but met at Anthony's Restaurant to decorate for the evening banquet. While unloading their boxes and bins in the restaurant, they conversed about their brief jaunts through the park to glimpse the festival bustle and events.

"I had to wait in line fifteen minutes to get a chicken-on-a-stick. I suppose it was worth the wait," complained Mary Cecil.

"I got a funnel cake with extra powdered sugar, like I do every year at the Prairie Arts Festival," said Trudy.

"Our book sale in the library was a huge success," said Katherine. "Many people came inside to get out of the heat. My assistant said strange people came into the library and wandered around, looking at our special displays."

Crazed Interruption

The ladies chatted while they adorned the tables with old photographs and festive candles. Trudy tied helium balloons around the room and on the entrance banisters.

"I drove around this afternoon and took pictures of our classmates and videotaped everything. My husband is at home putting together the PowerPoint show for tonight," said Trudy. "The crowd at Buster MacGinnis's house surprised me; everybody sat around and ate Mama Mac's fried chicken and potato logs. Nobody fished."

"It's too hot to fish," said Mary Cecil.

The blues band arrived to set up its sound system and instruments.

Katherine and Trudy laughed and talked about their classmates they had seen in town.

Deep in thought, Mary Cecil was silent. Then she grumbled, "I'm astounded that Lottie isn't here. I can't believe she left town for the weekend. I can't blame her for bailing out on us. I'd want to get out of town, too, if I had to work with someone like Lucy Jenkins. I don't hold a grudge against Lottie, but I do resent Lucy Jenkins's shirking her final obligations. It disturbs me that she isn't here to help us."

Mary Cecil continued her denunciation. "Lucy Jenkins could at least show up to decorate for the banquet. Her careless conduct on this committee is sickening. Lucy Jenkins has been unreliable and lazy."

"Lucy told me she had something important to do," said Trudy. "She said she would be here as soon as she could."

Katherine and Mary Cecil looked at Trudy with their hands on their hips and blinked their eyes at Trudy's naiveté. Trudy shrugged in unconcern.

The girlfriends worked diligently to trim the back room of the restaurant. However, Mary Cecil's resentment toward Lucy infected Katherine and Trudy. Their zest for the long-awaited banquet diminished with each mechanical motion.

Duress

As they gathered their belongings to leave, they looked out the picture window and saw Lucy whip her sports car into a parking spot. She slammed her car door and dashed into the restaurant.

"Are you girls leaving?" beamed Lucy, who had just gotten her hair highlighted.

"We put out the decorations without you," said Mary Cecil, "just the way we did *everything* without you. We couldn't wait until you got here this afternoon to start. You are uncivilized and ill-bred. You're always late! You're a selfish garble gut!"

Lucy laughed, amused that her presence so easily disgruntled Mary Cecil.

"You stay here with the band, and put the stuff in these boxes out on the table!" ordered Mary Cecil. "We always do your work, and we're tired of it!"

Lucy threw up her head at Mary Cecil and looked away to show that she ignored her rudeness.

"We have to dress for the banquet, and then we'll rush back," said Katherine.

"It'll be almost an hour before anyone gets here, Katherine. What can I do?" asked Lucy.

Mary Cecil interjected, "I already told you what to do, you asinine empty head. Stay here, and put the stuff in these boxes out on the table."

Lucy shot back a crude rebuttal, "You're an unpopular bossy snoot!"

"You vacuous female!" shouted Mary Cecil.

Lucy cackled in hilarity. "You're too much, Mary Cecil. I don't have a clue what you're talking about. Only an ill-tempered freak like you could come up with a mythological word like that."

Mary Cecil's aversion to Lucy intensified and prompted her to grasp Lucy's arms and rattle them. Uneasy with Mary Cecil's uncalled-for outburst, Katherine pulled Mary Cecil away and tried to calmly reiterate, "You may take the CDs and the trophies out of these boxes, Lucy, and set them on this registration table, neatly and in order."

Mary Cecil picked up a piece of paper and shook it at Lucy. "Use this list, and write name tags for everyone. Can you do that simple assignment? Or does one of us need to stay here and make sure you do it? And arrange them alphabetically. Light the candles in exactly thirty minutes," ordered Mary Cecil.

As the women walked out, Lucy stuck out her tongue and threw up her hip at Mary Cecil. She left a voice message for her police chief husband and told him, "The other ladies skipped out on me and left me here at Anthony's by myself to take care of everything. You'll have to come to the banquet by yourself." Lucy thought, *Don will love that message. He'll probably go by the station to delay his coming.*

Lucy amused herself by looking at the old photographs on the tables. She talked with the workers who busily set up the food line and then sampled bites from the buffet. She set up the welcome table and then thought to herself, *I'm not going to label those name tags. They can write their own names when they get here.*

Lucy moved to the beat of the blues band as she cheerfully lit the candles. Then she went to the bar to sip a vodka tonic. As guests arrived, Lucy welcomed everyone exuberantly.

When Trudy and her husband arrived, she asked, "How's everything going, Lucy?"

"Great!" responded Lucy.

"You don't have on your name tag. I'll get you one and make sure everybody gets theirs."

"Thanks, Trudy." Lucy looked out the window and saw Mary Cecil striding on the sidewalk toward the restaurant with Katherine and her husband. To avoid Mary Cecil, Lucy disappeared into the crowd and directed classmates to the food line and to the restrooms.

Duress

Mary Cecil doggedly hunted for Lucy among the crowd of guests. When she found Lucy, she immediately lashed out at Lucy in a venomous rage. Stupefied, Lucy opened her mouth at Mary Cecil's public tantrum.

"You're an obtuse twit! You're an embarrassment to our class!" yelled Mary Cecil. "You couldn't complete one simple task without someone holding your hand. You floozy! You hampered all of us with your witless effort. I can't stand your ignoramus excuses! If I hadn't kept an eye on you, the class reunion would've been ruined because of your stupidity! You're the dumbest woman I've ever known! You were born brainless!"

Then Mary Cecil noticed that her angry voice was the only audible sound. The room was quiet. She looked around and hushed immediately. Profoundly embarrassed, Mary Cecil confessed loudly, "I'm sorry. My reckless outburst is unforgivable. I shouldn't have raised my voice toward Lucy Jenkins on this special occasion. Please forgive me. I beg you to not hold my inexcusable behavior against me! I never behave like this."

But no one was looking at or listening to Mary Cecil. Into the room had walked a strange man with stringy black hair and a purple-splotched ashen face, who smelled like sewage.

Chapter 32

Ladies in Hades

The vagrant wore a flannel shirt and an oversized black suit coat. A greasy tuft of hair rose over his pointed head and cascaded across a squinting eye. With a rigid neck, he panned the room to study the crowd. Slowly he raised his trembling hands and arms upward and then brought them down to his side. He opened his mouth as if to speak, but smacked his lips. He thrust out his tongue to encircle his wet lips. In one quivering fist, he held a handkerchief that he swiped across his chin to catch the trickling saliva. He cleared his throat, making an annoying guttural noise.

His manners and appearance puzzled the roomful of people. Reunion guests rippled away from the intruder, stepping onto each other's feet and grabbing onto arms to maintain their stance. No one dared to look down or away, but they fixed their eyes on the grotesque person.

Seconds of silence passed. The class reunion attendees suspiciously wondered why this bizarre man had invaded their party and what his intentions were.

The stranger nervously turned his stiff body back and forth. His eyes widened in fear. Opening his mouth, he thrust his tongue in and out. His demeanor escalated to a frenzy.

Something terrified him. He pointed his twitching fingers and jumped around as if dodging something on the floor.

Words frothed out of his mouth. "Coiling, boiling! Snakes forsake! Escape! Escape! Snakes! Snakes! Pour under the door! Don't look!"

Many guests felt threatened by his deranged visions.

Abruptly, he slumped his shoulders and said, "Bones turn to stone. Depart in stark dark. No mark, the worst curse."

He lifted his eyes to scan the room in search of someone and then became agitated. "I foretell you'll dwell in hell! I can't see the upright saint. I may faint. I hate I had to wait. Is she here for me?" No one could really understand him because his words were enveloped in thick drool, which he gargled and swallowed.

"Hey, fellow or fiend. Halloween's next month!" yelled someone.

"Yeah, man. You're at the wrong party!" boomed another.

Snickers of laughter mushroomed. Classmates looked at one another and wondered if this was part of a crass skit for the evening, or whether a genuinely depraved reprobate had wandered into the room. Lucy laughed boisterously.

The eccentric person accelerated his words to a feverish crescendo. "Listen. Pay attention. You're to blame for my pain. I desire to burn her to save her!" He dragged an unsteady hand across his mouth.

The odd visitor raised his arms and looked upward to talk to God or someone. "Not save them from the grave? Yes. Use snake venom to send them to hell!"

"Ras-tus. Ras-tusss," hissed a classmate, reminiscent of school days, when boys harassed Rastus Webber. Whispers and murmurs ricocheted around the room as people recognized their old classmate.

"Let me persuade you. Let me save you!"

"Save me, Rastus! Save me!" jeered someone in the crowd, who burst out laughing.

Rastus smacked his mouth and tried to swallow his excess saliva. He used his quivering hand to push aside the stringy strand of hair that flopped over his sagging eye.

"You distort my message. You're wicked, not bless-ed!"

"Bless me, Rastus! Bless me!" yelled another classmate.

His weird utterances stirred fear in some guests; others thought the situation was humorous. A few unruly classmates riotously hooted.

"Wail for help! Yell and wail for help!" Rastus's arms erupted above his head, and then he pulled his fluttering hands and bony fingers down to his side, exhaling a deep breath. He pursed his mouth to speak and then opened wide to thrust out his tongue and swept it around. Before he could continue, another classmate derided him.

"Help, Rastus! Help me! Help me!"

The provocation ended in menacing laughter. The mockery vexed Rastus. He pounded his fist violently onto the closest square tavern table. Beverage-filled glasses overturned and shattered. Silverware collided and rattled. Liquids and food spilled onto the floor. Outcries from startled people peppered the room, followed by a buzz of chatter. Rastus looked intently at his former classmates and dabbed the corners of his mouth with his sleeve.

"I've come! Soon it's done! Moan and groan. Your bowels will become stone!"

Lucy and two other ladies fell over in booths and roared in hilarity.

Rastus fixed his gaze on Lucy and aimed a tremulous finger at her. "Women that wail. Destined for hell. Laughing ladies . . . in hades!" Slobber filled his mouth and garbled his speech.

"He's foaming at the mouth! Did he say 'rabies'?" asked an anxious woman.

Someone answered, "I think he said 'hades.'"

"Rabies! Lord, let me out of here!" responded the unnerved classmate, who ran out the emergency evacuation door in a panic. The alarm signal split the air as a crowd jammed through the exit, screaming, "Rabies! Rabies!"

Chapter 33

Neurotic Culprit

The piercing clang drilled Rastus's head and multiplied his headache anxiety disorder to produce stifling pain and confusion. He hacked a noise in his throat and pressed his ears to block the noise. Inhaling and exhaling sporadically, he churned his oscillating body.

Don Jenkins entered the room and surveyed the chaos; he immediately spotted the peculiar person. Rastus spun his body toward Don and spit judgmental words within inches of Don's face.

"Ungrateful fools, full of hateful rules. Where's the upright saint? They cast her out, no doubt. I don't see her. The upright saint's not here for me to sear." He looked around and pointed to the lingering guests. "You crapulent rats. Covered in fat. Filthy riffraff."

Don perceived that this stranger unnerved the guests, so he twisted Rastus's arm behind and said, "I think you better leave now." The police chief seized Rastus's stiff neck and guided him out the door and released him.

"That's my man. We're safe now!" said Lucy.

The remnant of classmates peered around the room and rubbed their arms to stave off the chill of the surprise confrontation. They rushed to Don and encircled him, demanding that Rastus be "put away" because he's dangerous and "crazier now than when he was in school." The crush of the remaining reunion attendees overwhelmed Don. Their shouts and demands overlapped in tangled words. The police chief realized he had turned a probable offender onto the streets. The guests finally withdrew from Don.

Everyone left the restaurant, except for the reunion committee and spouses. Since Trudy was denied her presentation of the sports trophies and the PowerPoint show, she wept in great disappointment. "No one got to tell about the great times they shared today."

Mary Cecil dropped her head and held her hand over her heart and throat as if in great pain. She walked to the reception table and stared in shock at the souvenir CDs, which she had punctiliously prepared. She placed her hand on the stack of her work and rubbed her fingers around the edges.

The dispirited ladies gazed incredulously from one side of the deserted room to the other. They all wondered, *What happened?* The plentiful buffet was abandoned. The blues band members hesitatingly put away their instruments. Katherine's tears dropped onto the check that she handed to the band. She strained to apologize for the short night of music.

The committee ladies gloomily crammed the banquet decorations into plastic containers, and packed the trophies and CDs into boxes. Trudy, Katherine, and Mary Cecil dejectedly left. Lucy and Don Jenkins were alone in the banquet room, except for the kitchen workers, who scurried in and out, removing food from the buffet line and cleaning Rastus's mess on the floor.

Don followed his wife around as she extinguished candles and dropped them into a bin.

He anxiously interrogated his wife about the emotionally disturbed person that he had just evicted. "Lucy, who is that guy, and what is his problem?"

Lucy laughed out loud. "His name is Rastus Webber. He was the class weirdo."

"I've never seen him before. Does he live in West Point?"

"When we were in school, Rastus lived with his father in a shack in the poor side of town. He disappeared at the end of our senior year. I don't know what happened to him. He had trouble in all of his classes, except for a burst of intelligence during junior literature when we studied mythology."

"Do you know why he left West Point or what happened to him?"

"No. Well, the Community Social Service people came and got Rastus before high school graduation. They said he was 'going away temporarily.' He was as peculiar as an opossum. Everyone avoided Rastus, except to heckle him. Oh, wait a minute . . . I forgot. Mary Cecil discovered that he lives in the mental institution in Claxton."

"If he escaped, I would have noticed a bulletin that he was missing or received an alert that he was coming here. What motivated him to come to the reunion tonight?"

Lucy looked at her husband mischievously, shrugging her shoulders and holding out her hands, and said, "Class reunion? Maybe he wanted to see his old classmates? Honestly, I don't know anything about Rastus anymore."

"How did he get here? Who brought him tonight? He looked like a vagabond, not the type of person to come to a banquet."

"I don't know how he got here. He looks and acts as weird as he did in high school."

"I surmise his classmates didn't welcome him to this reunion."

Duress

"Well, he wasn't Mr. Friendly or Mr. Courteous. It's hard to show hospitality to someone who stinks and yells, 'Laughing ladies go to hades.'"

"Do his parents still live here?"

"No, my man. His father disappeared about the same time that those Social Service people took Rastus. They may have taken his father away at the same time. They were both crazy." Lucy was amazed at her husband's bombardment of questions.

"What happened to his mother?"

"I'm not sure, but the rumor was that his father beat and killed his mother and buried her in their backyard. I don't know what happened to her, but she vanished from West Point. Everybody knew that Rastus's father abused him because he came to school burned and bruised."

"Was there an investigation into child abuse?" asked Don.

Lucy put her hands on her hips and said, "Are you kidding? No. That was years ago."

"Who's the 'upright saint' he mentioned?"

"Probably Lottie."

"Lottie!" exclaimed Don. "Why Lottie?"

"In school, Lottie was the only person who was friendly to Rastus. Nobody else tried to be nice to him. She shared her lunch with him. She let him come to her house after school to do homework or watch television. Almost every night, Lottie's dad took Lottie, Marilyn, and Rastus to the drive-in for hamburgers and then dropped Rastus off at his shanty house or the library."

"Did Rastus ever hurt anybody?"

"I don't know."

"You don't know?"

"Other kids probably hurt him more when they threw cafeteria food and playground rocks at him. In science lab, he never did what the teacher told us to do. He loved the

Bunsen burner. I always thought he would torch the school. He burned all of his lab partners and tried to burn me." Lucy laughed.

She enjoyed the conversational sparing with her husband. She had not had a spirited discussion with her husband in a long time, and she reveled in it. Conversely, Don was perturbed at his lack of preparedness for a neurotic culprit and irritated that his wife was in control of vital information. Don shamefully regretted he had not taken Rastus into custody.

Lucy told her husband, "I wonder if Lottie had been here . . . if she would have walked over to Rastus and taken him by the hand like she used to and . . . . No! He was a slobbering fool. Nobody wanted to touch him. Don, you need to go wash your hands. He may have a disease."

Don ignored Lucy's comments. "Did Lottie know he was deranged? Did she know he was coming to the reunion?"

Lucy sighed. "She knew he was in a mental institution but sent him an invitation anyway. I told her not to send him one. We had a list of the people who registered. But I don't remember seeing his name on our list. He could have registered late, and Katherine didn't tell us," said Lucy.

"Rastus was the troublemaker I told you that Lottie invited," Lucy reminded Don. "You should have asked Rastus your questions. Or maybe not. He can't speak clearly, and you would have gotten a face full of spit trying to drag a straight answer out of him."

"Lucy, you're right. I should have questioned him. I should *not* have let him leave the premises. He's on the streets of our town. He does not communicate normally. His excessive drooling and strange dress will frighten people. He displayed erratic and possibly demented behavior."

Lucy burst into laughter at her husband's revelation. "Yes, Rastus is still crazy."

Don's interest piqued. "I need to know if he has a criminal record or if he escaped from somewhere." The police chief agonized that he had not taken Rastus into custody. "I didn't expect to confront a mental case tonight. I need to check and see if the mental institution is missing a patient."

Lucy sensed her husband's fascination in Rastus. She shook her head and threw up her palms and shoulders. "Lucky Lottie. She didn't have to experience the ruined reunion."

"Yes," said Don. "She may be luckier than she'll ever know. I need to run to the station." He started to leave, processing the facts of the disturbance. Then he turned around to question Lucy again.

"Lucy, where's Lottie? Why isn't she here?"

"Lottie decided to fly away with her husband to his builders convention in Seattle. She had enough of Mary Cecil and her annoying hostility. Going out of town was a good excuse to distance herself from that hotheaded know-it-all. Lottie left the committee here to finish all the work. And just think . . . that blubbering fool probably came to the reunion to see Lottie."

"When will Lottie return to West Point?"

"Late Tuesday afternoon."

"That's in three days. I'll tell my men to be on the lookout for this man. I shouldn't have let him go. I wasn't prepared for the troublemaker that you warned me was coming."

As he hurried out the restaurant, he said to Lucy, "Don't wait up for me!"

Lucy rolled her eyes at her husband. *Are you kidding?*

Chapter 34

Endangered Deranged Person

*D*on and the officers on duty cruised around town Sunday, looking for Rastus Webber. The holiday weekend was quiet, except for a few fireworks and family barbecues. Townspeople felt safe as they saw the steady presence of policemen.

The police chief drove to the town's bridges and creeks, almost hoping to see Rastus's body floating. Since he was the last person known to talk to Rastus, and since he had forced him out on the streets of West Point, Don felt obligated to find him. However, no stranger was sighted. No irregularities were reported.

Early the following morning, Labor Day Monday, Don went to the station. He called in his assistant chief of police to discuss Rastus. "Tyrone, we don't know if this guy has left West Point or gone back to Claxton. I called the mental home to ask if he was missing. The grunts there say they can't give that information."

"Chief, I checked the data bank for missing persons, and his name isn't listed," said the assistant chief. "No bulletin's out about a mental home escapee. Nobody's reported a suspicious character matching his description in our town."

Don said, "He hasn't been seen since Saturday night, but I have a hunch he's still in West Point."

"Our men are watching for this guy. If he's spotted, we'll bring him in, Chief."

"All right, Tyrone. I need to know: Is he a threat to our community?"

"I'll keep you posted, Chief." The assistant police chief walked out.

Don sat at his desk, gnawing at his lack of information. *How aggressive is this guy? Has the institution not noticed he's missing? He must have escaped from the mental home. Nobody in his right mind would let a deranged person from Claxton come to West Point by himself. What's happened to his escort? I'm going to call Mike Cantile.*

Don had always admired his older peer in Claxton and valued his lifetime of experience in law enforcement. He fanned through his personal phone book to find the number, but hesitated calling the Claxton police chief's cell phone since it was a holiday. Don immediately apologized for disturbing him on Labor Day.

"No problem. I'm at the station in Claxton," said Mike. "I was about to call you."

"I think I know why, Mike."

"So you've met Rastus Webber?" asked Mike.

"Yes. Briefly. Did he flee from the mental home?"

"He *has* escaped repeatedly from the facility. This time, however, he was granted a temporary pass to come to West Point and has not returned. In my opinion, it was an unwise release," said Mike.

"Who accompanied him?" asked Don. "Surely he was supervised."

"He should have had a guardian. Somebody from the mental home called in a tip this morning that Webber's psychiatrist sent his patient to West Point alone because the doctor couldn't coerce anyone to come with him, and Dr. Affle didn't want to come, either. Unbelievable!" said Mike.

"I can't understand how Webber's psychiatrist thought that he had transformed his insane patient into a normal citizen," continued the Claxton police chief. "Allowing Webber to go anywhere by himself is insane. Rastus Webber can slither out of the facility as he pleases. The doctor insisted that Webber's attendance at an authentic function outside the facility in your town would prove his patient is rehabilitated."

"I should have been notified he was coming," snapped Don.

"Listen, Don, if I had known about Webber's release, I would have objected and intervened. Every time he sneaks out, he finds an innocent person on which to prey. Someone calls 911. Then his physician calls to warn us not to mistreat his patient. Afterward, the doctor, his lawyer, and the judge work out a deal," complained Mike.

"Just between you and me, Webber's doctor is the one who needs psychiatric help," blasted Mike. "That doctor claims that Webber is a 'helpless victim of his psychosis.' Dr. Affle warns us not to violate Webber's civil rights."

Don sensed that Mike ranted out of frustration with his repeat offender. He sympathized with the Claxton police chief, but Don wanted to speedily apprehend Webber. "Mike, is he armed and dangerous?"

"He's not armed with a gun, but I would say he's definitely dangerous. Listen, Don. You've got problems. Webber's physician filed an endangered missing person's report. He declares that 'foul play' in West Point deterred Webber's return. I'll fax you a copy. This cockeyed doctor will fault you for whatever Rastus has done. You'll be blamed for inciting Rastus's actions. His doctor will con you into believing that any wrongdoing is a medical problem and not a legal issue."

"Does he frighten or terrorize people?" asked Don.

The older police chief paused and then laughed uncontrollably. Don wondered, *What is going on? The lunacy of this patient has rubbed off on Mike.*

When he regained his composure, Mike apologized profusely. "Don, that question struck me as funny because that's exactly what he does. And I can't get a conviction. He freely reveals his offenses."

Mike explained, "Prosecutors have tried to convict him on 'diminished capacity,' which allows for a lesser charge with prison time. But his psychiatrist has expert witnesses who slant their testimony to prove Rastus is schizophrenic and doesn't know what he's doing. He gets acquitted. Declared innocent of any crime. Rastus and his physician are fishhooks in my butt."

"I'm sorry you haven't been able to resolve your legal difficulties. I intend to find him before he frightens or terrorizes anyone in my community."

Maybell came in and interrupted Don with her personal emergency signal of flashing her left index finger straight and then popping up the right index finger. She repeatedly snapped her index fingers up and down.

"Mike, I've got to go. We'll talk later." Don clicked off his phone.

"What is it, Maybell? I thought you were off for Labor Day."

"No sir. I had enough holiday yesterday. Officer Tate apprehended the man you're looking for, but the culprit fled on foot. Tate chased him behind some buildings and caught him again. When backup arrived, he became combative and resisted arrest. Four patrolmen are holding him at the Laundromat on Main Street."

Don grabbed his hat and his gun. "I'm on my way!"

He turned on his siren and raced to the Laundromat, dazzling passersby with the flashing lights of his patrol car. Don

Endangered Deranged Person

heard gunfire and barreled out of his car. He marched toward his men. Three of the policemen were telling Officer Tate, "Go to the emergency room! Go to the emergency room!" The assaulted officer had multiple misshapen protrusions on his bald head. Blood ran down his wet neck and forearms.

"Where is Webber?" asked Don. "I heard gunfire."

Officer Tate replied, "Chief, I saw a vagrant who matched the description of Webber. I approached him, and he ran. I pulled out my Tazer to charge it and intended to disenable him."

"Did you purposefully discharge your gun, or was it an accident?"

"Well, Chief, as I was saying," rambled Officer Tate. "I pursued him with my Tazer, ready to fire, and then he wildly ran back at me and slung a big snake on me."

"What snake?" asked Don.

"That one," said Tate, flipping his wrist toward the ground. Don walked over to look at the snake.

"You Tazed a snake!"

"Yes sir," said Officer Tate. "I thought it was a water moccasin."

Don squatted down and saw that a bullet had blasted off the snake's head, and the stun gun wires were exposed on the ground. He poked the snake. "Is that a rubber snake?"

"Yes sir. I thought it was real. It was big and came at me so quick, I had to react."

Don shook his head in disgust.

"Chief, I ran him down to handcuff him. But he wrangled and jerked one hand free before I got them both locked. He beat my head with the metal handcuff that was loose. Then he dug his pointed fingernails into my arms and neck. Sorry, Chief. It happened so fast."

"Where is he now?" demanded Don.

Officer Tate shook his head in puzzlement.

"I don't understand," said Don. "He doesn't weigh more than 140 pounds. He has no muscle mass."

"I've never had to arrest a psychopath," said Tate. "He slobbered all over me."

The other policemen snickered.

"That's enough," barked Don. "Go find this deranged 'endangered missing person.' Bring him to the station, and lock him up! Now!

"Tate, go to the ER, and get cleaned up. Get a tetanus or rabies shot. Then report back for duty, and file a report. Do I make myself clear?"

All of the officers responded in unison, "Yes sir!"

Don drove back to the station. Maybell followed him into his office to update the chief on new information. "The physician of the missing person called to see if you had located his patient. He said that he fully expects you to 'safeguard' his 'patient's civil rights.'"

Don wrinkled his brow and said, "What?"

"Umm hmm," started Maybell. "He says he's anxious to retrieve his patient and begin 'protocol procedures.'" Maybell fingered the direct quotation from the doctor.

"What does that mean?" asked Don.

Maybell shook her head. "He says he has a 'warrant for his confinement' and will return his patient safely to the mental home."

"'Warrant for his confinement?' We can easily confine him here. That doctor acts like he's picking up a delinquent child and carrying him to the house. Webber is an unstable adult and is responsible for posting bond," said Don.

A few seconds later, two officers brought in a jumping jack, handcuffed man who violently flung his head and stomped his feet to strike the policemen. Hearing the commotion, Don jumped up to follow his men who had apprehended Webber.

"Lock him up!" ordered Don.

Hanging shirttails, torn sleeves, and tracks of blood evidenced a defiant confrontation between the officers and Rastus.

Don picked up his phone to call Mike Cantile and then heard an embroiling disturbance. Someone yelled, "Get him! Don't let him get away!" Rastus streaked out the door.

Chapter 35

Perfect Hideout

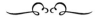

*D*on slammed shut his phone and ordered the two policemen, "Go get him, now! Bring him back, and lock him up!"

The police chief, the assistant chief, the dispatcher, and Maybell walked to the holding cell where Rastus was secured. A stunned jail trustee lay quivering on the floor by the jail cell door, moaning, "Ohhh. Ohhh."

"What happened?" asked Don, who put his hands on his hips and bowed his calves backward.

The jailer grabbed the bars of the cell and pulled himself to his feet, rubbing his neck and biceps. "He said he needed toilet paper in a hurry. He said he had to have a whole roll, a brand new roll. It wouldn't fit through the bars, so I opened the door and handed it to him. He reached for it and then spit on me. Then he clawed my arms and neck. I bet he files his fingernails sharp on purpose. It felt like little knife points stabbing me over and over again. Sorry, Chief. He surprised me. He didn't have a weapon," said the trustee, "so I thought it would be okay to give him a new roll of toilet paper."

Don said nothing. He walked to his office and shut the door.

Perfect Hideout

The Police and Fire departments united their efforts in search of Rastus Webber. Every shift wholeheartedly strived to locate Rastus. The hours dragged, with no sighting of Rastus Webber. At midnight, Don sat at his desk in misery, with his hands on his temples, pondering what to do next. Don asked out loud, "Where are you hiding?" The police chief finally went home for the night.

The next morning, Don arrived at the station and questioned the dispatcher about Rastus. Assistant Chief Tyrone Duncan walked up to the chief, wanting to tell him something.

The dispatcher explained, "No visual contact of Webber has been reported, but Officer Tate filed a report about a break-in at the library. Katherine Storey, the librarian, went in early this morning to get things in order after the holiday weekend."

"Yes, Chief," interrupted Tyrone. "I went down there, and I can attest that someone has definitely bedded down in the library. I believe it was Webber. It looked like a large mouse had gathered all the food and snacks from the lounge and made a nest in a corner between two rows of books and against a wall. Cellophane wrappers and empty plastic bottles were stuffed under an adjacent bookrack. An oversized dark suit coat was wadded up like someone had slept on it. And strangely, there was a backpack stuffed with rope, duct tape, and a rubber snake on an adjacent bookshelf."

"How did the intruder gain entrance?" asked Don.

The dispatcher, who felt ignored, said to Don and Tyrone, "I'll keep you posted." She turned her back on the men and attended to incoming calls.

The two men walked to Don's office.

"The suspect went in and out of the library through the window of the librarian's office," said Tyrone. "The librarian was hysterical that someone just climbed in, stepped all over her desk, and pushed her papers and pictures onto the floor.

She said she kept a twelve-pack of water under her desk, and it was gone."

"Why didn't the alarm trigger a break-in? Did he turn on the lights?" asked Don.

"There's no alarm system at the library. They can't afford one. A few lights stay on all the time, but nothing out of the ordinary was reported until this morning. The librarian said the library was locked early Saturday afternoon after the Prairie Arts Festival ended," Tyrone said to Don.

"Do you think the library is where Webber hid the past two days?" asked Don.

"Yes, Chief. Someone was there," said Tyrone. "The evidence points to Webber as the trespasser. The detective is dusting for fingerprints. I found a registration form and a check issued on behalf of Webber for that class reunion. We bagged up that smelly suit coat, the backpack, duct tape, rope, and the rubber snake and tagged them for documentation. Nothing else appeared to be vandalized or missing."

"Who would have thought that a centrally located landmark in town would be the perfect hideout for a mentally disordered offender?" asked Don rhetorically. "Anything else?"

"Well, Chief, there was some kind of glue gun or engraver on a shelf close to where he was bedding down," responded Tyrone.

"Were there books on a particular subject around his lair?"

"Yes, Chief. How did you know? There were books about Greek mythology scattered all around his area."

"I'm going to the library. I want to see for myself," said Don as he grabbed his gun out of his desk and put on his cap to leave.

Chapter 36

Unexpected Revelation

*A*fter a whirl of spa treatments, specialty seafood, and convention bustle, the mini-vacation for Lottie and Miles ended. The airplane touched down at the small-town airport the Tuesday after Labor Day Monday. They drove home, gazing at the sun as it dropped to the horizon against a red-streaked sky.

"Isn't that a magnificent Southern sunset? I've missed West Point and Little Rob," sighed Lottie.

"Yes. I'm glad to be back. I have to go to work early in the morning," said Miles.

"Our trip ended too quickly. It seems like we left West Point yesterday. I'm glad I went to Seattle with you, Miles. But I had enough of the big city." Lottie sighed again. "I can't wait to hear about the reunion and see Trudy's pictures. I can't believe I forgot my phone charger. I couldn't call anybody to find out about the reunion."

"You can talk to everyone as soon as we get home," said Miles. "I can't wait to get the new building supplies stocked. Most of them have a good profit margin," said Miles.

They arrived home to the ecstatic cheers of Little Rob, who ran to the pickup truck with open arms to meet his parents. Lottie showered him with convention trinkets and Seattle souvenirs, which Little Rob fervently handled.

Mrs. Edwards hugged Little Rob and told him, "Good-bye, Dearie." Then she spoke to Lottie. "Your message machine beeped that it is 'filled to capacity.'"

Miles thanked Mrs. Edwards, paid her, and closed the door.

"Miles, come listen to these messages with me. I don't want to be your secretary. Those contractors and painters could've waited until tomorrow to call you at the store."

Lottie and Miles stood and stared at the telephone answering machine as it relayed message after message about the reunion banquet.

"Girl, you missed an outrageous scene Saturday night! Call me as soon as you get home so I can tell you what happened," said Lucy.

"Lottie. This is Mary Cecil. Our class oddity showed up at the reunion banquet. He was disgusting. Everyone left the restaurant before the evening program." Mary Cecil choked, "We didn't get to distribute the reunion CDs." She coughed. "Please call me at your earliest convenience."

"Oh, no," lamented Lottie. She pulled up a chair and sat down. "Did she say everyone left the banquet before the program?"

Miles tilted his head and widened his eyes. Lottie pressed the "play" button and continued to listen.

"This is Katherine. Lottie, I can't believe you weren't at the banquet Saturday night." Her voice cracked. "It wouldn't have turned out so badly if you'd been here. One classmate ruined the reunion banquet. Trudy didn't present the trophies or show her PowerPoint program. We spent a lot of money on those trophies, the CDs, the band, and the buffet. Nobody there got to order Trudy's reunion DVD." Katherine started crying. "Give me a call soon. I'm so sorry, Lottie." She could hardly conclude her message. "We never anticipated a dreadful disaster!"

Lottie was dismayed. "Oh, no, Miles. What happened?" Lottie succumbed to the shocking news and sobbed in frustration. She wiped the tears from her eyes and face. "Oh, Miles. I can't believe those messages. I don't understand. How could everybody just leave the banquet and not stay for Trudy's presentation? Could I have prevented such a terrible catastrophe?"

Lottie stood and cried in distress. Miles hugged his wife to console her.

"Even if you had been here, you couldn't have stopped whatever happened." Miles pressed the answering machine button to continue.

"This message is for Lottie Arnold. Don Jenkins here. I need you to call me at the police station as soon as possible in regard to a former classmate."

"Police station!" exclaimed Lottie.

"Police station? Former classmate? Let me see," said Miles. "Umm . . . some bully showed up and wrecked the banquet. It's a good thing I wasn't there. I would have hammered him into the concrete floor."

"I can't imagine why Don wants me to call. Mrs. Edwards didn't say anything about Little Rob accidentally sending a false alarm." Lottie was troubled. "How could one person spoil the reunion?" asked Lottie. "Everyone signed up to come see his or her old classmates. Why didn't someone take control?"

"Don't worry, Lottie Love. I'm sure it wasn't as bad as they made it sound. The committee buckled from the pressure, and they want to blame you."

Lottie was too upset to hear her husband.

Miles decided to be funny and help his wife cope with the unexpected news. "I know. Mary Cecil had enough of Lucy and wrangled with the police chief's wife. Lucy pressed charges against her former classmate, and she needs you to testify for her side."

"Miles, don't be ridiculous. Listen to the rest of these messages."

"Who, ha, Rastus, ha, ha. Lottie, it was who, whooo, Rastus, ha, ha."

"Who is that?" asked Miles.

"I don't recognize the laugh. Did he say Rastus?"

"I'm not sure. Something was funny."

"Rastus Webber probably showed up for the banquet, and people made fun of him, like they did in high school."

"Who is Rattus Wetter?"

"Rastus Webber. He was the poor boy that my classmates mocked and taunted constantly in school. Nobody was nice to him, but I tried to be kind to him."

The last three messages were silence, except for bubbling and someone breathing.

Chapter 37

A Spook Outside

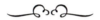

"One of your former boyfriends called to hear your voice on the machine," said Miles. When he saw the look on Lottie's face, he said, "I was joking. I believe *you're* the one who needs a secretary. Do you want me to bathe Little Rob while you call everybody?"

Lottie drew in a deep breath and then blew it out through her nose. "No, thank you. I had a wonderful vacation with you. I don't want to talk to anyone about the reunion." Lottie dabbed her eyes and breathed with resolve. "I left them with explicit instructions. I don't know what happened at the reunion, but at the moment, I don't want to talk about it. If I call everyone, I'll be upset and worried all night. Lucy and the others probably argued about who was in charge of what, and let it disrupt the whole banquet. Well, I want to spend time with Little Rob. I'll put him in the tub while you bring in our luggage."

"Don't worry, Lottie Love. It's not the end of the world. We're home safe. We've got Little Rob, the house, our health. We're okay."

Duress

"You're right. It couldn't have been as bad as they made it sound. I'll call everybody tomorrow. I don't want to deal with this tonight."

While Lottie helped Little Rob with his bath, the telephone rang repeatedly. Miles politely told the callers, "Lottie is busy bathing Little Rob." No one would talk to Miles about the reunion. Miles shook his head and thought to himself, *It must have been worse than a wrecking ball breaking off the chain.*

Lucy called every five minutes. "Is Little Rob still in the tub?"

Miles finally asked, "What happened at the reunion?"

Lucy started with the classmate check-in at the Prairie Arts information booth. She told Miles about the golf scramble, the tennis round robin, and the fishing and fried chicken at Buster MacGinnis's farm. Then she asked again, "Has Lottie finished bathing Little Rob?"

Miles sensed that Lucy would not tell him what happened Saturday night. Lucy chattered about the blues band and the food buffet. Miles interrupted, "I'll tell Lottie you called. Good-bye, Lucy."

The telephone rang again. Miles stared at the phone, deliberating whether to answer or not. "Yes," Miles said as he picked up the receiver.

"Miles, this is Katherine Storey. I'm so upset. I have to talk to Lottie. It's been a terrible weekend. And this morning, I went to the library and found where a tramp had broken in through my office window, camped out, and made a mess in the books." Katherine cried uncontrollably.

"I'm sorry, Katherine. Lottie's busy with Little Rob, and it's getting late around here."

"Of course, I apologize for calling late. Will you ask Lottie to call me in the morning?" She struggled to stop crying.

A Spook Outside

"I'll tell her, Katherine. I'm sure she wants to talk to you."

Miles set the house alarm and went upstairs. The bathroom door flew open, and out ran Little Rob. Lottie and Miles followed their son into his bedroom. They tucked him in bed, knelt beside him, and listened to his prayers. "Good night, Little Rob. We're glad to be home with you." They turned out his light and went to their bedroom.

"I'm ready to sleep on my own mattress," said Lottie. They quickly showered and got into bed.

"I almost forgot to tell you . . .," said Miles. "Katherine called and said a bum broke into the library this weekend and made a mess. She wants you to call her in the morning."

"Who would break into the library?" asked Lottie.

Miles shook his head. "I don't know, but Katherine's upset and wants to talk to you about it."

"Poor Katherine. Dealing with the reunion is hard enough. She probably feels violated. The library is her life."

"This wasn't a good weekend for your committee women. Even if you'd been here, you couldn't have prevented . . . whatever happened," said Miles. "Hmm. I guess the police were busy this weekend. I hope this isn't the start of an increase in crime in our town."

The telephone ringing interrupted their anticipated quiet and rest. Lottie said to Miles, "It may be an emergency call." She answered but heard no response. Two more times the phone rang, and she reluctantly picked up the receiver and heard clucking and bubbles or something.

Miles and Lottie anxiously lay down in their comfortable bed. Lottie rose up and said, "I almost forgot to call George with our 'phone signal.'" She quickly dialed his number, let it ring once, and hung up. Lottie whispered, "Oh, Lord, bless George and Victoria in their time of need."

The Arnolds' telephone rang once, and Lottie nodded, closed her eyes, and whispered a prayer.

"What are you doing?" asked Miles.

"George and I send 'phone signals' to each other. We let the phone ring once and hang up. I call him to signal that I've sent up a prayer for him, and he returns the call with one ring. George calls me at night to let me know when Marilyn gets home so I can pray for him and Victoria."

"They definitely need a prayer when Marilyn gets home."

The telephone rang again, but no one answered Lottie's "Hello." She heard inaudible garbled noises. "Who are you calling? With whom do you wish to speak? Hello. Hello."

"Lottie, don't answer that phone again tonight. Turn off the ringer. I've got to get some sleep. I've got to go to work early in the morning. What's wrong with these people who call so late?"

"Can we meet for lunch tomorrow?" asked Lottie.

"I've got a lot of catch-up work. I won't be able to leave. Why don't you grab some lunch for us and bring it to the store? We can eat there."

"Okay. I'll bring lunch to your office tomorrow. Miles, I don't know what happened at the reunion, but I'm glad I went with you."

"I enjoyed our little vacation together, Lottie Love." He pecked her lips. They both snuggled down, intent on immediately falling asleep. However, minutes later, a pandemonium chorus of yelping dogs in the neighborhood hindered their awaited rest.

Perturbed, Miles said, "Something's out there spooking the dogs."

"I've never heard the dogs bark like this," said Lottie.

They lay flat on their backs in their bed and stared at the ceiling while the menacing barks continued.

"It must be deer running across our yard. Or an armadillo," said Miles.

"I can't sleep with this noise," whined Lottie as she flopped on her side.

A Spook Outside

The dogs snarled and growled. "If those dogs don't shut up, I'll get my gun and shoot whatever's out there," said Miles.

"Something's out there," said Lottie.

"Crazy dogs! Shut up!" strained Miles. "I've got to get some rest. I have a long day at the store tomorrow."

"Miles, please go outside and see what's disturbing the dogs in the neighborhood. Maybe you can scare it away."

"Okay," said Miles in exasperation as he threw back the sheets and got out of bed. "Where's my handgun? The bullets are in the closet." Miles floundered around his bedroom to find his gun and to load the bullets. "All I want is some peace and quiet!"

He stomped down the stairs, carrying his gun. After Miles disengaged the house alarm, he went outside.

Chapter 38

Rastus Finds Lottie

"Poooig!" popped the pistol. Lottie heard the yip of dogs slowly migrate toward the main road. Miles returned inside the house and reset the house alarm. He climbed the stairs, two steps at a time.

"What was it?" asked Lottie.

"I don't know. I saw some teenager down by the mailbox who probably sneaked out while his parents were sleeping."

"You didn't shoot at a kid, did you?" asked Lottie, concerned.

"No. I fired in the sky. You should have seen him take off running," laughed Miles as he unloaded his pistol and put it in his nightstand.

"Are you going to call the police?" asked Lottie.

"No," said Miles. "I don't want any more disturbances tonight. I just want some rest." He quickly got into bed and laid his head on his pillow. They both sank into a deep sleep.

The next morning, Miles arose early, dressed, and hurried to his building supply business. An hour later, Little Rob sluggishly came down the stairs and sat at the table. He stared at his cereal and milk. Lottie packed Little Rob's

Rastus Finds Lottie

school lunch. She helped him dress and get his backpack ready for kindergarten.

Marilyn called as they were leaving. She asked Lottie to pick up George and Victoria and take them to school since she was already at the office and needed more time to finish her work.

"Lottie, I have an important proposal that I must complete this morning. I have to catch a plane for Atlanta this afternoon. My boss insists that I go. I shall attend an awards luncheon tomorrow. Nobody is supposed to know, but I'll be recognized as the Corporate Manager of the Year! Isn't that great?"

"Yes, Marilyn. Congratulations."

"Since I shall leave town on short notice, will you keep George and Victoria until I return tomorrow evening?"

"Sure. I'll get them this morning and pick them up from school this afternoon. No problem. I'll drive them to your place after you return tomorrow evening, if it's not too late."

"That's wonderful. I'm glad I don't have to call Mrs. Edwards to stay with them. She probably has another *sick aunt* to visit."

Lottie called Miles on his cell phone and left him a message, since he didn't answer. "George and Victoria will spend the night with us while Marilyn flies to Atlanta to receive her outstanding manager award. And don't forget, I'm bringing lunch to your office so we can eat together. And you have to sit down to eat. I don't want you walking around the store eating while I'm there for lunch." Lottie chuckled and hung up.

After Lottie set the house alarm, she and Little Rob drove to Marilyn's condo to get George and Victoria and their luggage for an overnight stay. They arrived at school as the bell rang. George let himself out of the car and immediately went to his class. Lottie and Little Rob walked Victoria to her classroom, which was full of chattering children. Lottie kissed her and said, "I'll pick you up this afternoon, Sweetie. You relax and have a good day. You'll be fine. Your Uncle Miles will play with you and the boys when he gets home this afternoon. Won't that be fun?" Lottie felt apprehensive for her niece. Victoria dragged her feet and stood hunched over her seat, pressing one hand on top of the other on her desk. Her face was pale, and her eyes were wet with tears. Lottie patted her shoulder and rubbed her head.

Lottie pulled Little Rob toward the door and said, "Let's go, Little Rob. Your teacher doesn't like you to be late." She hurried him down the hall.

"I don't want to go to school today, Mommy. I want to stay home with you."

"Little Rob, you'll have a great day at school," Lottie said as they reached his colorful classroom. When her son saw the boys in the room gathered around Carey Lee and a shoe box, Little Rob ran over to look. Lottie left quietly since her son was happily intrigued.

Lottie headed home. But on the way, she remembered she needed gasoline for her car. Then she had to run in the grocery store to pick up milk, bread, and fresh fruit. She finally arrived home and went inside to sit down and write a list of everybody to contact and of everything she needed to do. She looked through the mail that had come while they were gone.

Lottie gathered dirty clothes, carried them to the laundry room, and began sorting them. The front doorbell chimed. She unbolted and opened the door, but no one was there. Lottie thought, *It can't be a prank because the children are in school.*

She returned to the laundry room, and the doorbell rang again. Aggravated at the second interruption, she kicked clothes aside and traipsed to the front door. She looked on the porch to see if a package had been delivered.

"Hmm. That's strange." She went back inside and put clothes into the washing machine. The doorbell rang a third time. Lottie was exasperated. *I have a lot to do. Who's ringing the doorbell?* Lottie walked to the front door, and this time she saw the outline of someone through the etched glass door. She swung open the door and gazed at an eerie-looking man.

"May I help you?"

"I'm here. It's clear. The way I feel is real."

Lottie looked at the gray-splotched face and excessive bubbly saliva that rolled around the skinny man's mouth and tongue. She couldn't understand what he said.

"I beg your pardon?"

"Behold the upright saint. A bright light in the stark dark."

A twinge of uneasiness crept over Lottie. She intuitively closed the door with her left hand, ready to turn the deadbolt with her right hand. However, he grabbed the door with a bruised hand and flung it open.

In a raspy, excited voice, he proclaimed, "It's I, Rastus. I'm loose, thanks to Zeus!"

"What? Who are you?"

"It's I, Rastus. I see past us. We're cast together forever."

"Rastus? Rastus Webber? Oh, Rastus. I haven't seen you in years. I didn't recognize you. What? What's happened to you?"

"I mark earthly ones worthy of the divine sign."

Chill bumps prickled Lottie's skin. Rastus looked bizarre. He made Lottie feel uneasy. He didn't talk like the harmless Rastus she remembered. A bleak metamorphosis had mutated Rastus. "I have to go, Rastus." Lottie tried to slam the door on her childhood friend, but Rastus lunged through the door, clamped his cold wiry fingers onto the front of Lottie's arms, and bored his sharp fingernails into her biceps.

"Oh! Oh! Oh, my God! Stop! Stop!" Lottie screeched in shock. "What are you doing? Let me go!" Her body tingled with terror. The unexpected painful pinch paralyzed her. She was face to face with a gruesome man who reeked of body odor. In a panic, Lottie fought to pull away from his stinging fingernails that sunk into her arms, but Rastus had latched on.

Chapter 39

Send Help

Rastus held fast his pinching grip to her arms. He was edgy and fidgety, and loudly croaked, "Escape the fate of the snake! Don't look at the snakes. You'll never awake! Your bones will turn to stone!" His eyes darted toward the threshold of the door and then toward Lottie repeatedly. Rastus tip-tapped back and forth to dodge the twisting serpents he saw coming in under the door.

"Please let go! That hurts! Only one snake was in our yard last summer. You don't have to worry about snakes. Please let go! You're hurting me!" Lottie desperately wanted him to release her arms. She twisted to break his harrowing hold. *Oh, God, help me!*

Lottie trembled. She wanted to get him out of the house and away from her. She struggled to break away, but he firmly gripped her arms and tweaked her skin.

He spit more bewildering words. "Let's go inside to hide. I'll see you alone and whisper how feelings have grown . . . since I heard you on the phone."

His intrusion and assault horrified Lottie. "Rastus, stop. Please. Take your hands off me," pleaded Lottie.

He loosened his grip. "Ahh. That hurt." Lottie flinched in pain as she wriggled her right arm away from his pinch. She impatiently peeled away the fingers of his right hand that stubbornly locked on to her. She massaged her arms and stared where his nasty, long fingernails had pierced her.

"Oh, no. I'm bleeding." She squeezed bright red dribbles out of the slits in an attempt to expel the germs he had infused into her arms. Lottie was afraid.

Once more, she attempted to lure him out of the house and onto the porch. She did not want to be inside and alone with Rastus. Lottie thought that if she could get outside, she could run to a neighbor's house and call Miles or the police. He followed her outside. She strained to be calm and breathe naturally, although chills surged up and down her body. *Rastus makes no sense. Why did he claw me with his fingernails?*

"Can I call someone for you, Rastus? It's time for me to leave and meet my husband for lunch."

"Husband?" Rastus grimaced and pressed his head with his fingertips. He stumbled against the wall of the porch and opened his mouth, from which saliva dripped. "I had no clue until my letter came from you. I hoped it wasn't true. Your last name changed."

He smacked his lips, raised his shaking hands, and cried out angrily, "You took a mate! Why didn't you wait for me?" He grabbed Lottie's arms and shook her roughly. He shoved her against the porch rail and pushed her down.

"What does he do to hurt you?" Rastus wanted to know.

"No. No. Please stop. Don't hurt me. My husband's good to me and my son."

"Son!" Infuriated, Rastus clamped onto Lottie's arms, yanked her up, and shook her violently. She awkwardly stood. He sputtered in her face, "You have a son?" Rastus backed away in apparent disappointment. He reeled and wailed.

Send Help

Lottie was dumbfounded. *Oh, God. What should I do?* She sprinted down the steps to run away, but Rastus's gangling hands flew at her, and he latched on, twisted her arm, and then whipped her wrist.

Lottie fell to the ground in pain, worried that he had popped her elbow and shoulder out of joint.

He writhed in anguish and angrily shouted, "You run from me? Don't you see? Isn't it clear? I had to persevere to get here. Why didn't you wait for me? I'm the one to give you a son!"

Lottie lay sprawled in her yard, petrified. She couldn't move. She thought he expressed an unnatural infatuation for her. *What does he mean? Rastus has changed.* Shakily, she rose to her feet in shock and managed to walk up the steps. She rubbed her elbow.

The telephone rang and startled Lottie. "Excuse me, Rastus. I have to answer the phone." She dashed inside and locked the door. Lottie answered the phone with her voice quivering.

Lucy Jenkins immediately started. "Lottie, why didn't you call me? Everything was great at the reunion until Rastus Webber showed up Saturday night and freaked out everybody. Don's upset because that 'mentally disordered offender' got away."

"Lucy, I can't talk now. Rastus is here. I need someone to come and get him. He acts crazy. He clawed me and pushed me down. I'll call you back." Lottie replaced the receiver, turned, and bumped into Rastus.

"Ahhh!" Lottie jumped. "How did you get in here?"

"Zeus unloosed the door. Yearn for the burn. It's your turn!"

She thought, *I probably left the side door open.* Lottie went to the front door and walked out. She could not process her thoughts about what to do. She hoped Rastus would

Duress

follow. *I don't want to be alone in the house with Rastus.* He followed her outside again.

Lottie's teeth chattered, and her body shook in fear as Rastus conversed with her. "I freely give you mercy. I won't let you depart in the stark dark."

What's he talking about? "How did you get to my house?" asked Lottie as she looked at her arms and pressed on her cuts.

"I walked a mile to see your smile."

"You walked? It's a long way to walk. And it's hot. Let me call someone to take you home," offered Lottie.

"I'm home. Never again to roam." Rastus jerked his arms upward, smacked his lips, and thrust out his tongue. "I hate I had to wait for this day."

"Do you mean the class reunion?"

Rastus crinkled his forehead and scowled. "They're in the stark dark. They'll never receive the mark. Filthy ladies from hades."

The telephone rang again. "I have to answer that. Wait here, Rastus." Lottie flew through the front door and turned the deadbolt. She stumbled to answer the phone and then ran to lock the side door.

Trudy sobbed unintelligibly about the reunion banquet. She told Lottie, "Everyone left the restaurant before the awards were presented and before anyone could talk about the fun afternoon activities. My husband put together a fabulous PowerPoint set to music, and I didn't get to show it."

"Trudy, I'm trying to get rid of Rastus. I'll call you in a little while." She replaced the receiver and then picked it up to call Miles. The back door opened, and Rastus walked inside. *Oh, no. I didn't lock that door.* She replaced the phone on the base.

The telephone rang again.

"Stop the ring! Stop the ding! My heart, my brain. Every part's in pain!"

Send Help

Lottie reached to answer, and Rastus yelled, "No!" He surged at Lottie. She did not want him to touch her burning arms. Lottie pushed her palms back and forth at Rastus as if to urge him to stay back.

"I'll stop the ringing." She lifted the receiver and replaced it and turned off the ringer. Lottie walked away. *Is Rastus involved in a cult? I've got to get away from him.* Lottie hustled down the hall to escape out the side door.

Rastus stormed at her and clamped his bony fingernails into her shoulders at the base of her neck. He shouted, "You! You! Stop what you do!"

Why can't I get away from him? Miles's pistol is upstairs, but I don't know how to use it.

He steered her back into the kitchen. Lottie wondered how she could counter the coercion of Rastus. She persistently patted his hands, and he released his grip. She rubbed the fingernail pricks to her neck and shoulders.

"I have to go to my laundry room. I . . . I have to put dirty clothes into the washing machine." She looked directly into the yellowed eyes of Rastus and slowly backed down the hall. She thought about running out the door to the garage. *The garage door is noisy and rises too slowly. Rastus would catch me.*

She deliberately passed the laundry room and stopped at the alarm control panel by the door to the garage.

She thought to herself, *I can't get him to go away. He won't let me leave. He's holding me against my will in my own home. God, I'm scared.*

Facing the alarm keypad, Lottie thought, *Should I send an alarm to the police? The alarm's loud now. He may do something terrible to me if he hears the alarm. Wait, the duress code. It's the silent alarm that lets the police and Dudley know I need to be rescued.*

She tried to control her short, rapid breaths. *What do I do? How do I enter the duress code? What did Dudley say to do? Oh, God, help me remember!*

Chapter 40

Anticipated Rescue

"You! You! Stop what you do!" shouted Rastus from the kitchen.

Startled, Lottie gasped, "I . . . I thought I heard something in the garage. All right. I . . . I'm coming." She glanced around the corner to see if he was coming, but stood frozen in front of the security keypad.

Then Rastus walked toward Lottie and stopped. "Prepare to bear the mark before dark. Don't let Medusa's snake take our fate. Don't wait! Don't wait!" He turned and motioned with a spindly hand for Lottie to follow him, and he stopped to look for snakes coming in under the door.

His cryptic banter baffled Lottie. "Oh, my goodness," she wheezed. "All right, Rastus. Here I come! I'm coming!" Lottie leaned around to see if Rastus was watching her.

Her fingers trembled as she touched the numbers. *What was that duress code Dudley told me? Oh, God, help me remember. It was the last number that changed.* She entered the first three numbers of her alarm code: four, six, four.

Oh, God, help me. I add one to the last number, which makes seven. Lottie stared at the alarm keypad.

Rastus called, "Lottie, bring your body!"

Duress

Lottie touched the number seven to complete the sequence for the duress code. *Oh, no! I waited too long before I punched the last number.* She quickly entered the duress code for her alarm again: four, six, four, seven.

She fixed her eyes on the alarm screen. "That didn't work," she whispered to herself. Panic clouded her thinking. *I'll make the alarm sound. Maybe that will scare him, and I can run out the door and go to the Clarks' house.* Shaking, she pressed the policeman and the fireman pictures. Sirens and beeps boomed.

Lottie heard pottery and glassware shatter on the floor in the kitchen. She ran to see Rastus wildly flagellating his arms as he circled the room. He moaned and knocked her ceramic pitcher off the shelf. He grabbed the fruit-filled pottery on the counter and threw it down explosively.

"Stop, Rastus! Stop!" Lottie ran to the touchpad and pecked in her numerical code to disarm the alarm and silence the noise. Then she rushed back into the kitchen.

Rastus thrashed around the kitchen, shoving everything he could seize onto the floor. He raked off Little Rob's breakfast cereal bowl and juice glass, which splattered. Lottie saw her new designer vase that Marilyn had brought from Atlanta lying on the floor, cracked.

"It's off! Rastus, stop! The noise is gone. Please stop." Lottie barely touched his arm.

Rastus leaned over and dragged his coat sleeve across his mouth. He grabbed his head and winced in pain.

In a state of confusion, Lottie routinely proceeded to remove the broom and dustpan from her kitchen closet. She cried as she gathered the big pieces and swept up the rest. *Why is this happening?* Lottie wiped up the cereal and juice.

She remembered that the alarm company would phone the house and ask for her password, but she had turned off the ringer. She nonchalantly walked to the telephone and secretively turned on the ringer.

Anticipated Rescue

"You! You! What did you do?"

Lottie faced Rastus and said, "I . . . I have to clean the floor." She picked up the magazines, broken ceramic pieces, fruit, and her cracked designer vase.

The telephone rang. "I'll get it." Lottie quickly picked up the receiver.

"This is Deb at Stevens Security Systems. Is everything okay?"

"No, it's not."

"Is this Mrs. Arnold?"

"Yes."

"What's your password, honey?"

"I'm sorry. I can't answer today."

Rastus plucked the phone from Lottie's hand and placed it on the base. Lottie's heart pounded. She resolved to remain calm and to wait patiently for help to arrive. She knew that Deb from the security company would report their conversation to Dudley Stevens and that he would send the police to her house soon.

Rastus spoke firmly. "I must turn the tide. I must burn on the sign."

Lottie did not want to decipher Rastus's words. She concentrated on her imminent rescue. She sighed deeply, feeling the weight of anxiety lift. She expected Don Jenkins to send someone to her house immediately.

Her shoulders burned, and her arms throbbed where Rastus had hooked his fingernails. Lottie reached for the first-aid kit, which was high on a shelf. She cleansed the cuts with peroxide and applied ointment.

Lottie rambled about school days and ignored Rastus's outlandish statements. In the back of her mind, she persistently assured herself, *I didn't give the password to the security company. They'll send help even if the duress code didn't work.*

Lottie thought about Miles, who was expecting her. *He'll work through lunch and not think about me until he gets hungry this afternoon or until Dudley calls him.*

Minutes passed slowly. Lottie looked at her watch every few seconds. She thought to herself, *Where's Don Jenkins? He knows Little Rob didn't set off the alarm; school is in session. There's no way he could think this is a false alarm. Where is he? Where's Dudley? He fixed our system. I'm sure it works. Why isn't someone checking on me?*

"Lottie, are you in your body or out of your body? Lottie. Lottie?"

She wanted no emotional or physical contact with Rastus. Ominous jitters wrestled Lottie. Her arms twitched, and her teeth chattered without restraint. Her self-assurance and perseverance ebbed.

"You! You! Stop what you do!"

"Oh, sorry, Rastus. What did you say? Do you need something to eat? Do you want a glass of ice tea?"

"Hot tea for the bod-y."

"All right. Hot tea." Lottie nervously moved around the kitchen and made hot tea for Rastus to repress her bad feeling about her situation. She believed that the police or Dudley would arrive at any moment. *They'll come to my rescue soon, very soon,* she repeatedly told herself. Her arms pulsated with pain; her elbow and shoulder ached.

Lottie vacillated from positive anticipation of the police to wearied impatience of their disregard of her duress signal. Rastus's oppression puzzled Lottie, but she refused to think about his intentions or to understand them.

To dispel attention away from his freakish words and ghoulish stare, she unloaded the dishwasher, rearranged her shelves, and talked loudly so that she wouldn't hear Rastus's words or look at him. Lottie lit perfumed candles to mask the rotten odor of Rastus. She fought off the thought that the police and the security company had ignored the alarms.

Anticipated Rescue

How much longer? I need help. Where's Dudley? Why hasn't someone from the police station called? Where's Don Jenkins? I told Lucy I needed somebody to come get Rastus. Why hasn't Miles come home to see about me?

Oh, no. I have to pick up the children from school this afternoon. George and Victoria are spending the night. I need to leave and get the children. I don't want the children to be around Rastus. When will help arrive? Lottie was about to hyperventilate.

"I have a present for you." Rastus placed a matted nest of greenish, dusty, coarse hair on the kitchen counter. "A prize for your eyes."

"What is that?" asked Lottie warily.

"It's Mama's hair. Her hair was still there in the box under the rocks by the creek."

Lottie stared in shock. "What . . . . How do you know this . . . this is your mother's hair?"

"I know it's so! When I was a kid, I dug by the creek every week. One day I saw the edges of Mama's rug. I dug for days. I saw she was dead. Her hair came off her head. I liked Mama's hair."

"What . . . . When did you do that?"

"A few days before they made me go away. I saved Mama's hair. I loved Mama's hair. I hated my earthly father. I appealed to Zeus to strike him! He deserved the worst curse. Don't fail me. Don't tell my secrets. I'm lonely. I confess my secrets only to *you*."

Lottie felt weak and queasy. *Oh, my God! I need your help! This is more than I can bear.*

Chapter 41

Lottie Needs Help

The police chief sat at his desk, inspecting neat stacks of police reports to distract his attention away from the elusive Rastus Webber. Since Don had been police chief, his emphasis had been on training officers, obtaining grants for equipment, and initiating drug prevention in schools. His one indulgence had been to personally teach self-defense classes.

Don met Lucy when he came to West Point years ago to complete a rotation in his law enforcement curriculum. Because of his exceptional comprehension of the correctional system, Don was offered distinguished criminology positions. He turned down all of the prominent offers because he had fallen in love with Lucy and pledged himself to her. After they married, he resigned himself to stay in Lucy's hometown to ensure her happiness.

He thumbed through papers as he impatiently waited for a telephone call about Rastus Webber. The Claxton police chief's disclosure that Rastus preyed on innocent victims haunted Don. He didn't want Webber to assault anyone in West Point on his watch as police chief.

Lottie Needs Help

Maybell buzzed Don to tell him that the Claxton police chief wanted to talk. "Yes, Maybell. I'll take that call."

"Don, this is Mike Cantile. You already know it, but you've got problems. Webber has a list of offenses as long as a trip to Jackson and back. But worst of all, his doctor has filed a brief to expunge his records due to what his psychiatrist calls 'complete rehabilitation that demands full restoration of rights.' You want me to send you copies of his case narratives?"

"Yes, Mike. Yes. Fax me his records before they're expunged. He's committed fresh crimes. How can his doctor, in good conscience, try to erase his wrongdoings? If this fellow has a criminal history, the purging of that information would be a travesty, a gross misapplication of the legal system. In my opinion, Webber isn't ready for reintegration into society. I should've been notified of his release and his intent to come here."

"Like I said before, I didn't know about his release to West Point. I am utterly amazed that he was allowed to come by himself, with no one to oversee his arrival and departure," said the Claxton police chief.

"When I encountered him Saturday night," said Don, "I didn't know he had a criminal background. We had him in custody yesterday morning, but he got away. Also, we found proof that he hid out in the town library this weekend. And he's disappeared again."

"Hmmp. He's always had an affinity for libraries. The Claxton Library installed an alarm system specifically designed to prevent the breaking and entering of Rastus. Hmmp. Rastus will raise his ugly head soon. When he escapes, it's not just for a little walk around town. He never returns on his own. No. And his doctor always shows up to repossess his patient."

"The current charges I can pick him up on are vagrancy, disturbing the peace, and breaking and entering."

"You'll be lucky if his offenses are that minor. Don, I've tried for years to get a conviction on Webber or his physician. But his proceedings always come down to a concession between his lawyer and the judge, or else the case is thrown out on a technicality. I almost quit law enforcement because of Webber and his psychiatrist."

"Are you serious?"

"Yes. I nearly had a nervous breakdown. My advice is to gather your evidence carefully. Do everything by the book. Webber's psychiatrist and his lawyers know how to work the system to dodge charges and convictions. The main loophole they use is the one where the law says that schizophrenics aren't responsible for their actions. Psychopaths *can* be held accountable, and he *is* a psychopath."

"Thanks for the tip, Mike."

"Listen. I talked to Webber's psychiatrist. He's anxious to retrieve his patient. I'm sure he'll contact you."

"He's already called the station and told Maybell he would come and get Webber with a 'warrant for his confinement.' What is that?"

"That's his personal legal certificate that he's devised. It's useless, but it looks authentic. He says it gives him authority to take Webber into his custody. I'm positive he'll come to see you soon. I warn you, he has a slick tongue."

"I'm ready for him. This kind of doctor isn't capable of understanding dangerousness. Thanks, Mike."

"Let me know when you apprehend him."

Don leaned forward and folded his hands on his desk. He stared in deep thought. Then Maybell rang and said, "Your wife is on line two."

Don picked up the receiver. Before he could say a word, Lucy spouted, "Hello, my man! That crazy Rastus Webber is over at Lottie's house. He grabbed her, or something like that, and pushed her down. I'm on my way over there to push

Lottie Needs Help

him down and help Lottie get rid of him. Send a patrolman to her house now!"

"Lucy, how do you know Webber's location?"

"I told you that I talked to Lottie."

"No, you didn't say that you had talked to Lottie. How do you know he's at Lottie's house?"

Lucy was agitated at her husband's attention to her words. "I telephoned Lottie at lunchtime, and she told me he was there, and she wanted someone to come get him. She said he 'acts crazy' and that she couldn't talk, but she would call me back. Well, she hasn't called me and won't answer the phone, and I'm worried."

"Lucy!" said Don.

Lucy continued to talk. "I don't know what an insane person like Rastus Webber would do. I know he's still crazy. He's probably drooled on everything. I'm going over there and check on my best friend. What are you waiting for? She said she needed help!"

Chapter 42

Avoid Confrontation

"Lucy!"

"Yes, my man."

"Don't go to Lottie's house. The Claxton police chief informed me that Webber has a criminal record. He's mentally defective, and your intrusion could trigger fanatical behavior that could result in harm to Lottie and to you."

"What? Are you sure?"

"Lucy, I need you to come down to the station. I need to talk to you more about Rastus Webber and Lottie. Will you do that for me?"

Lucy hesitated. "Sure. Will you send an officer to check on Lottie and get Rastus out of her house?"

"Come to the station, and we'll discuss our options, Lucy."

"Uhh! Okay," said Lucy, unwillingly.

Don didn't trust Lucy to stay away from Lottie's house. He thought the best way to keep an eye on her was to bring her to the station.

Maybell buzzed Don. "Dudley Stevens is here from Stevens Security Systems."

"Ask him to come back later this afternoon."

"Sir, he's here about that emergency alarm sent from the Arnolds' house."

"What emergency alarm?"

"The one he intercepted and requested that our response be delayed until he verified if it was false or not," said Maybell.

"Hmm. Emergency alarm?"

"Umm hmm."

"Okay. Send him in."

Dudley timidly tapped on the police chief's door.

"Come in!"

"Uh, yes sir. Uh, a duress code went out from the Arnolds' house to Central Monitoring and to the police station. When I heard the beep and saw the flashing light on my little black box, I thought it was a malfunction. I ain't never seen my black box blink, except when I press the test button.

"Well, in actuality, two duress codes was sent. When the fire and police alarms was activated, I called as quick as I could to warn you not to gallop over there yet. Uh, you know, seein' as how you made some trips to their house that weren't real."

Dudley paused and looked at Don. The police chief wrinkled his brow and blinked his eyes at Dudley, waiting for him to continue.

"Uh, well, Deb at Central Monitoring called the Arnolds' house to make sure that it was a false alarm. But Deb said that Mrs. Arnold wouldn't say her password and didn't even make much sense. I got a bad feeling. Nobody's ever used the duress code."

Don drew in a deep breath. He folded his hands on top of his desk and looked from one side of the room to the other.

"Okay, Dudley. Knowing the Arnolds' record on false alarms, I can see why you reacted the way you did to obstruct the duress alarm. It may have worked out for the best that we didn't speed to the Arnolds' house in a loud clamor. I don't have enough information on Webber to anticipate his criminal inclination. A surprise showing of policemen could provoke him to violently attack Lottie."

"Uh, now say that again?"

"Dudley, there's an insane man, who may be dangerous, and he's with Mrs. Arnold at her house at this moment."

"Good God! Lord, forgive me. I didn't follow proper procedure." Dudley staggered and then crumpled into a chair. "My father will kill me. He left me in charge while he and Mama went to Florida. He told me I better not mess up things while he was gone." Dudley started crying.

"Dudley, get hold of yourself. We'll do everything we can to ensure Lottie's safety."

Maybell interrupted Don and said, "Your wife is here."

"Send her in."

Lucy threw open Don's door and confronted him at his desk. "When are you going to get Rastus out of Lottie's house? She said to send someone to get him. I wouldn't want to be alone with him, and I'm sure Lottie doesn't want him around!"

"Lucy, I need you to get Dudley some water and help him calm down. Ask him to tell you what he's done."

"Hello, Dudley. Why are you here?"

Maybell walked into Don's office with a stack of faxed papers. "These are from the Claxton police chief."

"Thanks, Maybell."

"There's a Dr. Affle on line one. He says that 'it is obligatory' that he 'speak with the person in charge.'" Maybell fingered quotation marks to emphasize the doctor's precise words.

"Yes, Maybell. I'll take that call."

As Maybell walked out of his office, Don said, "Maybell, get in touch with Miles Arnold, and ask him to come to the station. Tell him as little as possible. I don't want him to panic or rush to his house." Maybell nodded.

Avoid Confrontation

Don answered his call. "Don Jenkins here. Yes, Doctor. I saw Rastus Webber four days ago at an evening banquet. We had him locked in a cell yesterday morning briefly, before he escaped. He's currently holding a woman captive in her home."

The psychiatrist defended his patient. "Rastus is not involved in anything illegal. He is a psychologically handicapped schizophrenic, who experiences auditory and visual hallucinations."

The police chief's blood pressure rocketed as he listened to Dr. Affle.

"Let me interrupt you, Doctor. From my brief encounter with Rastus Webber, I assessed that he is a disturbed deviant."

"My patient is in need of therapeutic counseling to treat his depressed mental function," said Dr. Affle. "I must supply Rastus with specific prescriptions to control his psychoses. I demand that you avoid bodily abuse of Rastus. The law requires that you preserve his legal rights."

"'Police powers' in the U.S. Constitution allow me to take action necessary to protect and maintain the safety of law-abiding citizens," explained Don.

"You must delay your plans to confront my patient until I arrive," advised Dr. Affle.

"How long do you expect me to wait before I take action?" asked Don.

"Twenty minutes," answered Dr. Affle.

"Very well. I'll wait twenty minutes for you to get here, but no longer." Don slapped down the telephone receiver.

Lucy insisted, "Don, please go rescue Lottie from that pervert. Who knows what he'll try to do!"

"Lucy, I need you to take Dudley to the vending machines and get him something to eat and help him relax. I have to look at these incident reports so I can determine how to arrest Webber without endangering Lottie. Also, I need you to temper the situation when Miles gets here."

Lucy rolled her eyes at Don and extended her hand to Dudley. "Get up, Dudley. Let's go find you something to eat that will make you feel worse than you do now."

Chapter 43

Something's Wrong

*D*on grunted and shook his head as he read about Rastus Webber.

Maybell knocked on Don's office door. "Miles Arnold is here, and more papers from the Claxton police chief came over the fax machine for you."

"Thanks, Maybell. Take these first reports to Tyrone, and tell him to review them." Don accepted the new transmittals from her. "Send in Miles." Maybell nodded.

Miles walked into the office, shook hands with Don and Dudley, and spoke to Lucy.

"Dudley, get up, and let Miles have your chair," ordered Don.

"Uh, sure. Yes sir."

"Don, I don't have to sit. Keep your seat, Dud."

"Get up, Dudley. I need Miles to sit down," said Don.

Dudley slowly rose out of his chair. He hung his head and drooped his shoulders. He walked shamefully to the back of Don's small office and leaned against the wall.

"Miles, when did you last speak to your wife?" asked Don.

Duress

"She left me a message around eight o'clock. She said she would bring me lunch, but I haven't seen her or talked to her since early this morning."

"Are you acquainted with a man by the name of Rastus Webber?"

"Let me see. Is he the bully who ruined the class reunion banquet?"

Don did not respond. He folded his hands on his desk and looked straight at Miles.

"No, Don. I don't know him. Everybody was calling Lottie about that guy. I've never seen him."

Miles could see from Lucy's and Dudley's expressions that something was wrong.

"What's going on?" asked Miles.

"Your wife entered a duress code from your house alarm this morning. Were you aware of that?"

Dudley held up two fingers.

"Yes, Dudley. Correction: Your wife entered the duress code two times from your house alarm. Did you know that?" questioned the police chief.

"No. I've been glued to my desk today. We've been out of town, and I needed to catch up at work." Don, Lucy, and Dudley stared intently at Miles.

"Let me see. *Duress* code? Is that the special alarm you told us about, Dud? The one that's never used?"

"Uh, yes sir. Uh, in actuality, a police and fire alarm was sent from the house, too, but it was dee-activated from the house alarm keypad," said Dudley.

"I don't understand how or why alarms were sent. Little Rob's in school, so I'm sure that he didn't send them accidentally. I don't know who sent the duress code. I never understood that alarm myself. Dud, did you call Lottie to ask her about the alarms?"

"Uh, yes sir, Mr. Arnold. Deb at Central Monitoring talked to Mrs. Arnold."

Something's Wrong

Miles stood up. "Don, I apologize for another false alarm. I don't know how or why alarms were sent, but I promise that I'll have Dud disconnect it. We've never needed a security system living in this small town. I know it's a lot of trouble to send your men out to the house for no reason. Just send me a bill, and I'll pay for your time and trouble. I'm sorry. I'll make sure that an alarm *never* comes to the station again from our house."

Miles looked directly at Dudley and said, "I want you to disconnect our alarm *today!* We don't have problems with robbers and rapists . . . just repeated false alarms that cause trouble and screw a nail in everybody's life."

"Miles, sit down, please."

"Why? What is it?"

"I suspect this was not a false alarm."

"What? What do you mean? Dud said they talked to Lottie." Miles looked at Dudley. "What did Lottie say?"

"Well, Deb at Central Monitoring talked to Mrs. Arnold. When Deb asked your wife for her password, she wouldn't say it," said Dudley.

"Now, let me get this straight. Didn't you call me here to tell me my alarm went off accidentally again?"

"No."

Puzzled, Miles sat down on the edge of the chair. He gazed at Don to urge him to explain.

"The demeanor of Webber is consistent with that of a mentally disordered felon. Lucy talked to Lottie around lunchtime, and your wife claimed that Webber was at your house and had pushed her down."

Miles stood. "Pushed her down!"

"Be seated, Miles. Let me explain what we know. Someone, I believe it was your wife, activated a duress code through the alarm system two times. The alarm signaled Dudley's security office and our police and fire stations; however, Dudley called and asked that we disregard the alarms."

Miles stood to leave. "I'm going to my house to check things out. Why did you ignore the alarm, Dud? Why didn't you call me?" Miles waited for Dudley to comment on his reason for overriding the alarm.

Dudley timidly responded, "Well, seein' as how there was some false alarms in the past, I just wanted to check things out before the police and firemen went bustin' over there." Dudley broke down again. "I'm so sorry, Mr. Arnold. Please forgive me. Please forgive me! Please! We ain't never had a duress code, ever. I couldn't believe someone here in West Point could be held hostage."

"What? Hostage!" exclaimed Miles.

Chapter 44

Time of Need

"Miles, remain calm," encouraged Don.

"Hostage! Are you telling me that a class reunion wacko is holding my wife hostage in my house? And he pushed her down? And we're just sitting around talking about it? If you won't go arrest him, I'll go hammer his head into the sidewalk. I'm not afraid of a freak."

"Miles, sit down. Webber's physician will arrive soon. I have some grave concerns. We can't risk an immediate confrontation with Webber. First of all, I notice that the overall goal of his plan of care is 'to promote reentry into a community.' His effective rehabilitation depends on chemical restraint medications and mood-stabilizing drugs, which I have a hunch he hasn't taken since he left the mental facility. And my second concern is for your son. Do you know for a fact that he's not home with Lottie?"

"Little Rob's at school in kindergarten. Wait. Let me see. Lottie is supposed to pick up my son at 2:45 . . . and my sister-in-law's children, too. They're spending the night with us because their mother's going out of town."

Don looked at the big round clock on the wall, and Lucy and Miles looked at their phones. It was fifteen minutes past school dismissal.

"I'll go pick up the children," said Lucy. She grasped her purse and started to leave.

Miles's cell phone rang, and he quickly answered. His face fell when he heard Marilyn's voice. She yelled at Miles, "I demand to know why Lottie won't answer the phone or why Lottie hasn't picked up my children. Those incompetent educators at the school say they won't stay past 3:15 with my children. This wouldn't be a problem if Lottie would be responsible and do what she promised to do. I have a plane to catch!"

Lucy overheard Marilyn and whispered to Miles, "Tell her I'll get her children, too, and not to worry."

But Miles shook his head and hand vehemently at Lucy to tell her, "No."

"No, Marilyn! You be responsible for your children. I'm at the police station, and Lottie is tied up and can't help you this time. Why don't you call their father to pick them up from school?"

"I wouldn't call that man if he were . . . ."

Miles hung up. "Marilyn won't let anybody or anything come between her promotion and her flight." Miles looked at Lucy and asked, "Will you get my son and George and Victoria from school, and let Buster know? He can meet you in town and get his children from you. George and Victoria will be safe with Buster and Mama Mac while Marilyn flies to Atlanta."

Lucy was visibly shaken and could only nod her head as she took short, rapid breaths. As she walked out the door, Don called, "Lucy, do not go to the Arnolds' house for any reason! Your unsolicited intrusion could compromise Lottie's safety. Do I make myself clear?"

Lucy glanced at her husband and gasped for words. "I understand." Then she looked at Miles and said, "Don't worry about the children. I'll take care of them. I'll call Buster."

Meanwhile, Marilyn was infuriated with her brother-in-law. She twisted and clenched her hands in outrage as she sped down the highway toward the airport. *Who does Miles Arnold think he is? Nobody hangs up on me. I can't believe Lottie married that low-life builder. How could Lottie desert me in my time of need? What a dysfunctional family! They don't understand that my entire future corporate career hinges on this trip to Atlanta. This is my time, and I will not let them ruin it for me!*

Marilyn was unable to reach Mrs. Edwards to employ her child-care services. She did not know the telephone numbers of any parents of children from George's or Victoria's class. She couldn't think of anybody to call to go and get her children.

Marilyn called Miles's mobile phone once more. He answered immediately, hoping it was Lottie.

"Miles, I'm sure you're still at the police station. I don't know why, and I don't care. I don't have time for your pitty-pat problems. You're an impediment to my accomplishing my goals in life!"

Marilyn's voice pierced the air, and Miles had to hold the phone away from his ear. He bit his lip momentarily, but then reproved Marilyn: "The world doesn't revolve around you!"

Marilyn ignored Miles's rebuke and said, "My baby sister has proved herself to be irresponsible. I told her that I have to fly to Atlanta this afternoon, and she consented to care for my children until I return."

"I'm sorry to throw a wrench in your plans, but Lottie isn't available to take care of your children."

Duress

"Who picked up your son? Whom did you employ to care for him?"

"None of your business," said Miles, irritated at Marilyn's rudeness. "You are the most selfish parent I've ever known. Lottie is right; those children deserve to be with their father. At least Buster would love them and give them attention and a home life, which you're too busy to do. That's who should take care of George and Victoria—Buster. He would gladly meet their real needs."

"Do you mean Boyd? I wouldn't let my children stay with him if he were the last sitter in town."

"He's not a babysitter. He's their father. I already told Lucy Jenkins to get George and Victoria and meet Buster in town to give him his children, since their mother is too busy accomplishing her goals."

"How dare you interfere in my personal affairs! You have no right to . . . ."

Miles interrupted, "Marilyn, I have to take care of my own problems. I can't take care of your family problems, too."

"I'll have you know that I'm the one who provides everything for my children. I . . . ."

Miles clicked off his cell phone and looked at Don. "There's no point in telling Marilyn the situation. She wouldn't change her greedy plans for Lottie or anybody else. I'm worried about Lottie." He lowered his head to his knees and put his fists on his forehead. "My Lottie Love, hang on until I can get to you."

Marilyn was incensed. She thought to herself, *How dare that crappy husband of Lottie talk to me that way. I never liked him. Why did Lottie marry that idiot?*

I'm in a bind. What can I do? If only George were old enough, he could drive to school every day, and this wouldn't be a problem.

Marilyn finally got in touch with Mrs. Edwards, but she was obligated to tend to her sick aunt and couldn't help.

I can't miss my flight to Atlanta. I have to be at the luncheon tomorrow to accept my award and promotion. I'll have to let the children go with Boyd. I have no other choice. I'm sure he doesn't have anything to do but piddle with pigs on that nasty farm. Lottie is so irresponsible.

Chapter 45

Atypical Behavior

Maybell tapped on Don's door. "A Dr. Affle is here and demands to see you at once." She used her strength and large body to secure the door and purposely block the entrance. The short-statured physician tip-toed, stretched to see over Maybell, and pushed his way into the office.

Don ignored Dr. Affle and spoke to Maybell. "Thank you, Maybell. Please show him in. Will you bring a couple more chairs into my office for our good citizens? And will you ask the assistant chief to continue his effort to contact Mrs. Arnold and notify me if he succeeds?" Maybell nodded.

Dr. Affle stroked his thin hair from the top of his head down to his ponytail. He walked to Don's desk and thrust his face close to Don's. "I must enlighten this city's chief of police in regard to my rehabilitated patient, released to this city last Saturday."

Although the physician intruded the police chief's personal space, Don did not back away. "I am 'this city's chief of police,' and if you refer to a certain Rastus Webber, alias 'rehabilitated patient,' then you're in the right place."

Maybell opened the door, set two chairs in place, and said to Don, "Buster MacGinnis is on the phone and asked if he may be allowed to come in when he gets back from settling his kids at the farm."

Miles pleaded, "Please, Don, let Buster come in as soon as he arrives. He's family."

"Okay, Maybell. Send Mr. MacGinnis into my office as soon as he arrives."

Don politely stood and extended his hand to the psychiatrist, who held up his bandaged-covered fingers.

"I am unable to shake hands due to cuts I sustained from broken glass, which inadvertently fell into my pockets at the dry cleaners. My fingers were already sore due to my sensitivity to a chemical cleaner used in the institution."

"Okay," said Don. "Good afternoon, Dr. Affle."

"My name is Dr. Affle. You say 'waffle' and drop the 'w' for the correct pronunciation."

"Pardon me, Doctor. Let me introduce you to Miles Arnold. Webber is in his house detaining Mr. Arnold's wife against her will. This is Dudley Stevens from the security system company. Dudley received the alert that Webber is holding Mrs. Arnold under duress."

Dr. Affle showed no interest in preliminary office niceties. "Has the woman charged that he forcibly detained her? Is there factual evidence to prove my patient restrained her against her will?"

The police chief wrinkled his brow at Dr. Affle. "I'll let Dudley Stevens explain the alarm notification Mrs. Arnold sent and the status of the response to the alarms."

Then the office door opened slightly. Buster MacGinnis peeked in the room, and Miles motioned for him to enter. "Sorry, I just got here. Lucy said she would pick up my children from school and take them home to my mama."

Buster shook hands with everyone, except Dr. Affle, who held up his wrapped fingers. "I am Dr. Affle." The doctor explained to Buster, "My fingers are encumbered with cuts, which hinder me from shaking hands."

Duress

Buster shook his head politely and said, "Glad to make your acquaintance, Dr. Affle."

The physician rebuked Buster. "You say 'waffle' and drop the 'w' for the correct pronunciation of my name." Buster acknowledged his reproach. "Oh, excuse me. I'm very sorry."

"Dudley, since we're pressed for time, I'll tell the doctor what we know," said Don. Dudley blinked and sighed in relief at Don's offer to explain.

"Rastus Webber went to the Arnolds' house before noon. A female friend of Mrs. Arnold's called around twelve o'clock and was told by Mrs. Arnold that Webber was there and that he had grabbed her and pushed her down. Mrs. Arnold activated a duress code two times to signal that she was in a hostage situation, and then she entered police and fire alarms, which were canceled.

"Dudley Stevens called the station to postpone an immediate response until the accuracy of the alarms could be verified. The security company representative talked to Mrs. Arnold at approximately one o'clock to request her password to determine if the distress signals were real or accidental. Mrs. Arnold didn't give the correct password, which indicates there's a security problem that warrants investigation. Regrettably, we've received no further communication from her."

The physician stood up and prepared to exit. "It's advantageous for my patient that you didn't startle him with a surprise confrontation. The behavioral variables of his case demand that I retrieve Rastus and return him safely to the facility, where I will assess him further."

"Not so fast, Dr. Affle." Don also stood.

"You say 'waffle' and drop the 'w' for the correct pronunciation."

"Thank you for your enlightenment," said Don sarcastically. "Will you be seated? I have some questions for you.

And if you don't want me to file a 'guilty but mentally ill' charge in our county against your patient, you'll answer truthfully. Disturbed offenders typically receive harsher sentences and tougher punishment around here, especially if they're repeat offenders." Don and Dr. Affle sat down.

Shocked, Miles looked at Don and the psychiatrist as he heard them discuss Rastus.

Dr. Affle began, "The decision to release Rastus to attend his high school class reunion was made by a board of certified medical professionals, who maintain the best interests of my patient. My institution maximized his mental well-being through an extensive social, emotional, and cognitive skills program."

The psychiatrist crossed his arms and stared at the ceiling in a trance as he remembered meeting with the administrative assistant, the director of nursing, the activities director, the caseworker, and the certified nurse aide to determine if Rastus was competent to be released for a social function. The psychiatrist recalled that he governed the Temporary Release Committee meeting with extreme expertise.

Dr. Affle fondly remembered telling the staff, *I attest that Rastus is mentally stable. His chemical restraint medications and mood stabilizers have diminished atypical behavior. His improved mental well-being will allow him to accomplish his goal to reenter a community!*

Dr. Affle recalled that the caseworker argued that Rastus wouldn't be accepted, but Dr. Affle enlightened her that Rastus's hometown would provide the perfect setting to test his social rehabilitation.

Then the activities director made light of his peculiar manner of speech.

The doctor remembered telling her that this release was crucial to document Rastus's successful rehabilitation and that small-town people would tolerate his verbal handicap.

Baron, his nurse aide, rudely talked about Rastus's hygienic problems.

The newest employee, Nurse Dander, had challenged Dr. Affle. She incited the others to oppose the psychiatrist's noble endeavor. Dr. Affle thought, *I refused to deny him this occasion to prove he's capable of independently . . . .*

"Dr. Affle. Dr. Affle? Are you okay, Dr. Affle? Are you thinking about something of importance? We have a problem to resolve," said Don. "We must focus our attention on this difficult situation. You seem to be preoccupied in deep thought and not concentrating on our discussion of your patient. We want to apprehend him peacefully and not provoke him to irrational behavior. Are you okay, Dr. Affle? Do you need some water or coffee?"

"My name is Dr. Affle. You say 'waffle' and drop the 'w' for the correct pronunciation of my name."

Don looked straight up, rubbed his shaved head, and sighed. *Are there any sane people left in the world?*

Chapter 46

Past Charges Dropped

The psychiatrist inhaled and exhaled deeply to end his reverie of the fateful Temporary Release Committee meeting. He lifted and pointed his chin toward Don. "You wrongly attempt to label my patient as a mentally ill deviant. He's in treatment. He's not dangerous. He must be protected from manipulation and abuse."

"*He* must be protected . . . from manipulation and abuse? *You* have manipulated and abused the justice system." Don folded his hands on his desk and moved forward. "From the looks of your patient's notorious criminal history, he's a menace to society. He's committed serious offenses, for which you've allowed him to escape responsibility. You and your attorney finagled numerous acquittals."

"I beg to differ," said the braggadocio psychiatrist. "My patient has no criminal record."

Don leaned back in his squeaky chair and put his hands on his hips, astounded at the physician. "Yes, I understand you filed a brief to purge his record, but it won't be expunged for three days. You irrationally intend to erase the records of his crimes. Webber is a repeat offender who habitually breaks the law, and furthermore, he doesn't deserve full restoration of rights. He's paid no retribution for his many harmful acts."

"What harmful acts?" asked Miles. "What's he done? I don't want him to hurt my wife." Miles grabbed his head, closed his eyes, and prayed loudly, "Oh, God, Lottie needs Your help. Please protect my wife."

Don did not respond to Miles, but instead slid forward in his chair, folded his hands on his desk, and firmly fixed his eyes on Dr. Affle. "Now, you are trying my patience. I really don't care about the safety of your patient, but I do intend to protect my law-abiding citizens in this town, with or without your cooperation. Do I make myself clear?"

"My patient's plan of care inspired a high degree of recovery in his psychological and social functioning. You cannot abridge his privilege as a citizen."

"When his actions infringe upon the rights of an innocent person, I can."

Dr. Affle stood. "You cannot deny Rastus his equal protection of the law!"

Don stood with his hands on his hips. "With his repeated documented violations of the law against ordinary citizens, I can!"

"You cannot deprive my client of due process of the law!"

"Since his rehabilitation program has not deterred his recurring offenses against defenseless victims, I can!"

They both sat down.

Miles rubbed the curly hair on his head in exasperation. "How dangerous is this guy? Why is a weirdo with his problems out of the mental institution? Why won't somebody tell me what crimes he's committed? I'm going to rescue Lottie from this maniac. I'm tired of this talk." Miles walked to the door and spoke to Dr. Affle. "Your patient is dead if he touches my wife. I'm leaving." Miles opened the door.

"Miles, you must wait until we assess his tendencies of assault. For Lottie's sake, sit tight for a few more minutes," implored Don.

Buster latched on to Miles's arm. "Come on, Miles. Just wait a few more minutes." Buster patted Miles's shoulder to calm his distress and pulled him back to his chair.

"Dr. Affle . . .," started Don.

"My name is pronounced *Dr. Affle*. Say 'waffle' and drop the 'w' for the correct pronunciation. Mr. . . . . What did you say your name is?" asked the psychiatrist.

"Jenkins, Don."

"Mr. Jenkins. We share the same goal to return my patient to the mental facility as expeditiously as possible. I have the skill to recover him without bodily harm."

"No, we don't share the same goal. You intend to prevent bodily harm to him and return him to your bubble. I want to prevent physical injury to an innocent young wife and mother. His criminal records show that petty theft and felony assault charges were repeatedly dropped."

Dr. Affle twitched uncomfortably in his chair. Miles looked back and forth between Don and Buster in disbelief at what he heard. He sat on the edge of his seat, angrily grabbed the sides of his chair, and resisted the urge to pounce on Dr. Affle.

"I can't believe the number of times he received a suspended sentence. There isn't one injunction for supervised probation. Less than a year ago, he was arrested for . . . ." Don stopped and glanced at Miles, unsure if he should continue. The police chief spoke hurriedly in a monotone to avoid unnerving Miles: ". . . for murder, which was reduced to manslaughter, for which I see he was exonerated. I suspect that you're responsible for the dismissal of those charges."

"Murder! Manslaughter!" exclaimed Miles as he stood. "That's it! I'm out of here. We're wasting time. I can take care of this guy. What are you waiting for, Don? Let's go! I have a gun, and I know how to use it. This guy is obviously

Duress

crazy. Why don't we go to my house and check on Lottie? He's trespassing, and I want to press charges; isn't that a good enough reason to arrest him?"

"Miles, I know you're upset," said Don. "There are too many unanswered questions about the mental instability of Webber. We could prompt a lethal act against Lottie if we surprise him."

"If he's hurt other people, what's to stop him from hurting my wife? Sitting around here is pointless! She may already be dead. We all agree he's crazy. Let's go get the freak." Miles sprang to the door to exit.

Dr. Affle held up a hand with bandage-wrapped fingers to Miles, as if directing traffic. "Although he has a diagnosis of mental illness, that's not a sufficient reason to forcibly detain him and deny his deserved release. I have a letter from someone in your town who guaranteed Rastus an opportunity to experience friendly camaraderie. He was promised societal acceptance."

Don looked at Dr. Affle and shook his head. The police chief sighed in bafflement. "Nobody but you promised him anything."

Buster prodded Miles to return to his chair. Dudley suspiciously stared at Dr. Affle. Don shuffled papers on his desk, scribbled notes on one report, and then asked, "Why did you release Webber to come to West Point unsupervised? He's under state institutional care."

"Yes, he is," said Dr. Affle excitedly. "Here is my notarized Warrant for Confinement, which grants custody of Rastus into my professional and medical care."

Don briefly studied the paper, tore it up, and threw it in the trash. "I'm sure you're aware that dangerous mental patients may only be discharged by written consent from the State Board of Health. I'd like to see your legal documentation from the authorities who examined your patient and who they approved to supervise him," said Don.

Chapter 47

A Grave Fate

*D*r. Affle calmly explained, "A viable social outlet was necessary to demonstrate Rastus's successful rehabilitation. The timing of the reunion banquet prohibited me from obtaining the letter of consent from the Board of Health."

"Your excuse is unacceptable. The reunion wasn't planned last week. Your spur-of-the-moment decision to allow your patient to come to West Point unsupervised is unlawful."

"My patient's personal certified nursing assistant was assigned to escort Rastus, but the aide deserted his job responsibilities suddenly, without notice. I experienced an unavoidable, urgent family emergency, which prevented me from accompanying Rastus. However, my patient has a propensity for independence. Furthermore, my research proves that he completed a structured remedial program to maximize his mental well-being, which prepared him to reenter a community independently."

Annoyed at the physician's slush of words, Don asked tersely, "Why didn't you notify someone here that he was coming to West Point?"

Duress

"I mailed a form to a reunion designee that stated his intent to attend the reunion banquet. However, the registration may have been delayed since my decision to approve his outing was late. My colleagues and I determined that this social outlet was the perfect opportunity to prove his rehabilitation, especially since he received a letter, signed by a former female classmate, who personally invited him to come to the reunion."

Miles jumped out of his chair. "You fool! My wife sent that letter *personally inviting* every single classmate to the reunion. You let an insane person come here to test his rehabilitation?"

"Is Lottie your wife?" asked Dr. Affle in a soft tone.

"Yes! Lottie's my wife, and your crazy patient is with her in my house!"

"Rastus spoke endearingly of the woman named Lottie. I questioned her existence until Rastus received the signed invitation; therefore, I deemed that this was an appropriate time to grant a temporary pass."

Miles was livid. He again jumped to his feet and stood over Dr. Affle. "Appropriate time!"

"It's all right, Miles. Let Don handle this guy," said Buster as he gently pushed Miles down into his chair.

"Dr. Affle . . .," started Don.

"My name is *Dr. Affle*. Say 'waffle' and . . . ."

"Yes! And drop the 'w'!"

"Where *was* I?" said Don as he sought to regain his train of thought. "Yes, these records indicate that Webber frequently shoplifted hand-held wood-burning tools. Would you explain?"

"Rastus prefers wood-burning pen sets that come with interchangeable brass tips. He uses the tip point to make dots and the blade edge to make straight lines. The tips of a wood-burning tool may reach six-hundred degrees Fahrenheit."

"Couldn't you provide a tool set there at the facility so he wouldn't have to go out and steal one? But besides that, wood-burning is not a typical arts and crafts activity found in an institution, is it, Doctor?"

"On occasion, Rastus left the facility without authorization with the specific goal to obtain a wood-burning tool for his intended use."

"His intended use," Don repeated. "These reports say his aggravated assaults included burns to his victims." Don pierced Dr. Affle with his eyes. "Did Webber use the wood-burning tool to burn his victims?"

Dr. Affle momentarily squirmed in his seat, but his aptitude for verbal exposition empowered him to excuse his patient's actions. "The intent of Rastus is not to cause bodily harm. He applies a peripheral burn that he believes will save a select few from a grave fate."

Incensed, Miles grabbed the lapels of Dr. Affle's suit coat and shook him aggressively. "If that insane man burns my wife or hurts her in any way, I'll rip your fingernails and toenails off with pliers, one at a time, and you'll wish you could be burned instead."

"Sit down, Miles, and control yourself," ordered Don. Buster pushed Miles down in his chair and patted his jerking shoulders.

Don paused and called Maybell. "I need you to call Kellogg's Hardware and get Bucky on the phone for me." Don abruptly walked out of the office and came back with the assistant chief of police, Tyrone Duncan. A dispatcher followed with a tray of coffee for everyone; no one but Don accepted the coffee.

Don introduced the assistant chief to Dr. Affle. "This is Webber's physician from the Claxton Mental Home. This is the assistant chief of police." Tyrone smiled and extended his hand to Dr. Affle, who showed his bandaged fingers. Dr. Affle said, "I cannot shake your hand."

Duress

Don shook his head and said, "Tyrone, here are more reports for you to study. The mental uncertainty of this felon cannot be ignored. He poses a serious threat to Mrs. Arnold. I need you to continue your effort to contact Mrs. Arnold in her home and on her mobile phone," said Don.

"Yes sir. I haven't had a response yet. I'll keep trying. Let me look at these reports and find a weakness that will allow us to arrest this guy without a major incident." Tyrone walked out carrying the stack of papers sent from the Claxton Police Department.

Maybell beeped Don's phone. "Bucky's on line two for you."

"Thanks, Maybell. I'll take that call."

"Hello, Bucky. Someone came to West Point last weekend who likes to steal wood-burning hobby sets. Do you sell a wood-burning tool?"

"Why, yes. We always keep two or three in stock, especially when it's time for the Prairie Arts Festival. You need one, Chief? Do you want me to check to see if we have one for you?"

"Yes, Bucky. I'll wait while you check." Miles and Dudley fidgeted and snorted as they impatiently steeped in frustration.

Moments later, Bucky returned. "Chief, I know I saw two on the shelf Saturday morning, and they're both missing. No one remembers when we sold them. Why, they were real nice wood-burning tool sets with five interchangeable brass tips."

"Yes, I'm certain they were good ones," said Don.

"I may have another one in the back, if you want me to look, Chief," offered Bucky, "or I can order you one."

"No, that won't be necessary, Bucky. Thanks for your trouble."

"Glad to help, Chief. Anytime."

A Grave Fate

Don thought out loud, "One tool was found at the library. He may have another tool with him." The police chief looked directly at the psychiatrist and asked, "Dr. Affle (Don was careful to pronounce his name correctly), what motivates Webber to repeatedly steal wood-burning tools to burn his victims?"

"If you only consider external information, you will assume a pervasively negative interpretation of his purposes," answered Dr. Affle.

Don put his elbows on his desk. He dropped his head and pressed his fingers into his temples.

"Dr. Affle, you gush with words, but I deal with facts. Judges, lawyers, and psychiatrists use interpretive license. You have wasted valuable time. Now, answer my questions directly, or I'll charge you with obstruction of justice and lock you up in our no-frills, small-town jail. Do I make myself clear?"

"Rastus is on a mission to prevent particular people from dying and going to hell," explained Dr. Affle.

"Are you kidding?" exclaimed Miles. "Are you saying the devil himself comes to burn people to keep them *out of hell?* What kind of rehabilitation do you do?"

Don wanted to stay focused. "I see from this report that this nurse died after he burned her. I also see that the manslaughter charge was dismissed. Would you explain?"

Dr. Affle nodded and said, "Rastus attempted to securely immobilize the nurse to prevent excessive movement. He had to tape her mouth to halt her bites and stop her shrieks that triggered his noise-induced headache. In a state of confusion, the woman flung her head at Rastus, which knocked the heated point of the tool deep into her arm. In a reflexive motion, Rastus's hand and the tool flew up to her face and accidentally penetrated her left eye."

"Oh, my God!" said Miles and Buster, shaking their heads. Dudley blankly gazed at the psychiatrist.

Dr. Affle continued, "Notwithstanding, the nurse had a preexisting condition of ventricular tachycardia and diabetes. Her abnormally rapid heartbeat precipitated a cardiac arrest because she experienced a disoriented disturbance in the presence of Rastus."

Don glared at Dr. Affle, astonished at the psychiatrist's rationale. He buzzed his faithful secretary. "Maybell, I authorize you to call my good friend Michael Tillison, at the FBI office in Oxford, and apprise him of the hostage situation. We can't subdue Webber without his victimization of Lottie. He won't cooperate with standard approach and arrest procedures. Tell Mr. Tillison that I need him to activate the Special Response Team ASAP. If he has any problem with your request on my behalf, I'll talk to him. Do I make myself clear?"

Chapter 48

The Scar

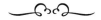

"I understand completely, sir," responded Maybell. "I'll call the FBI at once."

Don also instructed Maybell, "Tell Tyrone to send all patrol cars and two ambulances to the Arnolds' neighborhood entrance, and wait there as backup for the Special Response Team." She nodded affirmatively and promptly tackled her assigned tasks.

Don explained to Miles, "The Special Response Team invisibly penetrates a perpetrator's space and incapacitates him quickly. Webber's an unbalanced offender. The few times I've encountered psychopaths, I've found they don't think and act predictably. A blatant, deliberate rescue may not be in the best interest of Lottie due to the erratic traits of this guy."

"My patient is not a psychopath. He's a schizophrenic," said Dr. Affle.

Miles stood. "I won't wait any longer. That freak's in my house with my wife. I'm going home to throw him out. I can break his bones or just shoot him. You don't seem to care that he may have tortured and burned Lottie! We're talking about my wife, the mother of my son!"

"Miles, I know you want us to arrest him immediately and free Lottie. But we could provoke volatile behavior if we accost him by surprise. There're too many variables that I can't control. For instance, if he considers Lottie his prey, he'll protect her until he realizes he's lost her to you. And if he's suicidal, he won't think twice about killing her and then taking his own life."

"My God! Lottie! How can this be happening? I've got to do something," languished Miles.

"Calm down, Miles," said Don. "I gave you a dismal scenario to illustrate the importance of caution when apprehending a psychopath. Be seated for a few more moments." Miles sank into his chair.

Dr. Affle quickly articulated, "My patient is schizophrenic, not psychopathic. I am uniquely qualified to manage his behavior. I must intervene on behalf of my patient to alleviate his mental suffering. Rastus must not be subjected to an authoritarian confrontation."

Don sighed and shook his head. He bluntly said to Dr. Affle, "Your patient *will* be confronted, and he *will* be captured without your interference. I suggest that you go back to your institution with your expert psychological treatment techniques and revise your rehabilitation program. Your criminally committed patient has enjoyed his illicit obsession and has been repeatedly exempt."

"Let me correct you," said Dr. Affle. "Under the 'obviously ill standard,' my patient was *civilly committed*."

"Let me correct *you*," scathed Don. "If your patient harms Mrs. Arnold, the state attorney general will sue you personally for illegally releasing your *civilly committed* patient. You do not have discretionary freedom to release Webber without written approval from state authorities." Dr. Affle turned aside his head and shrugged, as if he were not worried.

Miles rushed at Don and pounded his fist onto the police chief's desk. "If something happens to Lottie, I'll never forgive myself for not going sooner to save her." Miles whirled in frustration and prayed, "God, help her. Oh, God, please help her."

Curiosity enticed Dudley Stevens to emerge from the back of the small office and to move to the front of Don's desk. "Uh, Police Chief?"

"Yes, Dudley. What is it?"

"Did, uh, did he say that man burned someone to death?"

"No, he said that the nurse had a heart attack when Webber tied her up, taped her mouth, and burned her, and *that* scared her to death." Dudley stared inquisitively at the police chief. The psychiatrist's distorted point of view had rankled Don. He continued sarcastically. "It wasn't Webber's fault she died since *she* had a bad heart and couldn't handle his fiery ritual. If *she* had not lunged at him and interrupted him, then *she* would be alive and simply have a scar from a bad burn."

"Oh. Will, uh, he . . . that man, try to burn Mrs. Arnold?"

Not waiting for the police chief's response, Dr. Affle explained, "My patient meticulously burns an artistic motif on a chosen person that's not life-threatening. The bodily locale for the mark is in an inconspicuous, yet a tender, area . . . ."

Miles lunged at Dr. Affle to push him, but Buster held Miles. "If that freak touches my wife, I'll grind you to fine powder and mix your dust in sidewalk cement and walk all over you!"

"Miles, sit down! We're going to apprehend this demented culprit in the safest way for Lottie's sake," explained Don. He asked Dr. Affle, "How does he select people to burn, and what characterizes the burn he inflicts?"

"Rastus suffers from delusions of grandeur, which are controlled through specialized medications. Through visions, he's instructed to burn a distinct mark on certain individuals to protect them."

"Protect them from what? Hell?" asked Miles impatiently.

"As I was saying, he has to mark an individual before he or she sees the snakes that are cut off Medusa's head. When he doesn't ingest his specialized medications, he sees snakes slide under doors that turn the beholders to stone."

Miles exclaimed, "What? What's a Doosa head? What snakes? Real snakes? Does he see snakes that aren't there? Like hallucinations?"

Dr. Affle explained. "Surely you remember the mythological story about Medusa, whose hair was snakes. If someone looked at the snakes, they turned to stone."

"What? He thinks fairy tales are real?" Miles could hardly sit still. He wanted to clutch Dr. Affle's neck and choke him. Miles sat in his chair, holding his clenched fists out from his body while Buster stood over Miles to hold him down with his strong hands. Dudley remained puzzled.

"Rastus experiences excessive mood swings. He flails his limbs. He speaks in associations that rhyme. I assure you his medications control his behavior. However, he suffers adverse reactions from his prescriptions," sympathized Dr. Affle.

The psychiatrist continued, "The most obvious side effect is the darkened gray, mottled appearance of his face. He must tolerate tardive dyskinesia, which causes involuntary mouth sucking, tongue-thrusting and lip-smacking. Rastus deplorably endures excessive salivation and slurred speech at times."

Defending his patient, Dr. Affle said, "Fortunately, Rastus has undergone optimal psychosocial treatment in combination with mood stabilizers and a chemical castration drug, which provides the same effect as castration but without the need for surgery. Regardless, his many medications render him impotent and depress his high sex drive."

Don cleared his throat. "Dr. Affle, does Webber have these medications with him, and does he regularly self-medicate, or does your staff dispense his drugs to him?"

"Police Chief Jenkins, I can assure you that the mental disorders of my patient are completely under control with his prescribed medicines, which he was given and instructed about clearly. However, since his Sunday morning return was *hindered*, he's had no opportunity to access his daily medications.

"Nonetheless, I believe there's a high probability that he retains a residual effect from his drugs. But it's critical that he consume his prescriptions promptly. Without the administration of his exact dosage, he's potentially at risk for delusional schizophrenia."

Don spontaneously blurted in disbelief at what he heard, "*He's* at risk?"

"Lottie doesn't deserve this," said Miles. "She would never hurt anyone. I don't want this guy to hurt Lottie. Why don't you go to my house and arrest him, Don? Or just shoot him. I can't sit here and wait while you and this psychiatrist talk about how crazy he is. We've got to go rescue my wife! If he sees things that aren't really there, he may see something that makes him want to hurt Lottie."

"I can see you are distraught," responded Dr. Affle. "You must not assume that he wants to harm your wife. I assess that he developed erotomanic delusions about the said woman, Lottie. He believes that she loves him, and he desires her affections."

"What did you say?" Miles lost control. "How could you let a nut with his problems out of the mental institution?" Miles grabbed Dr. Affle by the shoulders, but Dr. Affle pulled away. Then Miles swung to smack Dr. Affle's face, but the physician deftly flapped his elbows up and rolled his bandaged fingers into fists. Miles grabbed at Dr. Affle, who batted Miles's arm aside. Dr. Affle amazed Miles with

Duress

his defensive capability as he beat the air with his elbows and twisted his arms. Then his coat and shirt sleeve rose to expose a strange scar on his left posterior arm above his wrist. Miles saw it and gasped, "What is that?"

Don Jenkins locked onto Dr. Affle's arm and firmly turned it up to expose a peculiar healed wound. Dudley, Buster, and Miles crowded directly above the mysterious scar and marveled; they stood motionless and stared in silence.

Clearly visible were dots and lines on Dr. Affle's left wrist on the underside of his arm, an unmistakable scar from a burn. The edges of the dots were discolored, and the centers lighter. Faint ropy lines threaded evenly to the spots. The scar was well-healed and had obviously been there for a long time.

Chapter 49

Burn Procedure

*D*r. Affle wriggled and twisted his arm, trying to free himself, but Don maintained a strong hold on the doctor's wrist. Don asked, "Is that the mark Webber burns on his victims?"

"Yes, but let me explain."

"Okay. Everyone sit down so we can listen to the doctor explain." Don looked at his watch and hoped the explanation would not be lengthy.

Dudley moved an old rusty chair from the back of the office and set it beside Miles and Buster so that he could clearly hear the psychiatrist. He felt guilty that he had obstructed the alarms from the Arnolds' house. Dudley thought, *That was an irregular alert. Nobody's ever sent a duress alarm. I'm the one to blame for Mrs. Arnold's trouble. I need to do something.*

"We're waiting for your explanation, Dr. Affle," said Don. "I assume Webber used a wood-burning tool to burn this image on your arm. Is that correct?" asked Don.

"Yes, that's correct," answered Dr. Affle, as if replying to a lawyer.

"Will you explain the significance of this mark?" implored the police chief.

"Rastus believes he's a descendant of the Greek god Zeus, whose half-god son, Perseus, ventured on a quest to abduct Medusa's head. Instead of hair, her head wriggled with snakes. Perseus saved Andromeda, the one he loved, by holding Medusa's head for her cowardly suitor to behold and turn to stone," expounded the physician. "Rastus maintains that his mother mated with a half-man, half-god relative of Perseus's, and the union resulted in the birth of Rastus."

"What?" exclaimed Miles. "Myths are not true. How could you let him believe he's a fairy tale person?"

"Exactly what does this mythological story have to do with the burn on your arm?" asked Don.

"It's a perfect depiction of the constellation of Andromeda. Rastus is convinced that this mark protects chosen ones from the underworld of hades. Unfortunately, he also suffers delusions of snakes crawling under doors. However, his prescribed medications control his hallucinations."

"Miles exploded, "Snakes? How could you let someone come here who dreams he's seeing snakes crawl under doors?"

Dr. Affle continued his composed explanation of Rastus. "My patient believes that his father found out about his true parentage and forced his mother to leave but made Rastus stay."

Dudley's lips stretched back to form a dimple that disclosed his lack of comprehension. Buster blinked his eyes dubiously at the physician. Dr. Affle's strange revelation flabbergasted Miles, and he gushed, "That's utterly ridiculous! He's crazier than I imagined. He's so far out, it's absurd!"

Don did not want to lose control of his probe into Rastus Webber's motive. "Dr. Affle, will you enlighten us as to how and why Webber chose to burn you?"

Burn Procedure

"My name is Dr. Affle. For the correct pronunciation, you say 'waffle' and drop the 'w.'"

"Yes. Thank you for correcting me in regard to the correct pronunciation of your name. Now answer my question! Tell me exactly how and why Webber chose to burn you." *He's trying my patience.* Don looked at his watch and thought, *He's wasting critical time.*

"Rastus restricts his selection to esteemed individuals who consummate significance in his life. I gained the confidence of Rastus four years ago, and he elected me to receive the mark. He restrained me with ropes and performed the procedure painstakingly," said Dr. Affle calmly. "After Rastus precisely marks an individual, he treats the chosen person as an expensive, valuable trophy set high on a shelf as a prestigious possession."

"If that man ties up my wife and burns her, you're a dead man!" declared Miles to Dr. Affle.

"You're fortunate that I can use my expertise to intervene with Rastus and your wife. He accepts only me to administer his psychiatric treatment. Moreover, I am his personal social confidant. As his physician, I must spare him the negative impact of criminal complaints."

Don opened his mouth in astonishment and shook his head. "How can you say you want to spare *him* the negative impact of complaints? Do you believe that burning someone against his or her will wouldn't justify a criminal complaint?"

"His intentions are highly honorable in his desire to save a chosen one from hell. He merely inflicts a nonthreatening, expeditiously applied mark, which is painful only for a short time," stated Dr. Affle.

Exasperated, Don responded, "He does not save anybody. Can't you comprehend that he torments a person for his own personal fantasy? His agenda to burn someone causes the person mental anguish. How can a law-abiding citizen lead a normal life after enduring his painful procedure? He carefully and terrifyingly restrains his victims and cruelly burns them. Don't you see a problem with behavior that intentionally hurts innocent people?"

Miles begged, "Don, you've got to do something. I can't wait any longer. If that crazy man burns Lottie, I'm going to shoot him in a place that will inflict real and not imagined pain for a long time. Please go and help Lottie."

"Miles, I know you're upset, but we can't afford to surprise this psychopath, or we jeopardize the safety of Lottie."

"I don't care that you don't want to surprise him. I want you to go get him *now*, before he hurts Lottie!"

Dr. Affle protested, "My patient is a schizophrenic, not a psychopath. After he begins his procedure, it's in the best interest of the person not to interrupt. Superficial burns are far easier to overcome than deep, subcutaneous third-degree burns."

"My God! We've got to rescue Lottie. I won't wait any longer! I'm leaving! I'm going to my house!" Buster patted Miles's shoulders and encouraged him to wait.

Don ignored Miles's hysteria. "Is he easily provoked to hostile behavior?"

"His neural capacity is antagonistically affected by loud noises, such as sirens, alarms, thunder, or vocal outcries, which may induce hostility. At these times, he experiences intense pain in his head and uncontrollably thrashes his upper extremities."

"Why don't his victims run away? Webber doesn't appear very strong. How does he subdue his victims before he uses his burning tool?" asked Don.

"People selected to receive the mark have tried unsuccessfully to flee from Rastus. He's incredibly fast and has an inscrutable, strong, pinching grip. He communicates with the chosen ones, and they agree to be restrained before he proceeds."

Burn Procedure

Don thought, *You're as insane as your patient.* "Your rehabilitation has not deterred Webber's offenses. He may believe in his own mind that what he does is right, but it's wrong. You have tolerated wrong behavior and haven't corrected it. As Webber's responsible party, you have failed. I want you to understand that I will contact the attorney general at my first opportunity. I will personally file charges against you. You will be held accountable for his reprehensible behavior, which you try to justify."

Dr. Affle turned his head and threw up a shoulder. He had been threatened before. Lucy Jenkins burst into the room crying. "The teachers said Trudy Lee picked up the children. She got all three and said she would let Lottie know she was bringing them."

Buster blurted, "No! I should have gotten the children."

Don asked Dr. Affle, "Does he put his mark on children?"

"My patient has had little contact with young children; however, a baby that cried unceasingly was accidentally suffocated to terminate the intolerable noise."

Don buzzed Maybell. "Call Mr. Tillison in Oxford, and explain that we now face a multiple child endangerment threat. Tell Mr. Tillison to send the Special Response Team to the Arnolds' house ASAP! I'll watch for them there." The police chief took his Glock out of his desk and put it in his holster. "It's time to go." He put on his cap and walked out the door of his office.

Dudley cried, "Lord, Lord. Oh, God! The kids! The kids! What have I done? Miles, forgive me. Oh, God. My father's gonna kill me when he and my mama get back from Florida. He left me in charge. My father told me I better not mess up things while he's gone. Oh, God! I need help! I need help! What am I gonna do? I don't know how I'm gonna live with this. The kids! What if he burns the kids?"

Dr. Affle approached Dudley. "I can help you with your problem. Here is my card. Call me next week," the psychiatrist said as he left.

Miles glared at Dudley and defiantly pressed his lips together. He snatched the business card out of Dudley's hand and tore it into little pieces. Miles threw the paper fragments onto the floor and walked out.

The realization of danger to his wife and son panicked Miles. He raced to his pickup truck. Buster ran to catch him and said, "Don't worry, Miles. We can handle this guy. I'm coming behind you."

Miles managed only a nod to Buster, and then peeled away.

Don got into his police car and locked the doors. Dr. Affle saw that the police chief was about to leave and waved, as if hailing a cab. Don screeched away as Dr. Affle shouted, "Wait! Wait! Do not proceed without me. I don't know where to go. I'm his doctor. He needs me. Moreover, it was an excruciating experience, one I shall never forget! Only I can fathom his deep desire to save others! Don't leave without me. I'm needed to spare him . . . ."

Dr. Affle stood alone in the police parking lot.

Chapter 50

Roughen You Soon

At the Arnolds' house, Rastus slurred his quasi rhymes and repulsed Lottie. She felt isolated and abandoned. Her hope for help to promptly arrive had dwindled to despair. She slipped by the phone to turn on the ringer and wondered if she could dial 911 faster than Rastus could take the receiver from her. She strained to converse with Rastus. He refused to let her out of his sight. Lottie fought bodily exhaustion and mental despondency.

Rastus noticed that Lottie was not attentive. He pecked his nose in her face and clamped his fingernails into her biceps again.

"No! No! Stop! That hurts. Don't pinch me. It hurts. Let go of me."

He spit in her face, "Your eyes are full of lies! At night I dream you are upright, but it seems you want to flee from me!"

Lottie withdrew from his spew of words and the odor of his body. Rocking sobs shook her. Rastus loosened his grip, and his mood changed. He gazed at her face and unclipped her hair. "I like it unwound and down." Sliding his long, bony fingers down her arms to her hands, he softened his

Duress

voice. "We can go away, or we can stay. My entire being is on fire for you, too. I've waited years to make my feelings clear. Zeus is the one who's done this for us!"

Fear paralyzed Lottie. Fatigue numbed her senses. She wanted help to arrive. She could not stand Rastus's demented intimidation. Lottie turned away.

Rastus stepped in front of her. He sloshed his lips on hers and gored his tongue in her mouth. He pressed his skeleton against her body, but Lottie pushed him away with a shriek.

Unrestrained spasms, belching, and dry heaves erupted inside her. Nausea sickened her body as she tasted his bad breath and the rotten slime of his mouth. She ran to the kitchen sink and vomited. Lottie splashed water on her face and mouth to wash away the putrefaction. Gag reflexes undulated painfully from her stomach up her esophagus and stabbed her throat.

Rastus stretched his arms upward and spread his fingers and shouted, "Exaltation! Celebration! Zeus freed me to be me!"

Lottie wiped her face and mouth with a kitchen towel. She spit and sputtered to empty her mouth. Then she heard a familiar pound of little hands on the side door.

"Oh, no. It can't be . . . ." She rushed to the door, opened it, and felt chill bumps as her son raised his hand to greet her happily. "Mommy! Mommy! I'm home." He ran toward the den to watch television.

Tears poured from Lottie's eyes. Unrestrained shakes riveted her.

Sensing his mother was upset, Little Rob asked, "What's wrong, Mommy? Don't cry, Mommy. What's wrong, Mommy? Is Aunt Marilyn here?"

"Nothing's wrong, Little Rob," she said, struggling to control her emotions. Lottie wiped her tears and squelched her gags. "Little Rob, we have a guest."

"Rejoice in the boy's voice," said Rastus as he walked toward Lottie. "It's no mystery, Lot-tie. We're meant to be!"

Lottie disregarded Rastus's lewd words. She thought, *I have to concentrate on Little Rob and protect him.* Then she remembered George and Victoria.

"Little Rob, where are George and Victoria?"

"They're coming. They're slow. They're not fast like me."

Distress ravaged Lottie. She struggled to think. "Who brought you home?"

"Carey Lee's mommy."

"Okay. Little Rob," said Lottie as she strained to draw in a breath, "this is an old classmate of mine from my school days. His name is Mr. Webber. Can you say hello?"

Little Rob dutifully replied, "Hello."

George and Victoria walked in. Dread suffocated Lottie.

"Come in. One thin and two hefty. Let me feel them," said Rastus, reaching for them.

"No!" Lottie burst.

"No? *No?*" questioned Rastus in her face, and he shoved her against the wall.

"No. I mean they're not all my children. One is my niece, and the other is my nephew." She tried to tone down her negative response to avoid upsetting Rastus.

George's mouth and eyes opened wide in disbelief at the strange man and his rough treatment of Lottie. Rastus seemed more frightening with the children there. *How can I protect them? I don't know his intentions,* thought Lottie.

The Arnolds' home had always been a stable place for Victoria and George. Rastus reached for Victoria, but Lottie instinctively pushed him away. "Don't touch her!"

Rastus slung the back of his hand across Lottie's face. "Don't tell me, 'Don't touch her!' I'll touch as much as I want when I want!" Reeling backward, Lottie's body banged into the wall, crashing pictures to the floor.

Rastus placed his hands on Victoria's bony shoulders and said, "Does your father bother you?" She clasped her arms across her chest and dropped her head. Disquieted, she stood still as urine ran down her legs onto the floor.

Lottie staggered to Victoria and said, "That's all right, Sweetie." She pulled Victoria's shoulder away from Rastus. George and Little Rob froze. Rastus stooped to closely peer into the face of Little Rob; they quietly studied each other's countenance. Rastus remembered a time when he was young and innocent like Lottie's son.

Little Rob had never seen anybody who looked or smelled like Rastus Webber. The boy put his hands on his hips and cocked his head to one side as he curiously stared at the funny-looking man.

Giggles erupted from Little Rob. Rastus appeared delightfully hilarious. A twig of hair flopped back and forth across one of Rastus's eyes as he involuntarily swayed his body. Little Rob perceived that the tongue thrusts and the odd facial expressions were funny faces like he and his daddy did for fun. He cackled happily in naive amusement.

Rastus raised his arms up and spread his fingers in anger. He grimaced and gushed out a garbled, "Iiiiii!" which frightened Little Rob. The stranger reached out for the boy, who escaped to his mother's side. In a rage, Rastus struck the window of the side door with his fist and shattered the glass. Lottie screamed. Blood splattered on the door and the children.

"You laugh at me? I'll bury you in the steep bank by the creek!" Rastus smacked his lips, thrust out his tongue, and shook his bleeding fingers from his side to above his head. As he talked, saliva spilled out of his mouth. Rastus held his cut hand and faltered a few steps down the hall. He pointed his trembling bloody hand at Little Rob and said, "My hand burns with pain. You're to blame. Don't thwart my plan again." Little Rob's eyes widened.

Rastus frantically breathed in and out of his nose. He warned Little Rob in a screech, "You baby baboon, I'll roughen you soon!" Rastus reached for Little Rob, who jumped away.

Rastus gravitated toward George and Victoria and peacefully placed his hands on their heads, touching Victoria with his wounded hand. "These children will be my children." He looked up and said, "Prepare me to care for them. I'll save these from hades."

Chapter 51

Body Slam

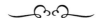

*L*ottie huddled the children close and opened the door to push them outside. "Run to the Clarks' house! Call Miles or Buster to come get you!" Her son rolled under his mother's push and took her hand. "No, Little Rob! Go with them!"

George and Victoria did not understand what was happening, but they obeyed their Aunt Lottie. George held his sister's hand and led her as fast as she would go toward the neighbors' house.

Little Rob hesitated and then started out. Rastus pushed Lottie aside and grasped Little Rob, who wriggled to get free.

"Little Rob, don't fight him," Lottie pleaded. "He's bigger than you." The boy stopped scuffling, and Rastus released Little Rob and studied the boy's face again. Rastus's mood changed. He said to the boy, "I'll do a good deed and meet your need."

"Oh, he doesn't need anything but an afternoon snack. Isn't that right, Little Rob? I'll make you a peanut butter and jelly sandwich." Lottie reached for Little Rob and pulled him into the kitchen to get away from Rastus.

Little Rob saw the matted hair on the counter. "What's that, Mommy?"

"Don't touch it. It's nasty."

Her son stepped from side to side and dipped his head up and down to inspect the bristly mass without touching it. She could not hold back her tears. Lottie wept. Little Rob held onto his mother's elbow. "Mommy, don't cry. Are you scared? Mommy, are you hurt? You okay, Mommy? He broke the glass. I saw blood."

Little Rob pointed to the hair. "What are you going to do with that stringy stuff?"

"Nothing. I'm not going to touch it, and I don't want you to touch it."

"Okay, Mommy."

Afraid to run out another door since her son was there, Lottie struggled to remain composed. Lottie had to figure out how she and Little Rob could escape. "Don't worry, Little Rob."

Her son said, "He's in there with all that blood and peepee."

"Yes, Little Rob."

"He needs a lot of Band-Aids, Mommy."

"Yes, Little Rob. We'll get bandages for Mr. Webber," said Lottie. She whispered to her son, "Go call 911 now!"

Rastus walked toward the kitchen. Lottie tried to stand in his view so he wouldn't see Little Rob on the phone. "I have a bandage for your hand. Let me cover your cuts to stop the bleeding." He said nothing. He held his hand out, but did not look at her. Lottie wrapped gauze tightly around his hand to compress the cuts and taped it in place.

Rastus raised his head and exclaimed, "Who's he talking to?"

"Oh . . . oh . . .," stammered Lottie.

Rastus pushed Lottie over, and she fell sideways. He dashed to Little Rob, who ran. This was an opportunity for

Lottie to escape, but she would not desert her son. She followed them to the den, where Rastus cornered Little Rob. When Rastus reached for the boy, he ducked and ran to his mother.

"Quick! Out the door, Little Rob!" They ran toward the side door and crunched broken glass underfoot. Lottie flung open the blood-splotched door and pushed Little Rob out. But Rastus grabbed them both, inattentive to his cut hand, and shoved them into the wall.

The mental patient stood over them, pointing his bandaged hand at Little Rob, and shouted, "You refuse me? Your mother is due me. You're of no use to Perseus, son of Zeus!" Rastus bullied Little Rob with his fingers on the boy's chest. He dribbled in Little Rob's face, "Where's your moan so bold? You'll die cold as stone."

Lottie wanted to get away from Rastus because he had become more erratic and crazy. *I'm afraid for Little Rob. I don't want Rastus to hurt my son.* Lottie pushed Rastus's hand off of Little Rob's chest. She secured Little Rob's hand and dragged him into the kitchen.

"He's mean. He's mean."

"Shhhh, Little Rob. Don't say that." Sweat drops popped out on Lottie's head and neck as she fought back retching. Rastus did not follow them into the kitchen. Lottie made a sandwich and poured a glass of milk for Little Rob, and attempted normal conversation with her son. She whispered, "Did you call 911?"

"Yes, Mommy. They asked a lot of questions I didn't know."

Lottie bowed her head, "Thank You, God." She told Little Rob, "Thank you, Son."

Little Rob was curious about Rastus and quizzed his mother. "Why's he fighting with us? Why's he smell bad? Why's his mouth runny? Why's he here? He broke the glass. Daddy'll be mad. Why's he mean? I won't let him hurt you,

Body Slam

Mommy. Is he still bleeding? Can we go see Daddy? What's Daddy doing? Is that a spider nest on the counter? Where'd you find it?"

Lottie heard her son's questions, but could not concentrate on one answer.

They heard Rastus in the laundry room. "What's he doing, Mommy?"

Lottie heard Rastus bumping around in the laundry room. She put her ear to the door and turned the knob, but it was locked. At that moment, she picked up Little Rob's hefty body and sprinted to the closest door, which was opposite the laundry room.

This was an opportunity to escape. She couldn't wait any longer for someone to come and rescue them. As she turned the knob, Rastus emerged from the laundry room. Lottie tried to run outside with Little Rob, but Rastus clasped his scrawny fingers tightly around Lottie's waist.

"Please, Rastus, let us go. I don't understand what you want, but you must let us go. Please!" Little Rob slid out of his mother's arms.

"Await! Don't escape. Annihilate those who forsake!" Little Rob shoved Rastus. He pulled on Rastus's hands to help free his mother.

Rastus released Lottie. He seized Little Rob's shoulders and thrust him brutally down. Rastus rasped his words, "I'll hold you and goad you. You're a wicked kid! I know what you did!"

Little Rob shakily stood, but Rastus knocked him against the wall, and he fell to the floor.

"Mommy! Mommy! Make him stop!" Tears splotched Little Rob's face as he suffered the unexpected attack from Rastus.

"I'll dump you in a pit and cover you with dirt and watch you squirm like a worm," sputtered Rastus.

Duress

"Stop, Rastus! Don't hurt my son! You're too rough. He's only a little boy."

Rastus ignored Lottie's plea. He pulled Little Rob to himself and shook him violently.

Lottie wanted to remember what Don had taught her in the self-defense class, but all she could think to do was push and kick to make him release her son. Rastus let go of Little Rob and clutched Lottie. He wrapped his wiry fingers around her body. He picked her up and slammed her head and body into the hard ceramic tile floor.

Chapter 52

Bad News

𝓑uster's mobile phone rang. He clicked it on and heard a young voice saying, "I need to speak with my father, Boyd MacGinnis. This is George MacGinnis."

"George, is that you? Are you okay?"

"Yes, Father. Yes. Aunt Lottie told Victoria and me to run to the Clarks' house and call you to come get us."

"Are Victoria and Little Rob with you?"

"Victoria's here. I don't know what happened to Little Rob. Aunt Lottie told him to come with us, but we didn't look back, and he's not here. A bad man is with Aunt Lottie. Will you come get us, Father? We're scared."

"I'm on my way, Son."

Buster pressed the accelerator to his pickup truck and sped to Miles and Lottie's neighborhood. He wanted to take his children to his home before he went to Miles's house. Buster called Miles to let him know that George and Victoria were at the Clarks' house, but not Little Rob."

Buster locked both hands around the steering wheel and strained forward in his seat. His mobile phone rang. He answered and heard Marilyn's bossy voice.

"Boyd, I'm almost to the airport. You and Lottie's husband are a hindrance to the biggest promotion and pay raise of my career. My own sister ignored me and defaulted on her promise to pick up my children from school."

"Trudy Lee dropped the children off at Lottie's house," said Buster.

"Miles said he asked Lucy Jenkins to get the children from school."

"Yes, Sugar Foot, Lucy drove to the school to get the children, but Trudy was there first and thought she would help by dropping them off at Lottie's house."

"Nobody does anything they say they'll do. I can't believe Lottie has such a dysfunctional family. She married such a loser."

"Sugar Foot, what are you talking about? Lottie's in trouble. Some mental home patient is holding her and Little Rob hostage in their own home. He may tie them up and burn them. George and Victoria escaped and ran to a neighbor's house."

"What are *you* talking about, Boyd? Lottie's never been in trouble or pain. She's such a baby. She's hardly had to work. But I don't understand why she broke her promise to me. She's never had a problem before when I needed her to babysit."

"They're *my* children, too. I'm almost to the house where they're waiting for me."

"Boyd, I need help. This is an emergency. You're my last resort. I have to attend that awards luncheon tomorrow. I can't miss my flight."

"Well, go on to Atlanta, and get your promotion. Don't worry about the children, your sister, or anybody else. It'll be my pleasure to take care of my children. I'm thankful they escaped from the crazy man. I'm taking them to the farm so my mama can watch them. I'm very disappointed in the way you've raised our children."

"What? You don't know anything about parenting," disputed Marilyn. "I've given them more than you ever could."

"Yes. You've given them things, but they need love and attention, just like you, Sugar Foot," reasoned Buster.

"Don't call me that," said Marilyn crossly.

"Sugar Foot, we once loved each other and had a good life. I always hoped that you would change and see that the best things in life can't be bought."

"I always hoped *you* would be the one to change," said Marilyn.

"Money can't buy real happiness. Your money has produced a crop of misery in our children," stated Buster. "You've neglected our children. They have no friends. George and Victoria are the most unhappy, insecure children I've ever seen."

"They have everything they need," argued Marilyn.

Buster shook his head in condemnation. "I'll do everything in my power to strip away your legal restraints that block me from my own children."

"We'll talk about this when I get back from Atlanta. You'll never get legal custody," said Marilyn.

"I went along with your selfish demands because I thought you would eventually come to your senses."

"Come to my senses? My children are fortunate to have a *mother* who can provide the finer things in life for them. How could a child profit by living on a pig farm?"

"The children could breathe fresh air and experience the joy of a family," said Buster.

"Oh, please. Save your sentimental rhetoric for the old farmers' society."

Marilyn arrived at the airport and parked her car. She rolled her bag inside the terminal and waved her ticket and identification in the security officer's face. After her small suitcase proceeded through the x-ray chute, she grabbed the bag and pulled it toward the airplane. Buster talked about

Duress

how happy the children were when they came to the farm to visit. "I'm going to let George and Victoria invite other children over to play."

Buster paused for Marilyn to respond. "Sugar Foot, you're not listening. I still love you, even though you've failed as a mother. I'm picking up the children now to take them to my home, where they'll be safe. Then I'll drive to Miles's house to be there when they arrest that insane man. Good-bye, Sugar Foot. Have a nice trip." Buster hung up.

"Boyd MacGinnis! How dare you hang up on me! Who do you think you are? Nobody hangs up on me!"

Marilyn thought about what Buster had said. *Boyd still loves me. I can't believe he . . . still loves me.*

Lottie and Little Rob are hostages? Boyd said George and Victoria escaped, and that crazy man may burn Lottie and Little Rob. Oh, that's why she didn't go to the school. She couldn't. George and Victoria don't need to be around a raving madman. He could scar my children and leave them disfigured. It's probably good that Boyd's taking them to that stinking farm. Hmm. I'll travel more once I get my promotion. It might be a good idea to let Buster babysit the children since it's so much trouble getting Mrs. Edwards or Lottie to help.

Uncharacteristically, Marilyn felt a twinge of hurt inside. Tears welled up in her eyes, and a lump crested in her throat. Several times, she coughed and cleared her throat to dispel the prick. She batted her eyes repeatedly to squelch the tears. *What's wrong with me? My hormones must be off.*

She stowed her suitcase in the overhead bin and sat down in her seat. Marilyn couldn't stop thinking about Buster and their failed marriage. *I can't believe Boyd still loves me. I've given him hell. But he should've stayed in school. After we married, he could've gone back to college. He and his mother should've sold that farm and moved up in life. I found him*

Bad News

a decent job that paid well that would've gotten him off that nasty farm, but he wasn't interested.

Suddenly, Marilyn felt somber and emotionally burdened. Again, she felt an ache pressing her chest and throat. Momentarily, she envisioned her children alone and friendless. Marilyn rubbed her hands through her hair to symbolically cancel the conjectured daydream.

I don't understand why I feel guilty. Everybody will be fine when I return tomorrow. There's no reason for me to feel bad. I have to fly to Atlanta for the awards luncheon. It's expected of me. This is my opportunity for the company executives to see me as a gifted and outstanding manager. Maybe they'll transfer me out of this redneck town to Atlanta or Dallas.

An urge to get up and go back to West Point overwhelmed Marilyn. She felt someone pulling her arms and lifting her out of her seat. *I mustn't think about going back to West Point. What's wrong with me? I can't miss that luncheon. I can't seem to think clearly. I have to go to Atlanta. Lottie and the children will be fine. I'll be back tomorrow. They don't need me in West Point.* Unexplainably, she stood up, removed her suitcase from the overhead bin, and headed to the secured hatch door. The stewardess confronted Marilyn. "Please take your seat, and fasten your seatbelt. The cabin has been prepared for . . . ."

Marilyn interrupted, "I can't go. I have to get off the plane."

"Are you ill?"

"Yes. I can't fly to Atlanta. Let me off. Leave, and don't hold the plane for me."

The flight attendant opened the flight deck door to notify the pilot of the passenger's request. The captain ordered the ground crew to push the exit stairs back to the plane. He instructed the stewardess to open the hatch door. The airline

Duress

attendant peppered questions at Marilyn, but the small-town native ignored her, anxious to deplane.

Marilyn almost tripped down the stairs as she exited the airplane. She ran across the Tarmac while her suitcase wheels swiveled in miniature "S" formations. A rush of elation like booming fireworks shot Marilyn sky-high.

What am I doing? I'm giving up the awards luncheon and defaulting on a promotion. This is incredulous. I can't believe how good I feel about this decision. I'm giving up the biggest career opportunity I've ever had. She recklessly and spontaneously cackled. For the first time in her life, Marilyn felt giddy. The awards luncheon didn't matter. She knew she was doing the right thing.

I'll drive straight to Boyd's farm. I'm not going to Lottie's house. I don't want that pervert to burn me. Lottie shouldn't have let him in. She always brought home stray dogs and cats when we were kids. She hasn't changed.

Fifteen minutes later, Marilyn turned onto the long country driveway near Boyd's house. *I hope I don't get my car muddy.* For the first time, she noticed the neat landscaping. Brilliant yellow mums bloomed on both sides of the road. Giant plumes of pampas grass accented the angles in the white fence. The country house came into view. Close to the house was an antique cast iron dinner bell that hung on a pole. Planted underneath were clusters of purple periwinkles. Bunches of daisies lined the sidewalk that led to the porch.

Marilyn walked up to the door and heard laughter and voices of children. *Could that be George and Victoria?* She reached for the screen door handle, looked in, and stopped. Mama Mac sat in a chair in the kitchen. George and Victoria embraced their grandmother. George stood with both arms around Mama Mac's head and neck. Nestled in Mama Mac's lap was Victoria, who had wrapped her arms around her grandmother's fleshy arm. The frail girl rested her head on

her grandmother's chest and gazed up into Mama Mac's face. Boyd's mother gently hugged Victoria and stroked her hair. Marilyn felt uncomfortable and shocked.
I've never seen them snuggle with another person.
"George! Victoria!"
At the sound of her harsh voice, the children jumped to attention. Their relaxing break from stress ended. George stood straight as a soldier who awaited inspection. Victoria almost fell out of her grandmother's lap and stumbled to stand. She hunched her shoulders, crossed her arms, and looked down while urine dripped on the kitchen floor.
"Victoria MacGinnis! You make me sick! Can't you control yourself? You're a poor excuse for a daughter. Do you want me to buy you baby diapers? You're a bad child!"

Chapter 53

It's Over

*U*naffected by Marilyn's venomous demeanor, Mama Mac pleasantly spoke to Marilyn. "Come in, Dear. The door's open."

Mama Mac stood and hugged Victoria. "There, there, precious one. Don't worry. I'll clean things up. You'll be fine." Then Mama Mac addressed Marilyn. "Would you care to join us after a while for supper?"

"No!" Marilyn toned down her stern voice. "No, thank you."

"Hey, Sugar Foot," said Buster as he walked into the room, surprised to see Marilyn.

"Don't call me that," snapped Marilyn.

"What do you want me to call you?" teased Buster.

"Marilyn. That's my given name."

"Marilyn isn't pretty or sweet enough for you, Sugar Foot."

"At least drop the 'Foot' part," said Marilyn.

"I thought you went to Atlanta to get your big award," said Buster.

"I changed my mind for some reason," explained Marilyn. "Something or someone pulled me out of my seat on the airplane, pushed me off, and pressured me to come here. I don't understand what happened. I lost my mind. I gave up the biggest promotion and raise of my life."

"That's awesome, Sugar F.... I've got to lock the door to my work barn. I'll be back in a minute. Wait for me, Sugar F.... I've got to talk to you," said Buster as he dashed out the door.

George stood stiff like a mannequin. His lower lip quivered, and he looked as if he was about to cry. Victoria's head curled down until her chin rested on her chest, and she clung tightly to her elbows. Silent tears rolled down her face and dropped onto her clothes.

"There, there," said Mama Mac as she stretched her arms out toward them both and drew them close. She rubbed their heads and patted their shoulders. "Everything will work out for the best. Now, don't you worry."

Mama Mac strained to get down on the kitchen floor to help Victoria remove her wet panties and to wipe her legs. Then she toweled up Victoria's accident.

Marilyn was uneasy and didn't know what to do. "Mrs. MacGinnis," said Marilyn as she stared at the older woman, "the driveway and the yard look pretty, and the house appears clean."

"My son is such a help around here. I couldn't live on our old home place if it weren't for Buster."

"I can't believe you call him 'Buster.' You're his mother. His given name is Boyd."

"Yes, Dear. The name on his birth certificate is Boyd, a fine name. He has his father's name. His daddy, bless his soul, called him 'Buster' when they wrestled and played together, and the name just stuck."

"Boyd was smart in school. He could've been a veterinarian, but he quit college and never went back."

"Things were tough after Buster's daddy died. Do you remember when Mr. MacGinnis suddenly passed away while you kids were in high school? I tried to take care of this place and make ends meet on my own. I couldn't run a farm by myself then or now. If Buster hadn't fixed cars and worked for other farmers to make money during high school, I would've lost this farm and all this land."

Mama Mac sighed, "He had to sacrifice college to come back home to work and pay off our debts. He knew my heart would break if I had to give up the home I loved. He's such a fine son."

"Boyd shouldn't have felt guilty about going to college just because his father died," challenged Marilyn. "I can't imagine what Boyd does all day on a farm or how he makes any money."

"My son is a genius." George and Victoria locked their eyes on Mama Mac. "He invents remarkable things. I love to see the sparkle in his eyes when he comes up with something good," glowed the grandmother.

"His newest concoction is amazing. A version for humans is put into nutritional formulas for the elderly. Buster figured out how to add it to the swine food. It's healthy for the pigs, and best of all, it takes away the pig poop smell."

George and Victoria giggled.

"Two businessmen from some big company were here again yesterday, wanting Buster to sign some papers . . . ."

Marilyn interrupted Mama Mac, "I hope Boyd didn't sign any papers. I know how these big companies operate. They offer small-town ignoramuses a token amount for a formulation and then market the product for millions."

"I don't know about that," said Mama Mac. "One of those men said, 'Your son is going to be a very rich man, ma'am.' I told those men . . . ."

Marilyn butted in again. "I need to read the small print on those documents. If they offered him a lot of money, they're banking on extreme dividends. Boyd mustn't sign any contracts; he could lose all rights to the formula. I can't

It's Over

believe Boyd is sitting on an agricultural golden egg. I can help Boyd get investors and apply for patents and . . . ."

"Sugar, come outside, *now*, please."

"Excuse me, Mrs. MacGinnis." Marilyn did not like for Buster to tell her what to do, but she went outside.

"Sugar, we don't have a lot of time to talk because I have to hurry to town. I wish I could make you see things my way. I still love you. My mama's gotten older, and she doesn't have anybody but me to take care of her. She loves the children and wants to be with them, too. I'll renovate this house or build you another house on my land. I need you, Sugar. Let's try to mend our marriage."

Marilyn stared. "I can't believe you still love me. I've given you a lot of grief."

Buster moved toward her until her back was against the white fence. Buster placed his muscular arm above Marilyn's shoulder. She felt his hardness against her body. "Sugar, I *still* love you." Buster embraced her affectionately in his arms and kissed her. She resisted at first but then relinquished and enjoyed the closeness.

"Boyd, I don't know if we can work things out. There's so much about you that I don't like."

"Like what? Tell me."

"This pig farm. It's a pig farm. What will people say when George and Victoria say that their father owns a pig farm?"

"Other people will say, 'I heard your daddy owns and runs the best pig farm in the South. You must have a blast living in the country on a big farm.' What else do you not like about me?"

"I don't know."

"Since you've said what you don't like about *me*, I'll tell you what I don't like about *you*. First of all, you're selfish. The children are unhappy and unhealthy. I'm surprised the teachers at school haven't reported you for child abuse."

"I do not abuse my children," said Marilyn defensively.

"Victoria is skin and bones. She looks like a starving child from some Third World country. George told me that you withhold food to punish her. That is physical abuse. And you've heaped mental abuse on both of them."

"What are you talking about?" asked Marilyn.

"I'll be honest with you. George and Victoria can't become normal children until you become a normal mother."

"We live in an advanced technological age. All mothers work except for lazy, unmotivated women. The 'normal' of yesterday is gone," argued Marilyn.

"You're wrong, Sugar."

Anger stirred inside Marilyn. "How dare you tell me how to raise my children! I want you out of my life and out of my children's lives."

Buster backed away in disbelief at Marilyn's attitude. "Okay. The children and I will get out of *your* life. You can pack your bags and move to Atlanta and enjoy your corporate lifestyle and be free of your motherly burden. Maybe I'll find a sweet stepmother for George and Victoria here in West Point since you'll be out of our lives."

"What? You can't take the children away from me," protested Marilyn.

"Watch me," said Buster. "It's over."

"They have a good life."

"Marilyn, Marilyn, there's no hope for you. The children and I will be a family, and I predict we'll be a happy family without you."

"You can't push me around. I have rights," argued Marilyn.

"Not anymore. Not with the children, and not with me. You're free to leave. Just leave." Buster turned his back on Marilyn and walked to the house.

Marilyn was furious with Buster and disturbed that he rejected her and claimed the children. She felt that prick again in her heart and a painful lump in her throat. She thought, *I'm really not happy. I'm just driven to accomplish my goals. I've never liked children, not even my own. And I need to help Boyd with his profitable ideas since he doesn't know what to do.*

"Wait, Boyd!" He didn't stop. "Boyd! Boyd! What do you want me to do? I can't change. I don't want to change."

He walked into his mother's old country home and let the screen door slam. He closed the wooden door. She walked to the door and knocked in hesitation. Buster opened the door and stepped past Marilyn, jingling his truck keys.

"Wait, Boyd. I'm confused. You can't write me out of the children's lives. I have lawyers."

"Call them. Get your witnesses ready. There's no evidence to prove you're a fit mother." Buster briskly walked to his pickup truck, with Marilyn trailing behind.

"How can you say that to me? You know nothing of the quality care that I've procured for my children."

Buster laughed and shook his head.

"How dare you laugh at me?" said Marilyn. "You make me feel as if I've done something wrong." She grabbed one of his hands from behind, shook it, and pushed it away, frustrated at her lack of control. "Talk to me. Don't leave me, Boyd."

Buster stopped and faced Marilyn. "What do you want out of life, Marilyn?"

"I . . . I don't know anymore."

"Do you want to be a happy wife and mother, or a rich businesswoman, always looking for the next promotion? I want us to be together as a family. I know you could be happy living by yourself, as long as you climb the corporate ladder. But it's clear to me that before we can come together as a family, you have to get professional help. I won't take you back unless you agree to go to counseling."

"Are you suggesting that *I* need to change?"

Buster slapped his knees in laughter. "Sugar, you can change. There isn't anything you can't do once you set your mind to it."

"I don't know if I want to change. I like my life."

"Yes, I know. But George, Victoria, and I don't like your self-centered lifestyle. You decide if you'll change your priorities to become a wife, mother, and working woman, in that order."

Buster explained, "We either work things out, or else *you* go away. But *you* have to change. If you won't come off your high-rise skyscraper, then you can live your life without the children and without me. So, Marilyn, that's the deal. Take it, or leave it."

"All right. All right. I'm willing to try. But you've asked me to give up everything that I've worked for!"

"Sugar, you'll get much more than you give up. We'll talk later. I've got to hurry to Miles's house. I need to be there when they rescue Lottie and Little Rob. Stay here until I come back." Buster passionately kissed Marilyn again and then strutted to his pickup truck.

Marilyn yelled, "Another thing I don't like about you is that pickup truck!"

Buster shook his head and laughed as he drove away.

Chapter 54

Pledge to Escape

*L*ottie opened her eyes and wheezed a breath over her throat. She couldn't move. Painful shards stabbed her body. She touched her throbbing head and felt a round protuberance. Her arms stung from Rastus's fingernail cuts. She lay on the ceramic tile floor disoriented and wondered why she was there. "Little Rob!" she whispered. Fear for her son's safety stimulated a flow of adrenaline. Lottie heaved to get on her feet.

From the laundry room, she heard Rastus chant, "I have reconsidered; I won't be embittered. I have reconsidered; I won't be embittered." Lottie opened the door and gasped. Her son sat in a chair with duct tape circled around his mouth and head. A bristly hemp rope bound his ankles, legs, and hands. Little Rob trembled in fear and twisted to free himself. Tears dripped over the tape. Moans diffused from his throat.

Rastus held a pen-shaped instrument and moved as if he intended to write on Little Rob's arm. He looked at Lottie and calmly said, "The sight of you, upright saint so true. I'm on fire with desire."

Duress

Lottie swallowed hard and determined that she would not let Rastus's suggestive words unnerve her. She was frightened for her son. "Rastus, what are you doing? Why have you tied up my son? Is that an engraving tool?"

Rastus thrust out his tongue, and saliva dripped down his chin. He clicked his tongue on the roof of his mouth. "Although not my son, it must be done. Then you and I can be one. Hear me! I'm weary! You didn't wait for me."

Lottie ignored Rastus's insinuation. "Please, Rastus. He's a child. Don't hurt him."

Rastus smacked and drooled. "Burn him with the mark. Turn away the stark dark. Look! Snakes pour under the door to take him to the floor!" He pointed with his bloody, bandaged hand that he shook hysterically. He saw heads of snakes boring their way into the house. "Snakes race into this place!" Rastus worked himself up into a frenzied state of mind. "It's a sign! I'm behind! There's no time!"

"There're no snakes. Are you going to burn Little Rob?"

"He yearns for the burn. Now, he won't cry and yell in the fire of hell. Medusa's snakes! Evil serpents slither under the door. Their eggs litter the floor. I must burn him and not let him turn to stone."

"Please, Rastus," begged Lottie. "There're no snakes. Please let my son go."

Lottie irritated Rastus, and he shouted at her, "Do not ask! Pain passes fast!" Little Rob shivered in fear.

"All right, Rastus." Lottie didn't want to provoke aggressive behavior in Rastus. Her head hurt. Her teeth chattered, and her body jerked spastically. Since no one had come to save them, she had to improvise a plan of escape from Rastus.

"I need you to do something for me, Rastus. Tie me up and start with me so that Little Rob can see what you want to do. Don't you think that would work, Rastus?"

Pledge To Escape

Lottie remembered that Don Jenkins said in his self-defense class, "Never let someone bind you because you decrease your chances of getting away safely. Help may not arrive to unfasten you. *But,*" he also said, "let them tie you up if it will buy time. Pull your hands and legs as wide as possible, without alerting the assailant, so that he thinks you are tied tightly."

Lottie continued to coax Rastus. "Let me untie Little Rob so you can tie me in this same chair. Then he'll see what you do and be more cooperative. Do me first, all right?" She steadied her trembling hands and voice. She must not agitate Rastus, and she must thwart the abhorrent procedure that he zealously wanted to perform on Little Rob. She hoped her rescuers would come before he tied her up with the rope.

Rastus laid his instrument aside and stepped back, acquiescent to her request.

Little Rob sobbed and whimpered as Lottie carefully unwrapped the duct tape from around his mouth and head. She slowly untied the ropes that shackled his ankles and arms. He clung tightly to his mother, who gently rubbed his arms and legs where the rope had roughened his young skin. Little Rob snubbed his runny nose and cried loudly.

Rastus pressed his hands to his head. "I need a pill to still how I feel. Stop the boy's noise. Stop his voice!"

Lottie fought to maintain control of her emotions. She didn't know how to reason or talk to Rastus. She held her son and then took Little Rob's head and whispered concise instructions into his ear. Her son positively shook his head and said, "Yes, Mommy."

"Are you sure you understand?" Lottie asked in a hushed tone. Little Rob nodded.

Lottie addressed Rastus in an effort to distract him from Little Rob. "Okay, Rastus. What do you want me to do? Do you want me to sit in this chair?"

Duress

Her son sneaked out of the laundry room and stood outside the door.

Rastus methodically began his familiar routine. He pulled the ropes tight around Lottie's ankles and arms, even though he had one bloodied hand from punching the glass. He secured her arms to her right leg with her left palm up. Lottie strained to spread her ankles and legs and arms to allow some slack with which to escape, but Rastus tightened the knots and pulled the rope taut. Panic gripped Lottie. She shuddered and cried out, "Oh, my God, help me!" Spontaneous sobs of fright burst forth from Lottie.

She suspected that she had made a terrible mistake. How could she possibly think that he was dumb enough to leave the ropes loose so that she could free herself? He obviously knew how to tie reliable knots. Rastus unwound the duct tape to place over Lottie's mouth.

"I mustn't hear you cry when I sear you by and by." Rastus almost sang his words cheerfully.

Lottie labored to control her breathing the way she had learned during natural childbirth classes. She forced herself to speak unhurriedly and intentionally. "Rastus, that won't be necessary. I pro-promise you that I can be quiet. I wo-won't make a sound. Please don't put that ta-tape over my mouth. Please. Please, Rastus."

"I mark in silence to bridle defiance."

"I'll be quiet. I pro-promise you that I'll remain still for the entire ti-time. The duct tape isn't necessary. Please, Rastus." Fear jolted the inside of her body. She struggled not to faint.

He laid the tape down and began to fondle the woodburning pen. Rastus drew the instrument close to his face to feel the heat and to gaze at the hot tip. He sighed contentedly.

Oh, my dear God, help me. Oh, God! Nobody else can help me but You!

Lottie moved her ankles together and then out slowly. She moved her knees apart and then slowly back together. She felt looseness in the ropes! With purposely contrived words, she spoke to Rastus.

"My mouth's extremely dry. I need a glass of water before you start. Would you please get me some water? Little Rob can lead you to a drinking cup. You can bring me some water and afterward start your procedure. I'll call Little Rob." Rastus paused and looked at Lottie.

"Little Rob." Lottie called softly for her son. She did not want to aggravate Rastus with a loud voice.

Her son promptly appeared. Lottie instructed Rob. "Little Rob, I need you to lead Mr. Webber to a drinking glass so that I may have some water to drink. Do you remember what I told you earlier?" Little Rob shook his head up and down.

Rastus exhaled heavily. He was prepared mentally and adroitly for his task of 'marking' Lottie. He was unprepared for her mundane request; however, he set his tool aside and followed Little Rob into the kitchen.

Little Rob walked around in slow circles in the kitchen to prevent Rastus from immediately fulfilling Lottie's request, and then the boy pointed to the dishwasher. When Rastus started to remove a glass, Little Rob said, "No, no. Those are dirty. Don't drink out of dirty glasses."

Then Little Rob led Rastus to the formal china cabinet and touched the door. Rastus could not get the antique cabinet door to open at first, but when it opened, he removed a glass. Little Rob said, "No, no. Those are special. Put it back."

Rastus slung the crystal on the floor, shattering the glass. "You! Stop what you do! I'll return to burn on the mark." He stamped his foot and turned to go back to Lottie. Little Rob grappled with Rastus's arm to stop him. "Don't hurt my mommy!"

Lottie emerged from the laundry room and cried out, "Little Rob, run! Run away!"

Little Rob loosed his grip on Rastus to run away; however, Rastus seized the boy, who kicked and bit. Rastus shook Little Rob violently, whacked the boy with his uninjured hand, and knocked him to the floor. Little Rob groaned, "Quit it; quit it."

Lottie ran into the kitchen to find something to use as a weapon. Her son struggled to drag himself into the kitchen, with Rastus tugging at his arm. Lottie grabbed the cracked Melanie Groner designer vase and screeched as she forcefully smashed Rastus's head. He let go of Little Rob, who pushed himself away. Rastus looked at Lottie with contempt while blood oozed through the cuts. She snatched a ceramic cookie jar off a shelf and threw it at Rastus's shoulder and chest. Candy flew over the room.

Rastus gritted his teeth savagely. He clutched Little Rob and wrapped the boy's arms behind his back. "Death for the unworthy!"

Lottie realized that she had to incapacitate Rastus before she and Little Rob could escape. She drew in a breath of determination and whispered a prayer, "God, help me. Help me remember Don's self-defense stuff."

Rastus shook Little Rob and yanked on his arms, as if trying to break them loose. Approaching Rastus from behind, she latched onto his ears, and twisted and pulled with all her might. Rastus released Little Rob, whirled around, fastened his hands around Lottie's throat, and choked her. Lottie drew her fists to her breasts and thrust her knuckles forcefully into Rastus's chest. He collapsed forward to catch his breath. Lottie doubled her fists together and struck the back of his neck.

Rastus raised his head to look at Lottie. He angrily clawed at her. Lottie stomped his shin and then stepped on his foot to trap it (as she remembered Don showing her how to do in a critical situation), and shoved him down, which should have broken his ankle. But Rastus wailed in pain and limped to his feet.

"You wicked woman!"

Oh, no! That didn't work, thought Lottie. "Run out the door, Little Rob! Run to the Clarks' house!" Little Rob didn't want to leave his mother. Lottie lifted her foot and drove her heel into Rastus's kneecap. The impact threw him off balance, and he fell to the floor in pain. He held a chair to pull himself up.

Lottie opened her broom closet in the kitchen and grabbed the mop. She gouged and poked Rastus, squeaking and grunting with each whap. She again yelled to Little Rob, "Go, Little Rob! Run to the neighbor's house. Call your daddy!"

She hammered Rastus unrelentingly with the mop. He grabbed at the handle, which Lottie bobbed up and down. She hit him on his head, on his shoulders, and in his stomach. He finally cringed from the blows and cowered away. She plucked a can of Pledge from the closet and sprayed it in Rastus's face. He crumpled to the floor in discomfort, maniacally scrubbing his eyes and face with his hands and sleeves.

Little Rob ran out the side door. The Special Response Team crouched outside the door, ready to strike. Little Rob screamed when he saw the darkly dressed responders. The expert unit appeared gargantuan in their head and vest gear, loaded with bobbles of equipment on their belts.

The closest one of the special force seized Little Rob and covered his mouth. "I'm here to help," he said in a low voice and then removed his hand. The terrified Little Rob yelled, "Help! Help! Help!"

"Little Rob! Little Rob!"

The boy recognized his father's voice and ran to his dad.

"Daddy! Daddy! Help Mommy! A bad man's hurting Mommy!"

Chapter 55

Awful Psychiatrist

*F*ather and son followed behind the heavily equipped patrol to check on Lottie. Don yelled, "Wait, Miles! Don't go in yet! You'll contaminate the crime scene. Stay outside!" Determined to help his mother, Little Rob ran toward the door anyway. Miles latched on to his son and held him back.

The Special Response Team pounced on the frazzled Rastus. With coordinated precision, they grabbed his arms and legs and flattened him on the floor. His hands and feet were shackled in deliberate swiftness. In less than a minute, the skillfully trained team carried Rastus out the door, as if they toted a lightweight human stretcher.

Emergency medics rushed inside to get Lottie, who refused to be strapped onto the gurney. "Let me out of this house," pleaded Lottie. A medical technician braced Lottie as she tripped down the steps. The EMTs insistently checked Lottie and Little Rob and found minor cuts and bruises.

The Special Response Team stuffed Rastus into the backseat of a police car as he twitched and convulsed in defiance. Officer Tate told them, "No! Put him in the other cruiser. I just cleaned my vehicle."

Dr. Affle emerged on the scene. He whirred around the sentinel specialists like an irritating horsefly. The psychiatrist demanded, "Do not abuse my patient! He lacks capacity to discern wrongful conduct. I'll return him safely to the facility myself. You must allow me to administer his medications to halt untimely regression." The special responders ignored Dr. Affle and securely restrained Rastus in the patrol car.

Dr. Affle found Don Jenkins and said, "I appeal to you to release my patient into my protective custody. Due to his mental disease, he lacks self-control. I'll return my patient safely to the facility."

"You're not taking him anywhere," declared Don. "He's guilty of his offenses, and you won't obstruct justice this time!" Don commanded his officers, "Take him directly to the station, and lock him in a jail cell until I get there. Do I make myself clear?"

"Yes sir," the men responded in unison. The two officers got into the patrol car and locked the doors. Dr. Affle held onto a side mirror and beat the front and side windows of the police car. He yelled, "I demand that you open these doors and give me *my* patient! He's under *my* authority and *my* medical care. You're not qualified to address his complex needs! I order you to release my patient!"

Assistant Police Chief Tyrone Duncan tapped his fist on the driver's window and told the policeman, "Go on to the station, and lock him up. Don't pay attention to this guy." The officer backed around and rocked the car enough to loosen Dr. Affle's grip, then drove through the yard to bypass the blocked driveway and to dodge Dr. Affle.

Meanwhile, Lottie draped herself on Little Rob and sobbed in relief that their ordeal had ended. "Where's my husband?" asked Lottie as she looked for him through tears.

"I'm here," said Miles as he wrapped his arms around them both. Lottie and Miles embraced. They walked out in

Duress

the yard to get away from the police and detectives going in and out of the house. "Are you all right?" asked Miles. "I was so worried about both of you."

Lottie wept. "Where were you? I thought you would come to our rescue. I sent the duress alarm, but no one came. Did the alarm not work? Why didn't you come, Miles?"

"I didn't know he was here until this afternoon. I wanted to come. I tried to tell Don . . . ."

Lottie interrupted, "Rastus knocked us both down, and he almost burned Little Rob and me. He tied us up with ropes and put duct tape around Little Rob's face and head. It was *awful*."

Dr. Affle walked up. "You must be the woman, Lottie, who personally invited my patient to come to West Point."

"Lottie," said Miles, "let me introduce you to Dr. Awful, the man who allowed Rastus to come to West Point."

"My name is Dr. *Affle*. You say 'waffle' and drop the 'w' for the correct pronunciation. I certainly hope you'll excuse the unfortunate psychotic episode of my patient. He suffered a minor setback in his psychosocial treatment. I trust you won't press charges since that could violate his rehabilitative progress."

Don Jenkins saw Dr. Affle with Lottie and Miles. He marched over to them. "Don't talk to this man," instructed the police chief. He turned to Dr. Affle and spoke in his face. "I think you better leave now." He twisted Dr. Affle's arm behind him and steered the doctor down the crowded driveway, with the psychiatrist sputtering, "Let me go! You have no right to treat me like a criminal. My lawyer will hear about this!" Don pushed him to the street.

The police chief returned to Lottie. "Don't let that man intimidate you. Neither he nor Webber will bother you again. You and Little Rob should go to the hospital now. I want you both to ride in the ambulance to the emergency room and get a physical examination. I'll need the medical evaluation to ensure his arraignment," said Don.

"I have a dreadful knot on my head where he threw me to the floor. And my arms are throbbing where he clawed me with his fingernails. He wildly shook Little Rob and pushed him down cruelly."

Little Rob looked at his mother and smiled. "I've got a knot on my head, too, Mommy."

"It was terrible. I wanted to escape, but I couldn't get away from him. I sent alarms, but no one would come and see about me. Don, did you think it was another false alarm?"

"We knew you needed help," said Don, "but apprehending a demented culprit like Webber was a threat to your safety. The more I learned about him, I realized that a conspicuous rescue would incite him to harm you."

"Miles, I thought you would check on us."

Before Miles could respond, Don said, "I couldn't let him jeopardize your safety." Don took off his cap and slapped it playfully in his hand and said, "Miles wanted to barrel out to your house. I had to handcuff him to a chair at the station. Buster MacGinnis had to hold down the chair to stop him from dragging it out the door to rush over here."

Lottie and Miles laughed and felt relief from some of the tension. "Looks like I won't have to charge you with abuse of emergency services this time." Don broke into a smile, which he rarely did. "I need you to go to the emergency room *now*. We can question you later about what happened and the assaults you sustained."

"*I* can take Lottie and Little Rob to the emergency room," volunteered Miles, "if that's all right."

"No!" said Don. "The EMTs have to document the extent of the assault and battery. All evidence must be preserved. You can follow the ambulance to the hospital and meet them there." Miles nodded, and Don went inside to check on the crime scene investigation.

Lottie hugged Little Rob. "You were so brave, Son. You're not 'Little Rob' anymore. You're my heroic son, Rob."

Miles put his arm around Lottie. She could hardly stand. "Lottie, can you walk?" asked Miles. She teetered. Miles lovingly picked her up in his arms and carried her to the ambulance. Little Rob held onto his daddy's pant leg.

"I'll follow you and Li . . ., I mean Rob to the ER."

"Okay," said Lottie as she stared at the gurney and the waiting medical technicians.

"Oh, no," said Miles.

"What's wrong?" asked Lottie.

Miles looked around and said, "My truck's blocked in. I can't get around these vehicles."

Police cars, the crime scene van, an ambulance, and a fire truck formed a blockade in the driveway. Miles wouldn't risk driving through the yard because he knew there were too many holes and stumps that would tear up his truck.

Buster MacGinnis lurched to an abrupt stop on the road at the entrance to the Arnolds' drive. He jumped out of his pickup truck and ran to the Arnolds. Lottie clutched Buster's strong arms.

"I'm sorry I didn't get here sooner, Lottie," said Buster. "How are you and Little Rob?"

"We're okay. Did you get George and Victoria?"

"Yes. They're with my mama. They're doing fine. Don't you worry about them."

"My truck's blocked in. Can you give me a ride to the hospital, Buster?" asked Miles. "They won't let me ride in the ambulance with Lottie and Li . . ., I mean Rob."

Detectives and policemen scurried in the house with work cases and cameras. Dr. Affle walked up the driveway toward the house and entangled himself in their work path. The disquieted psychiatrist redundantly cried out, "Police Chief Jenkins! Police Chief Jenkins!"

Don Jenkins marched toward Dr. Affle. "Are you still here?"

"Police Chief Jenkins, my patient needs an ambulance. I must protest. I believe this woman named Lottie used excessive force to wound my patient. Your men didn't exercise restraint in handling him properly. Rastus has clearly been physically brutalized and savagely restrained in a patrol car as if he were a common criminal."

"Dr. Affle . . . ."

"My name is Dr. *Affle*. You say 'waffle' and drop the 'w.'"

"I don't care what your name is or how you say it. Your patient has committed crimes, for which he will be prosecuted."

Dr. Affle sidestepped constantly in front of Don Jenkins's face and complained. "Your men subjected my patient to cruel treatment. Your policemen and that woman are guilty of causing bodily harm to my patient. You're negligent. You've denied his right to adequate medical care."

The police chief put his hands on his hips and glared at Dr. Affle. "Hmmp." *Mike Cantile warned me about this doctor and his lawyer getting charges dropped. I don't want to risk a dismissal of his case due to a technicality involving his criminal rights. I need to be careful to not deny him access to medical care.*

Don used his radio to contact the men who had Rastus in the police car and said, "Bring Webber back to the house. Let the ambulance technicians take him to the hospital for a medical assessment. When they finish with him, I want you to transport him to the station and follow standard procedure for felons. Do I make myself clear?"

Then Don confronted Dr. Affle. "After your patient gets checked at the emergency room, he will be jailed until you post bail and have proper documentation for his monitored release. My chief investigator will file an affidavit showing

Duress

cause for a criminal complaint against Webber. A probable cause hearing will be scheduled as soon as possible, at which time we will file formal charges and issue a warrant for his arrest. And furthermore, I've had your request to purge Rastus Webber's records *suspended*. Do I make myself clear?"

Highly irritated, Dr. Affle swung his body around and said something again about contacting his lawyer.

Don rolled his lips as he studied the psychiatrist and spoke loudly to him. "When Webber's proceedings are finished, you're going to need a couple of good lawyers to defend yourself at your own court hearings, Dr. Affle."

Chapter 56

Confession

The patrol car returned with Rastus. The officers drove through the rough yard to get close to the house. The policemen got out of the vehicle and opened the back doors so that air could circulate and so that the EMTs could easily access Webber. Rastus remained buckled in his seat belt, securely fettered, with his hands cuffed behind.

Dr. Affle immediately accosted the ambulance staff to enumerate his patient's particular medical needs.

Lucy Jenkins and Dudley Stevens arrived simultaneously at the Arnolds' house. Both of them had to park down the street.

Lucy jumped out of her car and screamed, "Lottie! Lottie! Wait! Wait! Are you all right? Lottie!" She ran to Lottie, who stood at the open doors of the ambulance. Lucy threw her arms around her best friend and sobbed loudly. "Girl, I didn't know what he would do to you. Don wouldn't let us come rescue you. He was afraid that Rastus would hurt you or kill you if he saw us. I hope he didn't drool or spit on you."

"Uuuhh. I don't want to talk about it."

Lucy couldn't stop crying. "After I talked to you, I told Don to send someone to rescue you. I told him you said that pervert grabbed you and pushed you down."

"I said he *clawed* me and pushed me down. Look at my arms where he *clawed* me."

"Yuk. That looks painful. Did he hurt Little Rob?"

"We're all right, now that it's over. My son was a brave man. We're calling him Rob from now on. He's not 'Little Rob' anymore."

Lucy hugged and kissed Little Rob. "Okay, *Rob.* I'm glad you were here to help your mommy."

Dudley Stevens took his time getting out of his red van. He felt guilty that Mrs. Arnold and her boy had been in a hostage situation and that he had told the police and the firemen not to respond. He wished his dad had been here to tell him what to do about that duress alarm. He anxiously thought, *What if reporters are here? I ain't answering questions. Nobody's takin' pictures of me, either.*

He twirled his mustache and rubbed his hands over his head to smooth his hair. He grinned in the mirror to see if anything was stuck between his teeth, straightened his belt buckle, and made sure his zipper was zipped. Then he got out, put on his cowboy hat, and walked up the driveway, scuffing his heels with each step.

Dudley's hat hung low on his brow. He kept his head straight, but cut his eyes from one side to the other. He watched the constant scuttle of people around the house and noticed the patrol car with both back doors open. He discreetly stooped to look in and quickly stood up. *That must be the crazy guy that burns people. He can't get away. They got him now.*

Dudley eased his head around so he could look at Rastus. He pushed his hat up. Since Rastus appeared to be securely restrained, Dudley felt safe to peer into the police car. *I want a good look. I ain't never seen a crazy person.*

Confession

Dudley stared at Rastus, as if he were a specimen under glass in a museum. First, he noticed the odor. "Pew, you stink." Next, Dudley saw the cuts, bruises, and bloody bandage on Rastus. "You been bleedin' like a stuck pig." Then he realized that bubbly saliva drooled out of Rastus's mouth. "Whoa. You're foamin' at the mouth. Rabies! That's why you ain't right!"

Rastus turned stiffly toward Dudley. He ejected his slimy tongue and swirled it around his mouth. "Go wail in hell!"

Shocked at the movement and utterance, Dudley quickly stepped backward, but stumbled. He lost his balance and fell on the pavement. His hat flew off his head, and he bruised his bony butt and skinned his elbow.

Tyrone Duncan bolted to Dudley to help him stand. "What happened?" he asked Dudley. "What did he do to you?"

Dudley shook his head and said, "I'm okay. Ain't nothin' wrong with me." The other officers checked Rastus's restraints. Dudley picked up his cowboy hat, slapped it on his thigh, and put it on his head. He walked back to his van.

Dr. Affle walked to the police car and asked, "Who inhumanely handcuffed my injured patient? I demand that you release him!"

The assistant police chief nodded to the emergency medics and the policeman. An officer unbuckled Rastus and removed the handcuffs, but Rastus lunged at Dr. Affle, forcing him to the ground. He punctured the doctor's neck with his fingernails and then pounded the physician's gut with his elbows. In a fiery rage, Rastus divulged his true desires toward Dr. Affle.

"You don't deserve the constellation. You deserve condemnation. I'm going to burn it off! You deserve pain, not fame. I'm going to roll you in a deep hole and cover you with dirt. I want to watch the earth rise when you draw in

Duress

your last breath and meet the same death . . . as my earthly father."

Officer Tate fired his stun gun at Rastus, who grunted in agony and rolled off Dr. Affle instantly. The EMTs and the policemen worked together to strap Rastus onto a gurney and to load him into the vehicle. The ambulance personnel wagged their heads sideways as they drove away with Rastus.

Don saw the Arnolds standing by the ambulance. The police chief walked down the driveway to encourage them to leave. "Lottie, you and your son are safe. Webber's in custody. I need you and your son to go to the ER in an ambulance *now*."

"All right," said Miles. "They're about to leave."

Don held up his hand and said, "Go to the hospital *now*."

"Okay, Don," said Miles.

"Very good. I'll be in touch," said Don.

Lucy cried, "I'm glad you're okay. I was worried about you." Lucy walked over to Don and hugged him. He put his arm around his wife's shoulders and squeezed her. Lucy kissed Don. Then he stood militarily "at ease" because he wanted to look professional on the job.

As the medical technicians helped Lottie and Little Rob onto the gurneys, Buster said, "After you get through at the hospital, maybe ya'll can come out to the house. Mama's cooking supper for Marilyn and the kids and me."

"I'm hungry," whined Little Rob.

"Wait a minute," Lottie said to the ambulance workers. "Buster, did you say Marilyn is in town? I thought she flew to Atlanta to receive an award," said Lottie.

"She was headed to Atlanta to get her big promotion and raise, but she got off the plane before it left the runway," said Buster.

"What happened?" asked Lottie.

"She couldn't explain it," commented Buster, "but I think her conscience prodded her to make the right decision."

"Do you mean that Marilyn is at Mama Mac's house?" asked Lottie.

"That's right. She didn't fly to Atlanta. We want to work things out and become a family."

"You and Marilyn and your kids are going to become a family?"

"That's right!" said Buster.

"George's prayers are answered! He prayed for you and Marilyn to get back together and for all of you to become a happy family."

One of the workers interrupted. "Mrs. Arnold, we have to leave."

"Okay," said Lottie. "Just wait one more minute, please."

"I think I'll build Marilyn and the kids a new house, and we'll live in the country on my farmland," said Buster.

"I can't believe what I'm hearing. But I know that I don't want to live in our house. I'll never be able to walk into my laundry room and not think about Rastus or stand in front of my kitchen sink and not want to vomit."

"I'll make you a deal on some good farmland. You can build a house in the country near us. Then our families could be close," beamed Buster. "The children could play together. My mama would love to cook for all of us. We could be a real family."

"Ummm," said Miles, "sounds good to me."

"My mind's playing tricks on me. That hard bump to my head affected my understanding. I know you didn't say what I thought I heard you say. Did you tell me that my sister, who loves big corporate dealings, intends to move to the country and live on the farm with you and the children and Mama Mac?"

"That's right, Lottie," said Buster.

The EMTs loaded the gurneys with Lottie and Little Rob into the ambulance.

"And did I hear you invite us to build a house on your farmland?" yelled Lottie.

"Yes. You heard me!" Buster smiled in genuine ecstasy. "I talked to Marilyn. She's willing to change. I gave her the option to change and live with the children and me, or not change and live without us."

The emergency crew shut the ambulance door and quickly drove away.

Don Jenkins alerted the emergency room staff to be ready for Lottie and Little Rob. The police detective photographed every cut, bruise, and contusion on the mother and son. Little Rob was especially cooperative; he helped the investigator find every possible wound on his body.

After a barrage of x-rays, medical procedures, and examinations, Lottie and Little Rob were discharged. Neither one had a concussion or a serious injury. The doctor prescribed an antibiotic for Lottie's infected arms and pain medication for her throbbing headache. Two nurses pushed Lottie and Little Rob in wheelchairs out the automatic sliding doors.

Miles helped Lottie into Buster's pickup truck while Buster watched Little Rob pull himself up into the backseat of the truck cab. Everyone was tired. Lottie lay on Miles's chest while he sympathetically held an ice pack on her head. Little Rob dozed as they drove to the country. He awoke to his father's voice: "We're at the farm!"

Little Rob climbed out of the truck and ran to Mama Mac's screen door. He flung it open and let it slam as he entered the kitchen of the quaint country home.

Lottie held on to Miles's arm and walked slowly toward the house in physical distress due to the bruising she weathered from Rastus's body slam.

Marilyn walked outside to greet her sister. "Lottie, you look awful."

"I feel worse than I look."

Miles and Buster walked around to the back of the house to let the sisters talk.

Marilyn breathed in deeply and sighed indignantly. "I need to say something to you that I can hardly articulate. Lottie, I'm sorry. I've been harsh with you and the children. I guess I may have been a little selfish. I suppose I may have taken advantage of you and taken you for granted."

"Wow! That's unexpected. Buster said you were willing to change. Well, it's all right, Marilyn. We're family. I guess it's my turn to forgive you."

"Boyd said I had to swallow my pride and apologize to you. I'm not sure I really feel sorry. I'm doing this at Boyd's request. I don't really want to change."

"It's okay, Marilyn. Change takes time. And patience is not one of your virtues."

"Boyd thinks I need help. I've been successful without anyone's help. I don't want somebody telling me what I need to do."

"Nobody's going to tell you how to make more money. A counselor will suggest ways to help you become a *successful* wife and mother," said Lottie.

"Uhhh!" huffed Marilyn.

Buster paraded around his yard, while Miles trailed behind. He pointed in the distance and fondly said, "Just over that hill are four acres of land that is the closest thing to the Garden of Eden you'll ever see." The men walked into the house in a fervent discussion of future house plans.

Chapter 57

Changes

Marilyn and Lottie sat on Mama Mac's porch swing, while Lottie cried and hugged Marilyn. Lottie's tears flowed freely to dissolve the strain of the past.

"You're still a crybaby," reproached Marilyn, shaking her head at Lottie. "Crying is immature."

Focusing on herself, Marilyn said, "Boyd says I *have* to go to counseling. Do you honestly think I need professional help?"

Lottie cocked her head, put her hands on her hips, and raised her eyebrows at her sister. "Some Christian counseling couldn't hurt. And I think you'll learn to like Buster and the kids."

Marilyn said, "Uhhh" in exasperation, and turned her head. Then she changed the subject. "I'm quitting my job, Lottie."

"Are you serious? Marilyn, are you all right? You sound as if you're the one who had your head bashed into the floor. You've always been a corporate businessperson. You love business trips. What will you do? You can't make money if you don't work."

"I'm not giving up business trips or making money. I have a new job. Mrs. MacGinnis brought to my attention the

Changes

extraordinary inventions of Boyd. He's a creative genius! We're destined to make a fortune with his ideas! I have to apply for patents and file for corporate status as soon as possible. And with my connections, I can market his farm products internationally."

"Oh, Marilyn. I believe you'll be a happy farmer's wife," said Lottie. They laughed. "You're the perfect person to help Buster achieve his goals."

"You mean *Boyd?*" asked Marilyn. They giggled. Then in a hushed tone, Marilyn said, "I'm beginning to find Boyd attractive."

Lottie rolled her eyes. She sighed and thought about the events of the day. Then she teased Marilyn. "I know what I want for Christmas."

"Okay. Thanks for the early notice. What do you want?" asked Marilyn.

"Well, Rastus knocked the designer vase you bought me onto the floor and cracked it. I had to use that vase to smash his head."

"I'm impressed," said Marilyn.

"Oh, that didn't work," continued Lottie. "My rescuers didn't come, so I had to throw my cookie jar at him."

"All right! I'll buy you the vase and the cookie jar for Christmas."

"That didn't stop Rastus; he kept coming at me. I tried to remember what I learned in Don's self-defense class. I stomped on his foot to trap it and shoved him down to break his ankle, but that didn't work. I kicked his kneecap, but that just aggravated him. Then, I whacked him with my mop handle over and over again."

Marilyn was unaccustomed to jovial conversation. Her body twitched inside and out. The thought of her baby sister kicking a man and pushing him down and beating him with a mop struck her as uproarious. She quaked in silent hilarity.

Her mouth opened wide to roar, but the cackle was stuck. Tears rolled down her cheeks.

"Marilyn, are you okay? What's wrong with you?"

Finally, an audible noise escaped. "You kicked his knee . . . . You beat . . . . You beat him with . . . with a mop?" Sidesplitting exhilaration swept through Marilyn. She uttered a loud cackling noise for several moments, unable to stop. She laughed uncontrollably. Marilyn hugged Lottie and quivered.

"I wish I could have seen you. No, I don't. I wouldn't want to be around that pervert. I wouldn't have used a mop. I wouldn't have wasted a Melanie Groner vase. I would have found a long, big knife and . . . ." Marilyn pretended to brandish a knife. They snickered like teenagers.

"You mustn't let a stranger come into your home," joked Marilyn. "I hope you've learned your lesson."

"I have. My new house will have shatterproof glass windows, deadbolts on all of the doors, and the loudest burglar alarm in the state."

Marilyn was euphoric from laughing. "I've never felt this good in my entire life. I feel so relaxed."

Buster opened the screen door. "Hey, girls, come on in. Mama's got some good food on the table."

They walked into the kitchen to behold a table brimming with bowls and platters of freshly cooked food. Mama Mac sat at her place with Victoria's arm intertwined in hers. George stood with one hand wrapped around Mama Mac's head. He held something in his other hand and took a bite.

"George," snapped Marilyn, "what are you eating with your fingers?"

"Vi-ee-nies! My daddy eats Vi-eenie sausages, and I'm going to eat them and be big and strong, just like my daddy!"

Everyone laughed.

"Yes, George," said Marilyn. "You're going to be just like your daddy."

CPSIA information can be obtained at www.ICGtesting.com
Printed in the USA
LVOW112055101012

302170LV00001B/4/P